VILLA
FORTUNA

For Audrey

—my brave and loving companion in this as in all our adventures.

*Tu proverai si come sa di sale
lo pane altrui, e come è duro calle
lo scendere e 'l salir per l'altrui scale.*

(*You shall find out how salt is the taste
of another's bread, and how hard a path
the going down and going up of another's stair.*)

DANTE ALIGHIERI, **THE DIVINE COMEDY**
PARADISO XVII, 58

VILLA FORTUNA

An Italian Interlude

GEOFFREY LUCK

NH
NEW
HOLLAND

Published in Australia by
New Holland Publishers (Australia) Pty Ltd
Sydney • Auckland • London • Cape Town

14 Aquatic Drive Frenchs Forest NSW 2086 Australia
218 Lake Road Northcote Auckland New Zealand
24 Nutford Place London W1H 6DQ United Kingdom
80 McKenzie Street Cape Town 8001 South Africa

First published in 2000 and reprinted in 2000.

National Library of Australia Cataloguing-in-Publication Data:

Luck, Geoffrey.
 Villa Fortuna—an Italian interlude.

 Bibliography.
 ISBN 1 86436 604 4

 I. Title.

A823.3

Publishing Manager: Anouska Good
Project Editor: Jennifer Lane
Designer: Peta Nugent
Cover Illustration: David Carroll
Typesetter: Midland Typesetters, Maryborough, Victoria.
Printer: Griffin Press, Netley, South Australia.

Every effort has been made to trace the original source material in this book. Where the
attempt has been unsuccessful, the publishers would be pleased to hear from the
author/publisher to rectify any omission.

CONTENTS

PREFACE

There are always two countries. The visitor comes to Italy to admire the richness of its art heritage—perhaps two-thirds of the world's treasures—conveniently and compactly arranged in a picturesque landscape little more than a thousand kilometres long; to gape at the surviving massive constructions of ancient civilisations and wonder at the ingenuity of men without our engines and technology; perhaps to study, from their many surviving monuments, the progression of thought, idea and design that led the world out of the dark ages and which underpin our modern culture. And with all that, to enjoy the warmth and hospitality of the people, and not least, their cooking.

But most of these things (other than the food) are only a proud backdrop to the lives of ordinary Italians. They are far more concerned with the rising tax burden, high unemployment, the kaleidoscopic changes of impotent governments, illegal immigration, the ubiquitous corruption and urban criminality, an ever-increasing cost of living. And day by day they must wrestle the strangling tentacles of incredible bureaucracy—the far less picturesque historical legacy of the Bourbons who believed all citizens were there to serve the state, not the other way round.

Expatriates live with a foot in each of these countries, enjoying the benefits as a visitor, suffering the incompetence and inefficiency along with the natives. The one advantage they have is that they can always pack up and go 'home' to wherever they came from.

But perhaps the outsider suffers more frustration than the Italian because of the inevitable comparisons he makes. In his mental baggage is the knowledge that so many things can be done—are done—better in other countries.

Campanilismo, the traditional home-town parochialism that has been the butt of so many Italian jokes, extends to a national cultural xenophobia, a chauvinism that in so many fields impedes the adoption of better ideas. Paradoxically and seemingly perversely (but probably defensively) most of the national defects have been elevated into virtues. Complacency, that debilitating characteristic tattooed on the national psyche by survival of centuries of local oppression and foreign tyranny, is the overwhelming sin of the Italians, and ultimately their last refuge. The final paradox is that it is precisely their softness, their admirable but often infuriating *flessibilità*, that has made the Italians so attractive to those of us from the rigidity of '*anglosassone*' backgrounds.

This is the story of an Australian couple's experience of living in both Italies.

1. A VISITOR FROM THE PAST

It began as another working Sunday in the garden. Grubby jeans, calloused hands, aching back. Not *bella figura*. Definitely not Italian. I took no notice when a car stopped in the road; Sunday sightseers were always pausing on our hill to admire and photograph the view of the lake. Or perhaps out of curiosity at the strange foreigners who defied convention by not dressing up and going out, to see and be seen. Then I became conscious of the woman staring at the house, and shyly, tentatively, advancing up the driveway. I straightened up and called 'Can I help?' thinking that she probably wanted to use the phone.

'I didn't want to disturb you...' she hesitated, then pointing to the open window of our music room, blurted out: 'I was born in that room'.

I stuck the fork in the ground and looked at her more closely. Probably in her early forties, but I had always found it difficult to tell; with their beautiful skins, Italian women seem to age so slowly. Typically conformist conservative dressing in her dark skirt and check jacket. Elegant expensive shoes, obviously a city person, which explained why we had not seen her around Paciano.

'So you must be Signor Liscio's daughter!'

Domenico Liscio had been the last *contadino* of Varacca before the farm and the house were abandoned, thirty-five years before. We might have bought the house, we might have restored it to life again, but to everyone around Paciano, it was still *'La Casa Liscio'*; local custom ordained that these farmhouses were known by the name of their last occupant. The first time I learned of this practice, I had made a mental note that one day, we would make sure that the house carried our name. It was the woman's turn to be surprised.

'Si, sono Giuseppina.'

This was a stroke of luck. I knew a little about Liscio, but all my attempts to find out more had run into a dead end. When we first arrived I went looking for him. I wanted to ask what it was like for him, Domenico Liscio the share-cropper and his family, to live here on this hill, in this little hamlet of Varacca. I wanted to ask him about the house. It's not important in a National Trust sense, but it's one of those picturesque dwellings, in stone and warm brick, that are dotted across the Umbrian countryside, many like ours, now restored, others still in ruins. They're all part of the history of rural Italy. History that I can see and feel and touch excites me—not the dry stuff of books—and is one of the best reasons for living in Italy.

I had traced Liscio to the village of Badia, ten kilometres

away, where he had retired. But he had died some years before, and nobody seemed to know what had happened to the family. And there I had run across a curious attitude in the locals I turned to for information. Why was I asking about him, they wanted to know. They couldn't understand why anyone, least of all a foreigner, would be interested in delving into the past. Their past had been hard, often tragic, for them completely unromantic. It was over. Liscio was gone, and that was that. Now, *fortunatissimo*, his daughter had turned up on our doorstep, so to speak. She could answer all those questions I had wanted to put to her father.

Giuseppina had been ten, she said, when the family left Varacca. She had never been back, but she could remember everything as if it were yesterday.

'What happened to the big *sambuco* tree on the bank?' she wanted to know. 'And where is the stone drinking trough for the pigs?' Alas, I had to admit, the builders, lacking a sense of history, had destroyed them both.

'Tell me about your father,' I began to dig, 'the family was settled here, you had this big house, he farmed these lands. Why did he leave?'

From the enthusiasm with which Giuseppina launched into the story, it was clear that nobody had bothered to ask her about it before. I had triggered a release of memories, offered a brief moment to recapture her country childhood.

'He thought he would be here until he died' she said, 'but then the war came, and after that, everything changed. The Biavati family owned all the land around here, they bought it last century from a Count Danzetta. It had been in his family from mediaeval times. You know how the old system, the *mezzadria* system worked...' It was more a statement than a question. 'It had been going for centuries, my father never thought it would change. The Biavatis owned everything— land, animals, this house too. All my father had were his hands and his strong back. He worked the land for them, the harvest each year was shared, half and half.'

I felt the touch of recognition; 'That is how many dairy farms in Australia were worked, when I was a schoolboy.'

'Every year', she continued, 'my father and the Biavatis signed a new agreement, called the *patto colonico*, the farmer's contract. They had to make an *accordo* on what crops to grow, how much would be spent on seeds and animals. They had some bitter arguments, but the *contadino* was always going to lose, wasn't he?'

'But in the end, what happened?' I persisted. 'Did the Biavatis evict him?'

'No, it was not dramatic at all, although around here, other landowners did kick out their *contadini*. There was a big agricultural revolution after the war. The Socialists and Communists demanded a bigger share for farm workers. The *padroni* refused to pay, and closed their farms. Many of my father's friends had to leave, and went to work in factories, in Milan or Turin. We were worse off. Our farm was really poor. Prices were low and our family was growing. My father decided that if he didn't leave we would starve. He was already fifty-seven, too old to learn factory work. So he went to work on another, bigger farm at Badia.'

'And after that?'

'When he died, our family moved to Rome. It was difficult at first, but life was much easier than here, on the farm.'

As she was telling this simple story, I couldn't help thinking of the gulf between our comfortable life in this beautiful countryside and the harsh existence of the last family to live in the house, all in the span of my lifetime. Her childhood knew little joy. If I had ever had lingering romantic notions of the idyllic pastoral life of the simple peasant, Giuseppina would destroy them in the next hour.

Italians have a childlike curiosity, and there's no beating about the bush. The directness of the questions our friends fired at us when we first arrived in Paciano had caused some sharp intakes of breath. Audrey, my wife, had been startled to find herself facing an interrogation: 'What time do you go to bed and get up? How much did your car cost? Where did you get those flowers? What do you eat for lunch? Why do you speak to each other in English at home?' But by now I understood the social acceptability of the personal question. Also, that there was a fine line that was never crossed. Personal questions never became too personal. After the initial embarrassments, my wife and I had also learned that nothing charms the curious Italian more than to offer a tour of *la casa*.

Of course, this is what Giuseppina had really hoped for, and so with a wink to each other, Audrey and I were delighted to oblige. It was a learning experience for both of us. She was amazed at the transformation and the modern facilities in a house she had known only as primitive; through her eyes I looked back on the tough life a peasant family lived only forty-five years ago. Right to the last days of their stay, the house had been little more than a shell. They never had running water. It had been one of her tasks to carry water from the well, fifty metres away, now in our neighbour's garden. Obviously, with no plumbing there had been no bathroom, no lavatory, although in later years a privy had been tacked onto the back of the house in ugly modern bricks.

Light came from oil lamps, burning their own olive oil, or smoky home-made candles her mother made from animal fat, when a cow was killed. Around here, the older Italians still call electricity '*la luce*', the light, because that is all it provided. When *la luce* at last arrived at Varacca, Giuseppina remembered, it was strung to two rooms only, on little porcelain insulators hammered into the roof beams. She looked up, there they were still. We had left them as part of the history of the house.

What is now our upstairs lounge room had been the Liscio kitchen. But much more than a kitchen, Giuseppina explained—everything in the family happened there. It had only two appliances, if we could call them that—a sink, hand-carved from a single slab of marble, and an open fireplace with a low hearth. The fire never went out, summer or winter; again, it was the children's job to see there was always wood stacked ready. A large iron pot swung from a pivoting arm in the chimney so there was always hot water; her father dried his boots over the embers at the end of the day. When I first saw it, the room was festooned in cobwebs, and also with lengths of rusting twisted wires. I had always wondered what they were for. 'Mother used to hang her tomatoes there to dry', she enlightened me. 'Corn and onions too, at times. And alongside them, when she made sausages, her *salsicce*.'

We went round the house upstairs, as Giuseppina checked it room by room for me. What is now our bathroom was the farm *granaio*. At harvest-time, the barley, wheat and corn were hoisted up through the small window to be stored in the dry. My study, with its computers and fax machine (and its distracting views to Paciano and across farmlands to the lake) was once the bedroom for the older children, once they had grown too knowing to share their parents' room.

Giuseppina was surprised at our large bedroom. It had been a kind of family rumpus room. At times when heavy snow or mud made the road impassable and the hillfolk were cut off from the village, it was a social centre for the neighbourhood too. There are seven dwellings in the jumble of buildings that make up Varacca. With all the extended families, the hamlet once had a population of over forty people.

'How many happy nights I remember here', she said, 'with all the people from Varacca, and from Pietreto on the next ridge, dancing and playing cards'. When we bought the house, the entire floor of that room was missing—beams, bricks, everything—leaving a huge cavern seven metres high, from the ground to the roof.

'Even before rock'n'roll, the dancing must have been pretty fierce to destroy the floor', I said. But she laughed, 'No, no...it must have been pulled out after we'd gone, so the *padrone* could store more hay'.

Finally, we came to that room she had come to see, the room where her life began. Giuseppina half-closed her eyes. She could still see, she said, the big iron bedstead of her mother and father, the cot for her baby brother, and the rough *armadio* for their clothes. Apart from those pieces of furniture, they had nothing. The room was warmed in winter by the kitchen fire on the other side of the wall. In summer everyone sweltered under the oven-heat of the ceiling of *mattone*, the terracotta bricks laid under the tiles. There was only one tiny window facing south, catching the full blazing heat of the August sun.

Now the walls are lined with bookshelves and there are comfortable chairs. I sat her down. 'I want to show you something special.' I put a CD of a Bach concerto derived from a Vivaldi work on the hi-fi. The great organ of Arlesheim in Switzerland swelled and reverberated in the room, reproduced as if we were in the cathedral itself. 'This is something you didn't know about the house', I said. 'The brick ceiling and thick walls have left us a marvellous legacy—perfect acoustics.'

We went downstairs, but this was of course, unrecognisable to her. It had been exclusively animal territory. The cows spent their lives in the big arched *stalla* we had converted into a kitchen–dining area ten metres long. Their heat helped warm the humans upstairs. For Giuseppina, this part of the tour was a catalogue of surprises. She went to look for the room where the pigs had been housed and found it is now the main guest bedroom. The little holding yard outside where she penned them as a barefoot child has changed into a private wisteria-covered terrace. The guest bedroom at the front of the house, now looking out from a Juliet balcony onto the front courtyard, had been the haystore. The farm's tools were stored in a room at the back; now it is the downstairs guest bathroom, with a modern laundry beside it.

She came back to our dining room to stare at the changes in disbelief. On the wall, I had mounted the series of photographs of the house I had taken when we first saw it. This was the home she had known. There was the old fireplace of so many family evenings together; there were the mangers in the *stalla* with its lime-washed walls—pale blue up to chest height, white above. Only the animals were missing from the picture. Giuseppina turned to us. I guessed what was coming next. 'Why are you here? Why do you come all the way from Australia, to restore this old farmhouse? Perhaps your parents were Italian?'

These are questions I've been asked hundreds of times by curious Italians as well as by even more puzzled Australians. It's not all that much of a surprise to the Italians. They readily understand why anyone would want to come and live in their *bel paese*. For hundreds of years, they've been accustomed to foreigners raving about the place. Goethe was one of the first German tourists, two hundred years ago. Byron, Keats and Shelley sang so sweetly of Italy that English romantics have followed their tunes to this day. A little later, Robert Browning went right over the top with:

Italy, my Italy
Queen Mary's saying serves for me.
Open my heart and you will see
Graved inside of it, 'Italy'.

Those same English romantics colonised Tuscany and converted its vine-clad hills into Chiantishire. Florentine villas became centres of culture. The English still come—but no longer on the Grand Tour—to escape British weather and British politics.

With their rising affluence, Italians are more canny now than last century. Judging by what I see around me in Umbria, they now extract a market price for each piece of their heritage. They have also turned a tolerant memory on the atrocities of the last war, and welcomed a huge influx of deutschmark-powered Germans as tourists and settlers.

Australian reactions, on the other hand, have ranged from gasps of envy from the Italophiles to almost amazed contempt for anyone who would want to leave the lucky country of sun, sand and surf. So what could I reply to Giuseppina? I told her the truth, but gave her the simplest of many possible answers. Twenty years before, we had spent a month in Italy during a long family holiday caravanning through Europe. We wanted to come back at leisure and see more. We could have gone to live in Britain, where my roots were, but we wanted to spend a lot of time on the Continent. Italy was the easiest country for a non-European to buy property in, the language was probably manageable because I had once, long ago, studied Latin and French. It was well-centred for European travel, we loved the light and the countryside, we would never exhaust the wealth of history, art and architecture.

The whole truth, of course, was rather more complex. In choosing Europe, I was turning my back on all the comforts and efficiencies of a modern Australia, but I was also escaping its confining insularity. The country suffers a tyranny, not so much of distance as of time zones. So many of the decisive and important events in the world happen when Australians are asleep. Their clocks may be half a day ahead, but they will always be behind Europe and America. And despite all its resources and all the talents of its people, the country seemed to be focussing too much for my taste on a stultifying quest for national identity which merely revealed a national insecurity. In the pursuit of Asian markets and a pseudo-democratic multiculturalism, it was becoming *de rigeur* to deny our European heritage. So for me, it was an opportunity to escape, to return, at least for a time, to an area which I felt to be close to my cultural and linguistic origins.

Is this just a selfish cop-out? Francesca Duranti is a greatly under-rated Italian writer who outraged national xenophobes when she exiled herself to find stimulus and freedom in New York. On a visit to Australia, she explained the move in a way that put words around sentiments I had struggled to express: 'I want to be in a place that is not my place. So if I feel that the politicians are very, very stupid, I couldn't care less, for a while. I want to be on holiday, a sort of moral, political and cultural holiday.'

It had been another Italian writer, Luigi Barzini, the distinguished journalist and author, who had first excited my interest in the country. Thirty years ago he wrote *The Italians*, a textbook analysis of his country and his countrymen. From my years as a foreign correspondent I knew that it is necessary to live in a country to know it. So my journalist's antennae twitched at the prospect of getting beyond the stereotypes of an ancient and fascinating country, trying to understand what Barzini called '…the absurd discrepancy between the quantity and dazzling array of the inhabitants' achievements through many centuries and the mediocre quality of their national history'.

I could also see other interesting similarities to my own country—the 'tall poppy' syndrome has run through Italian history; there was a 'Ned Kelly' attitude of resistance to authority. In the Italian countryside, the old Australian axiom 'if it moves, shoot it; if it doesn't, chop it down' still rules. As a ridiculous little car travelling at an absurdly dangerous speed cut me off one day, it was clear that Italians had added another: 'If it's on a road, pass it!'

But there was a big difference in one of those puzzling characteristics that I hoped to get to the bottom of. While Australians now try to clean up the world, Italians still litter their countryside. When Goethe made his famous journey into Italy in 1786 and asked his innkeeper where he could relieve himself, he was told, with a wave of the arm at the courtyard: 'Why, anywhere you like, of course!' And today, at any time on an Italian road or *autostrada*, you may see a car on the shoulder, the driver beside it, passing his water.

I found one attempt to explain the Italian's civic selfishness in *Getting it Right in Italy*, William Ward's essential manual for resident foreigners. He wrote: 'Systematic lack of respect for others becomes paradoxically a form of civil liberty; the right to "do your own thing", however destructive or pointless, is tacitly accepted as greater than the duty to observe by-laws.' This illusory sense of freedom has always been part of the charm of Italy for foreigners, but it seems to me that for Italians it's a matter of survival. Oppressed by centuries of tyranny and today by more than eighty thousand laws and regulations (whereas Germany has only eight thousand and France gets along with seven thousand), evasion has always been the Italian's only recourse. A popular aphorism pokes fun at the national differences: 'In France, everything is permitted except that which is prohibited. In Germany, everything is prohibited—except that which is permitted. In Italy, everything is permitted, especially that which is prohibited.' The entire population has embraced this credo so enthusiastically that avoidance, subterfuge, prevarication, the lie and the excuse have become second nature, and first port of call in an emergency.

But there was another very important reason for being here—the excitement of a new challenge, a third career instead of an indolent decline into old age. And I would be kept busy. I had been asked to write on Italian affairs for Australian newspapers and to report on major developments for national radio. This would propel me to learn a new language. Then there was the thrill of salvaging and restoring to new life a ruined house built around the time of first European settlement in Australia, the task of turning an overgrown acre into a productive *oliveto* and orchard, the satisfaction in all this of becoming a small, a very small part of the history that is all around.

. . .

The adventure began in December 1986. I had been attending a Partners' meeting of my management consulting firm in Bermuda and flew home via Europe to decide, once and for all, whether the idea of a house in Italy was a pipe dream or not.

Our eldest son, Antony, who was living and working in London, had done the initial research. He contacted Brian French and Associates, one of the most experienced British agents dealing with property on the Continent, and sent us lists of houses for sale from the Alps to the Abruzzi. The first problem was that his descriptions were largely incomprehensible. What could I make of an entry like the following:

> 'Traditional *casa colonica* for restoration. External stairs to covered *loggia*. Five rooms above with brick and beamed ceilings, plus four animal rooms and *cantina* with arch. External breadoven. Structure generally sound. 3000 sq m land with some olives. *Strada bianca* 2kms to village. LIRE 40,000,000. STG L20,000.'

I could not picture such a house. The price, equal to about forty thousand Australian dollars might seem cheap, but I had no idea what I would be letting myself in for.

The second problem was that I could afford to spend only a little over a week in Italy, obviously not enough time to check out the whole country from top to bottom. I had to find a focus, so I telephoned Brian French in Yorkshire. He had been selling property in Italy for fifteen years; I asked him to define a target area. 'Umbria!' he said at once. 'Forget Tuscany—it's over-built and over-priced. Never, never get into those valleys in Chianti—no matter how picturesque they look on a holiday, they can be a three-quarter hour drive on dangerous narrow roads to get to the station.'

'But where specifically?' I asked. 'Stay east of the A1 *autostrada* and the main Rome–Florence rail line. The communications are better. The area around Lake Trasimeno is the dress circle of Umbria—anywhere in sight of the lake, you can't go wrong.' I could not have got better advice. He recommended going straight to one of his agents, a young Englishman who had bought a ruined farmhouse himself two years earlier and restored it. He now worked out of Castiglione del Lago, he said, and described the village with its mediaeval castle on a spur jutting out into the lake we now know so well. Many, many centuries earlier, he explained, the promontory had been the lake's fourth island.

We flew to Milan to pick up the rental car I had booked. The AVIS desk was apologetic—they didn't have any of those cheap little Fiat Pandas left. 'Would you mind taking an Alfa Romeo 75 at the same price?' Would I mind?! I covered the four hundred kilometres to Castiglione del Lago in four hours, at night and through torrential rain over the Apennines. Driving is one of my passions, and I decided that this venture was off to a good start, (although my cramped ankle took hours to recover from the traditional simian Alfa driving position). My wife, who had been in the back seat for the ride, was not so sure. She still harbours dark thoughts about motoring in Italy.

Still waiting for us by the fountain in Castiglione's *Piazza Mazzini* at 9pm was David Newman. Our handshake marked the beginning of a long association. I've always been a little apprehensive about salesmen, so initially it was a cautious relationship but it developed as he became our agent, translator, facilitator, project manager, confidant and friend. Tall, built like a rugby five-eighth, with a shock of dark hair and an infectious chuckle, he was already merging into the local community. I thought that after only two years, he seemed more Italian than Anglo-Saxon in his appearance and his relaxed style. Italy had been just the anti-stress medicine David had needed. For years, he had travelled through East Africa and the Middle East as a sales director of a trading company. In 1985 at the height of the Khomenei revolution, the Iranian military arrested him as a spy. It was the experience of being questioned with the muzzle of a sub-machine gun in his mouth that decided him on a quieter life. But I didn't learn all that till much later. My immediate interest was what he could show us.

'What is the market like?' I asked.

'You've come just in time', he said. 'Only a few years ago, you could have bought half of Umbria for a song. Prices have risen, but it's nothing to the way they'll explode when people realise that soon there won't be any of these farmhouses left', he grinned, 'because they aren't making them any more!'

The next few days passed in a blur, and not only because David wheeled us around the Umbrian countryside at a great pace to more than twenty houses. That December a dense fog which lasted longer than anyone could remember enveloped the whole of Central Italy. For a fortnight there was absolutely no wind. We were in the Val di Chiana, the broad fertile plain that stretches from Umbria almost to Siena, a natural basin, once a huge malarial swamp, where the fog settles thickest.

He had booked us into the Miralago Hotel, then a run-down provincial hostelry with surely the most uncomfortable beds in Italy. A corner of the bedroom had been partitioned off to make a cramped en suite, and there we discovered the significance of the little pull-cord that comes out of the wall in every hotel bathroom. A thoughtful Italian government, concerned that tourists might bleed to death from a shaving cut or drown when their toe became stuck in the plughole, had legislated for a nation-wide alarm system. I have often wondered how many *albergatore* hours have been wasted running upstairs to the succour of curious foreigners who couldn't resist pulling the cord to see what it operated.

The only attraction the Miralago offered was a splendid view over the lake from its windows, but the fog denied us that. Every morning, it was a question of groping our way from the hotel to our car. By midday, visibility had usually improved to a hundred metres! In a swirling white soup, David guided us unerringly to ruin after ruin. We had absolutely no idea where we were. There must have been countryside around us, but we caught only glimpses of it. As we travelled, he gave us a running commentary on the territory, its history, its agriculture and customs, and a wealth of information about the purchase and restoration of the old farmhouses. I'd brought my dictating machine, and recorded everything as we went. It was just as well. When I transcribed the tapes later, back home in Australia, I was amazed at how much detailed information I had collected, and how much I had forgotten.

David certainly had sales flair. His psychology was to combine honesty with challenge. Our first visit was to a group of houses that he had just heard was coming on the market—so recently they were not yet in the Brian French catalogue. Up a steep gravel road just outside Paciano, we came upon the little hamlet. At the highest point, standing alone and a little aloof, was a large double-storey house. It was nothing like its neighbours, picturesque peasant-built houses with out-of-plumb walls and odd-shaped extensions that chronicled in stone and brick the successive additions to the *contadini* families who had lived there. Rather, it was severely proportioned, vaguely Georgian in style. There were no outside steps or porch. A central main doorway, arched in the local grey sandstone led to an internal staircase to the upper floor. 'Unusual in this district', said David. Windows and doors were symmetrically placed. Large blocks of stone had been set as quoins to strengthen the four corners of the building. I could see that the house had been architected, not just built.

But clearly it had fallen on hard times. Windows were missing altogether or their broken frames left swinging; the planked doors were cracked and rotting; two centuries of weathering had washed away most of the lime stucco that once covered the walls; the roof timbers had warped under the weight of the tiles and now the roof sagged like a sway-backed donkey.

'There', said David, 'if that doesn't put you off, nothing will'.

I took some photographs, put the house out of my mind and we went on to the next on his list.

In the following days, we drove from one end of Umbria to the other. I clambered up to crumbling mediaeval towers still keeping watch over ancient valley routes (but far beyond the reach of electricity and telephone) and tracked across ploughed fields to windowless ruins down on the freezing plain. There were old farmhouses for sale everywhere, but none seemed right. Maybe the fog was getting to me; gloom was setting in. A day before we were due to fly out, I sat down with Audrey to go over our notes methodically, and found ourselves rejecting one house after the other. It looked as if it had been a wasted trip; I thought of how better we could have spent our time in Italy.

Then I remembered that first house, the one that was supposed to put us off. When David Newman dismissed it so casually, I hadn't even bothered to put it on the list. It didn't have rustic charm, but it had a sort of…well, character is the only way I could describe it. And it might be more suitable for conversion into a modern liveable house than many of those romantic peasant rabbit warrens we had been looking at. We still had time. We decided to go back to Paciano and have another long quiet look at the house, by ourselves.

Varacca is three hundred and seventy metres above sea level, and a long climb up a 'white road'. I would never have found it in the fog but for my memory of two huge Tuscan pines standing guard at the turnoff from the *Via degli Etruschi*. This is now the main road into Paciano, but six centuries BC, it was the mule track between Chiusi and Perugia, when they were two of the twelve great towns of the Etruscan federation.

As we reached the house, the afternoon sun burnt through the fog, and all the colours—of the tiles, the stone and the old bricks—seemed to burst into life. Already it seemed a different proposition. We explored. The first thing was to check the integrity of the structure. The walls were as sound and solid as the day they were built, without a crack. The corners, always a give-away if poor foundations have allowed subsidence, were straight and true. It wasn't difficult to get inside. The *stalla* hadn't seen a cow for more than thirty years, but the rough-hewn mangers were still there, and the animal odour was still in the walls. The floor was brick-paved, sloping to a drain to run the urine out under the door. And there was the arch—a magnificent arch of hand-made bricks, a perfect semi-circle half a metre thick and two and a half metres (eight and a half feet) high. By now we had seen many arches in farmhouses up and down Umbria, but always they had been mean and ill-proportioned.

Upstairs, the rooms were big, and bare. The great rough-hewn oak *travi* (the beams that supported the floors) were sound, and so were most of the roof timbers. There was only one place, near the chimney, where water had penetrated. A secondary beam had rotted and collapsed, but the thin bush timbers that served as rafters were still holding, so the tiles had not yet fallen in. However, we could see that this room would soon be open to the sky, the rain would rot the timbers and wash the soft mortar out of the rubble walls. Deterioration would accelerate so that within a few years the building would not be worth saving.

It was soon obvious that a very minimum of internal reconstruction would be necessary. There was lots of space, and solid walls, level floors, high ceilings and almost all the original timbers, seasoned over two centuries. Of course modern facilities—electric light and power, plumbing, heating, kitchen, bathrooms and laundry—would be needed. I shivered as the damp cold oozed through the broken windows and wondered if Italy knew about double glazing. But my mind was leapfrogging all these details, racing ahead to a dream of a new home created from this wreck. A wreck it might be, but solid, seasoned, just waiting to be given new life that might last another two hundred years. If we were going to think seriously about this house, I told my wife, we needed to note down everything about it. We went around again, recording the positions of doors and windows. We hadn't brought a tape measure, so the only way to estimate the size of the rooms was to pace them out. That night, back in the hotel, we converted the figures into the first sketch plan. Much later, when the official plans were drawn up for building permission, we were pleased to find that our rough and ready measurements were less than five centimetres (two inches) out.

There was however, one serious objection to the house which told us we had to put it out of our minds. The road from Paciano to San Donato and Moiano, the *strada bianca*, dusty white in summer and muddy grey in winter, ran right past the house. 'Right past' meant two metres from the front door!

The school bus, the neighbours at Pietreto and up the hill on the *Via Po' del Vento* meant steady traffic, plus about twenty cars a day going to the nearby *fonte*, the spring of cool filtered water that for six hundred years had drawn people from miles around.

We went to David Newman for commiseration. Of all the houses we had seen, this was the one, but for that road. We hardly expected his response: 'I can fix that for you, if that's your only problem.' *La signora* Biavati, who owned the house, had just agreed to give the *Comune* of Paciano, the local council, a strip of her land to make an access road to an old farm building it wanted to convert into a small hostel, he explained. In return, she had exacted a promise that the *Comune* would move the road some ten to twenty metres away from her houses at Varacca, obviously to make them more saleable.

Great news! It seemed that we were destined to have the place. We went home to Australia to think, promising to call David with our answer after Christmas, but with our minds ninety percent made up. We had found what we wanted, and had gathered all the information we needed about laws, taxes, and building costs. The last objection seemed to have been removed. We were not to know that the issue of 'the road' would continue to haunt us, a running sore through our lives for the next ten years.

2. Buying a ruin—and a road

Buying a property in Italy is not difficult—if you have an honest agent. I have now heard so many horror stories of fraud and deception at the hands of incompetents or tricksters that finding David Newman seemed like striking the jackpot at first pull. It was a surprise to find that almost all of the fraudsters were non-Italians—English or even Australian citizens who hit the market in the boom times of the 1980s.

In those years, the Italian bureaucracy was so lax anyone could set up a real estate agency, without qualifications and without registering. There were a number of ploys a dishonest agent could use to fleece an unwary buyer, whose time in Italy was usually too short to find out the real market value. One was to persuade a landowner to give the agent an irrevocable mandate for a set period to sell the farmhouse at an agreed price. An unscrupulous agent could then inflate the price to the purchaser without either the buyer or the landowner being any the wiser, and pocket the difference. I have two Australian friends who were taken down by one of the other favoured tricks—'warehousing'. The agent bought up derelict farm-houses for a song and re-sold them for two to four times as much. It is illegal for an agent to sell as a principal, but who was to know, especially if the agent was unregistered?

Unlike Australian solicitors, Italian lawyers normally don't do conveyancing. Fortunately, I was warned of this early when Brian French told me that unless I had studied Italian law, I wouldn't make it through the purchase process without the guidance of a good agent. It's not that it's complex, there are just so many unaccustomed details. One English buyer arrived for the final settlement without a fiscal card, the piece of plastic essential for every serious financial transaction in Italy. The incompetence of his agent could have cost him his deposit if the vendor had exercised his right to abort the sale.

While in London, I had followed Brian's advice and taken the first steps to open a local bank account, through the international branch of one of the principal Italian banks, the Monte dei Paschi di Siena. It is the oldest bank in the world, established in 1472 and, along with Queen Isabella, it helped to finance Columbus' first voyage to America. (The records seem to show that the loan was never repaid.)

At the time of our purchase, Italy had strict foreign exchange control regulations, and funds coming in from abroad for purchase and restoration had to be quarantined in a special 'foreign *lire*' account. I could withdraw from the account to spend, but was not permitted to re-deposit any amount locally because our money would then have been magically transformed into 'domestic *lire*'! To activate the account, the first thing I had to prove was that I was a foreign resident. It seemed a little strange that my Australian passport, driving licence and address would not suffice—no, I had to have a certificate from our local council at Mosman, authenticated and duly stamped by the Italian consulate.

Once I had signalled our decision to go ahead, David was to have the first contract document drawn up by a lawyer in Castiglione del Lago on behalf of the vendor, Anna-Maria Biavati. I found it interesting that this was called the *compromesso*, the same word for compromise. The implication clearly was that the paper represented the outcome of a haggling process between seller and buyer. This seemed appropriate, except that we hadn't even started haggling. In Sydney, the consulate had recommended an accredited translator, Luigi Mastellone, to prepare an English version of the draft *compromesso*. When I saw the original, I was horrified. It consisted of a page and a half of handwriting on ruled notepaper, describing the property, and giving the details of vendor and purchaser, but little else. It bore no resemblance to any legal document I had ever seen, and worst of all, it was incredibly vague on key issues such as the road.

Luigi shook his head at it—'It's an amateurish document, with too many loose ends. I warn you, if you get into a dispute, it will take five years to have it heard in an Italian court!' Our daughter Fiona, who is a lawyer, wanted us to drop the whole project immediately. I'd been learning Italian at evening classes of the Dante Alighieri Society in Sydney. Suddenly the textbook came to the rescue with my first Italian proverb, which I shall never forget. *'Fidarsi è bene'* I wrote to David, *'non fidarsi è meglio.'* This translates loosely as: 'It's nice to trust people, but it's better not to!' So Italian!

I insisted that he sack the Castiglione lawyer. Before we signed off on anything, I wanted a real lawyer to negotiate our requirements with *Signora* Biavati, and to draft a contract that gave us the legal protection we needed. I figured this would also signal to the Biavatis that we were not just stupid foreigners prepared to sign anything they served up. Through Fiona's contacts, I found Vincenzo Vigoriti in Florence. A professor of law at Siena University and a practising litigation *avvocato*, he kindly agreed to act for us although, as he said, it was outside his practice and his area.

With Professor Vigoriti as intermediary, argument about the phrasing of the road deal went back and forth for weeks, but finally rights and obligations were pinned down to mutual satisfaction. He also found proper expression for the rest of the contract, checked that the house was not subject to *Belle Arti* (National Trust) restrictions and won concessions such as the offer of a water supply that would be needed for the building work. Adjoining farmers have pre-emptive right of purchase of farming land, but since the Biavatis owned everything around, this was not a problem for us. However, the entire negotiation took three months, and I was on tenterhooks the whole time.

At the signing of the *compromesso*, a deposit of twenty per cent was payable, and from that moment, our money was at risk. We would forfeit our down-payment if we pulled out of the deal, but under the *caparra* (deposit) provisions of the Italian Civil Code, the vendor would have to refund us double if she should default. That penalty effectively prevents 'gazumping', and keeps vendors honest. For I soon found that however willingly they seem to go into the sale of one of these old houses, Italian landowners frequently harbour retrospective regrets. The first time we met Paolo Biavati, powerful Perugia notary and Anna-Maria's brother, he upbraided us.

'So you are the people who bought my father's house!...My sister had no right to sell our patrimony!' I subsequently learned they no longer spoke to each other.

In many cases it's simply a case of envy and greed. Often, when Italians look at the reconstruction the foreigner has carried out, they can see the added value that could have been theirs—with a little foresight and imagination. In any case, Italian interest in the country life is a belated one. A property developer friend who has worked in Italy for two decades says the young city dwellers of the postwar generation deliberately turned their backs on the countryside to erase all memories of their parents' shameful *contadino* origins. Only today, as the cities become more foul and unsafe, are they starting to buy back the farmhouses.

The signing of the *compromesso* in mid-May that year marked the beginning of a period of frantic activity. The completion of the purchase—the ominously-termed Final Act—had been set for early September. There was much to do if the restoration was to start that summer. First I had to give David our personal details so he could obtain our fiscal cards. Another trip to the Consulate to have passport photocopies certified. And I learned the importance of '*nato a il…*' on every document. In Italy, identity depends as much on the place and date of birth as on one's name. Apparently there are hundreds of Luciano Pavarottis, but only one who was born in Pavia on a certain day in 1935. I was warned to take great care when first registering our information because a misspelling in the official records could never be corrected. There would be endless trouble if a discrepancy should be detected later.

The *Codice Fiscale*, issued by the Finance Ministry, identifies each individual through a unique combination of 16 letters and figures. A system that would have impressed Smersh codemasters takes the first three consonants of the surname, the first, third and fourth consonants of the first name, the last two digits of the year of birth, a letter code for the birth month, numerals 1-31 for a male's birth day but 41-71 for a female's, and a specific code for the *Comune* or council area of residence. So my fiscal card reads: LCKGFR31R07z700Q!

My wife's card of course encrypted her maiden name, because women in Italy don't acquire their husband's surname on marriage. This means, as we discovered later, that you can never find a friend in hospital if you know only her married name. An Italian wife keeps her surname, but adds 'in' and her husband's surname. We joke that my wife is described correctly, Italian-style, as Audrey Taylor in Luck.

We had a bank account, but a clean quick system for making payments had to be set up. The Castiglione del Lago branch of the Monte dei Paschi had neither telex nor fax machine to receive my instructions but, after some tricky negotiations, I persuaded the bank's headquarters in Siena to accept the receipt of a faxed letter with my registered signature as authorisation. Siena would then telephone the Castiglione branch, instructing it to release the funds. Throughout the reconstruction, this system worked perfectly.

By this time, Signor Brugnoli, the Legal Consul in Sydney, was getting to know me. So he wasn't surprised when I reappeared with my draft of a Power of Attorney, the *Procura Speciale* needed for David Newman to sign documents, make payments and commission work on our behalf. He would also represent us at the Final Act before a notary. Brugnoli had always been most helpful; now he pulled up his typewriter and re-wrote the *procura* for me as it needed to be.

On the other side of the world, David had set in train the *frazionamento*, the sub-division of the property for the land registry; applied for conversion of the house from rural to urban classification (apart from being necessary to seek development approval, urban land attracted a lower rate of transfer tax); commissioned a surveyor to prepare outline plans for submission to council, and lined up a builder to start the moment we owned the place.

He phoned one night. 'Good news and bad news', he announced cheerfully. I groaned. Our budget was already tight. The good news helped—he'd got a ruling that our work would come within the Trasimeno district *'recupero'* plan. This, he explained was a concession system to encourage restorations by reducing the IVA (Italy's value-added tax) on all building materials from eighteen per cent to two per cent.

'Great!…And the bad news?'

'Ah—Paciano will levy you something called the *Buccalossi* tax, a charge for changing the purpose of the house from a farm building to a residence.'

'How much, David?'

Pause. 'About two million lire.' The IVA gains were wiped out.

All the other *comuni* in the area chose not to impose the *Buccalossi* tax, but Paciano, being the smallest council area in Umbria, and one of the smallest in Italy, with a total population of only nine hundred people, had few sources of revenue, and looked for every *lira* it could collect.

Meanwhile, we had been working hard on the plans. David had checked and corrected the original rough measurements, giving us also ceiling heights and other details. From all these I scaled up new drawings, and marked the changes we wanted to make. Several windows were to be re-opened, and eight door positions changed, including some to be made into arches. We worked from these plans throughout the project, modifying them as new ideas arose, and superimposing details of lighting, heating, kitchen and bathroom layouts.

I had done a lot of the work on our first home in Sydney myself, and we had gone on to restore a derelict Federation home in the years before turn-of-the-century houses became really fashionable. So I felt we were capable of doing the architectural design of Varacca ourselves. We would have to engage a *geometra*, a surveyor-draughtsman to submit the plans but would save an architect's fees. We would provide the 'what' but rely on the builders for the Italian 'how'.

By the end of June I was able to mail David Newman an eight-page document plus plans, explaining our concept and giving detailed specifications. I wrote 'It is important that we recognise and keep the traditional style and character of the house externally, taking advantage of its site, positioning and the area of land around it. We also want to retain all the best features of the interior, but it is going to be a fully modern house. We are building for the next century, not the last.' We saw no reason to have fewer mod cons than in our house in Australia. This was to produce some surprises for the local Pacianese. When they saw it finished, they were amazed at what they insisted on calling 'the kitchen of the twenty-first century'—just because it had a wall oven, microwave, dishwasher and range hood.

The decision not to try to alter the exterior was wise. The Trasimeno Planning Commission was taking an increasingly tough line on external modifications; they rightly wanted the historic appearance of these farmhouses retained. They allowed us to open windows that had been blocked up, and did agree to our building a covered *terrazza* at the back of the house because there was evidence of a previous pergola structure. But if I had asked to install picture windows to take advantage of the views, I am sure it would have been stamped on. As for the interior, they didn't care what we did.

From an architectural point of view, one of the difficulties in modernising an Umbrian farmhouse like ours was its layout. The rooms were no more than a series of boxes without passageways. When it was built, hallways represented waste space and extra cost; and with the landowner paying, *contadino* convenience and privacy didn't count. He and his family just had to go through one room to reach the next. We were fortunate that the house was big enough for us to slice hallways off the centre rooms at the rear, opening passageways to reach those at the corners.

Early on, I realised we had to have a foolproof way of describing the house to someone half a world away. There were five rooms on ground level and five upstairs, so I numbered them clockwise on the plan G1-5 and U1-5. When hallways were added, they became GH and UH. In this way I could save a lot of time on the telephone by referring to the front downstairs bedroom for example, simply as G3.

David had engaged a building team of two brothers-in-law, Piero Passaglia and Leonardo Pascale. Piero and his wife Anna-Maria lived down on the plain at Pucciarelli, Leonardo and Nila not far away up on the ridge at Villastrada. Both places were only a ten minute drive from the job, a big plus since they would be able to go home for lunch. By the time all the documents were ready for the Final Act, they were champing at the bit. They had anticipated the successful purchase by moving their crane onto the site, ordering truckloads of sand, and stacking bags of cement downstairs.

The two sisters could not have been less alike. Anna-Maria was short, plump and continually bubbling; Nila was tall, dark and rather more reserved. Their husbands too. Piero was a local

Umbrian, with dark brown eyes and the most beatific smile which never seemed to leave his face, even when things went wrong. Leonardo on the other hand was regarded as a *forestiero*, a stranger in the district, since he came from '*Ndrangheta* country, in Calabria. With the build of a boxer, he had the gentlest of touches when it came to setting a window frame, but there was always the hint of powerful emotions just below the surface. Not a man to trifle with, I decided.

Leonardo had had his own brush with the '*Ndrangheta*, the Calabrian Mafia. When his father died, he and his brother Giuseppe put the coffin in Piero's truck and the three of them drove the body five hundred kilometres back to his home village for burial. This was quite illegal of course, and the local undertaker wasn't too pleased at missing out on such a lucrative round trip. So he tried a little extortion, refusing to handle the interment without a special payment—until Leonardo hit him. Just once. When the time came to return north, the brothers were given careful advice on the best road to take for the quickest trip home. Leonardo hadn't grown up in the area without learning something. He took a different route and got home safely.

The section of the A1 *autostrada* the Calabrians had recommended is probably the most dangerous in Italy for hijackings and robberies. A few years later, a little American boy, Nicholas Green, was shot dead on that stretch when a '*Ndrangheta* gang fired into his parents' vehicle in a brazen daylight car-jacking. (The Green family donated Nicholas' organs to give new hope to half-a-dozen Italian children, a gesture that drew a personal commendation from the President, and reduced half of Italy to tears.)

I had thought of flying to Italy to be present at the Final Act, but David fortunately persuaded me to save the money for the restoration. What seemed a momentous event for us would have turned out to be an anticlimax. It was a brief, dry meeting in front of a notary to hand over the balance of the purchase price, pay the appropriate taxes, and sign the contract. It is the *compromesso* that is the key document.

The transfer of all property in Italy, from the most luxurious villa to a battered second-hand car, must be signed off by a notary, to authenticate that all relevant taxes have been paid. As can be imagined, this gives the *notaio* an endless, guaranteed workload and a licence to print money. The office is carefully handed down from father to son.

For most of the postwar period, Italy had been 'cowboy country' for property sales. Prices were understated by fifty per cent or more, for mutual benefit. The buyer reduced his transfer tax and the vendor saved on his income tax and capital gains tax. The government at last awoke to the huge fiscal evasion and put pressure on the notaries to enquire more diligently into the sale prices they were confirming. And it introduced spot checks.

So I was warned that cosy arrangements were a thing of the past and advised to declare the correct purchase price. And since capital gains tax was levied on the difference between the total restored cost and the ultimate sale price, this would be to our benefit if we ever came to sell.

Nevertheless, strange things could happen. One of our friends, Peter Hurd, a cousin of Britain's former Foreign Secretary, received a summons for under-declaring the purchase price of his house. Peter was a lawyer, absolutely honest, and had been meticulous in declaring the full value. But when the case came to court, he found himself confronted by an admission that the vendor had agreed to falsifying the price. Peter asked the woman why she had admitted to it, when she knew it was not true. She just shrugged. She had been so terrified when questioned by the pistol-packing *Guardia di Finanza*, the finance police, that she thought it better to admit to their allegations than be dragged before the magistrates. On principle, Peter fought the injustice, and won—after two years through three levels of the court system. No Italian would have done it. As I was to find, Italians are so contemptuous yet frightened of their justice system they will often admit to offences they didn't commit to stay out of court.

With the house now ours, work could begin. The first step was to repair the roof to secure the structure against the weather. Piero erected his tower crane, swung the jib over the building and began stripping the tiles. I was surprised that a small-scale cottage builder would have such a piece of equipment, but it seemed that every little firm had its crane.

'Aha', said David. 'Apart from the Italian's fascination with machinery, there's a sound financial reason.' The government offered artisans concessional loans to buy working equipment, he explained. They could invest their savings in government bonds paying high rates of interest, tax-exempt. So they could make a nice profit borrowing from the government, and really afford to buy any equipment they needed, or fancied.

The original roof had thousands of hand-made *coppi*, the semi-tubular tiles to be seen on roofs all through the Mediterranean countries. They are tapered so they fit snugly together. On one row they were laid on their backs, so to speak, to form a vertical gutter down the slope; in the adjoining rows the *coppi* were turned upside down to form little ridged roofs which shed rain into the others.

Over the years, hundreds of the tiles had been broken and would have to be discarded. In addition, these roofs were very heavy, and Piero was going to replace each second row with the much lighter flat-pan tiles known as *tegole romane*. A few of these must have fallen on heads from time to time—the expression for 'like a bolt from the blue', Leonardo told me with a grin (carefully checking the roof at the same time) was '*come una tegola dal cielo*'—'as a tile from the sky'. Under the *coppi* a layer of hand-made terracotta bricks rested on slim rough rafters, to form the ceiling. They too had to be removed (and stacked carefully) so that the skeleton of roof timbers was now exposed to the sky and could be thoroughly checked for rot or borer damage.

However, before the roof could be restored, the walls had to be strengthened. No matter that they had stood without moving for two hundred years. Italy is an earthquake zone; we had to comply with the national anti-seismic regulations, and Paciano was most strict in their application. The *Comune* required us to cast a continuous reinforced concrete beam around the top of the outer walls to keep the roof structure intact if a tremor should shake the building. It was an unwanted expense at the time, but we blessed the regulations when the big quakes that so damaged Assisi and destroyed similar old houses in Apennine villages left us shaken but not stirred.

Fortunately few timbers needed renewing, and the ceiling bricks were quickly replaced. Over them Piero and Leonardo poured a layer of lightweight concrete reinforced with steel mesh. This would have the effect of taking the weight of the tiles off the ancient wooden beams, transferring it out to the massive perimeter walls. Next came sheets of foam insulation and over that a bituminous waterproof membrane before the *tegole* and *coppi* were laid to complete the operation.

We followed all this from the distance with mounting excitement. Every day, David Newman visited the site and photographed the work. Every week a stream of prints or negatives arrived in the mail. By the end we had an album that was a complete pictorial record of the reconstruction.

Once the workmen moved inside the house, we had some tough decisions to make.

'What are we going to do about the floors?' David telephoned. The upstairs floors were laid with terracotta bricks, nothing more than kiln-fired clay, but they were in poor condition. Some people prefer to keep them for their authenticity, notwithstanding the undulations. However, they are porous, needing constant applications of wax to seal them. Many an Italian housewife has spent the best years of her life polishing her *cotti* to a shine to make them impervious to grime and grease. This was not for us! I thought it was better to be able to admire their texture from downstairs, as a ceiling, especially as David assured me that sand-blasting would remove the whitewash and restore their original beauty. So I decided to leave them in place, with a reinforced concrete surface poured over them and new floor tiles laid on that.

I had to consider that a modern home has a lot more furniture than a *contadino* family's. So apart from the advantage of creating a level floor, all the weight would be taken off the wooden beams and carried out to the half-metre thick walls.

As for tiles, we decided to search out Italy's best through the warehouses of Sydney importers. Our choice fell on interesting tiles from the magic hills of Impruneta in Tuscany. Exceptionally hard, varying in colour from burnt biscuit to deep terracotta, they had random impressions in their surface which gave them a hand-made appearance. And they were glazed, which meant easy-care. Brunelleschi dug the clay for the tiles to roof his great dome of Florence's cathedral from the same pit at Impruneta. It seemed a nice touch that our floor tiles carried the Brunelleschi brand. Helpfully, the importer gave me the address, and a telex query to Impruneta brought a quick response with the name of the nearest retail supplier, in Perugia. I passed it on to David, another problem solved. Restoration by remote control was certainly requiring a good deal of ingenuity.

Downstairs, there were only earth floors in most of the rooms, although the *stalla* did have brick paving. Tons of earth had to be dug out by hand to a depth of half a metre so that new suspended floors could be laid on pre-stressed concrete beams. This left a space below for air to circulate, minimising rising damp. None of these farmhouses had dampcourses in their walls, nor were there foundations or footings for the walls as we would build them today. We were fortunate that like all the buildings at Varacca, the house stood on a rock ridge that ran down the hill.

Restoring the animal rooms of an Umbrian farmhouse for human habitation raises a major technical problem. Over the decades, if not centuries, animal urine has saturated the ground and permeated the stones and mortar of the walls. The contained ammonia salts will attack and blister any plaster and paint applied over the top.

The most common solution is to 'skin' the walls by building a new thin brick wall inside, with a slight airspace between. Apart from reducing the size of the room, this creates a new problem of thickness around doors and windows. I especially wanted to retain the marvellous aged timber lintels, so I dithered and dickered. It was just as well that I held off. Some weeks later, David came back with the news from our paint supplier of an American chemical treatment guaranteed to seal the walls against moisture and salts. The three-stage process was expensive, but quicker and far less costly than building completely new internal brick walls.

With issues like this, I ran up an enormous telephone bill over the weeks as questions and answers flew back and forth. At that time, there was not a fax machine within forty kilometres of Paciano, so all documents had to go by mail. The Italian postal system proved totally unable to cope with our needs. Any airmail packet from Sydney regularly took two to four weeks to reach Paciano; David had to abandon the more costly express service to us because it took longer! It always seemed that the little red 'Express' sticker on the envelope was like a red rag to some bull of a mail sorter.

The work went on, and the money flowed out. The builders had never seen me. I reflected that they had only David's word that I existed at all, let alone could be relied on to pay from twenty thousand kilometres away. I tried to imagine what would have happened if an Italian had flown to Australia, commissioned a builder and then returned to Europe, promising to send money for the progress payments. But we had come to an area of old-fashioned rural values as well as first-class workmanship. I was finding to my suprise, that if I didn't ask for an account it wasn't sent. Sometimes it's worse than that. Stefano Grilli, the local earth-moving contractor, did some excavating for me. It took four years to get the bill out of him.

As the weeks went by, what was worrying me most was the difficulty of estimating the final cost. We had fixed quotes from the electrician and plumber, but Piero and Leonardo, as well as the tiler, plasterer and painter were really employed as sub-contractors, and paid on a day-labour basis. Fixed price contracts for such work are rare, because builders seem to have no skill or experience in estimating, or managing a project to a cost. I've spoken to friends and neighbours who did have fixed contracts. They found the work stopped when the builder said he had used up the money; they had to put their hands in their pockets to continue, so it was really no solution.

At the beginning, David and Piero estimated that the roof work, for example, would work out at ninety thousand lire per square metre. But I could never get Piero to relate his bills for time and materials to that section of the job. Hence I don't really know how much the roof cost.

Provided the builder is honest, this might not be too important for the homeowner, but it becomes serious at the national level. It emerged from the great corruption investigations of the early 1990s that there was no professional estimation or cost control on any public project. As a result, it was only too easy for the cost to escalate through bribes paid to politicians to vote extra funds.

In Milan, the new airport, the extensions to the underground system and a new theatre ended up costing from three to nine(!) times the original 'estimate'. The revelation encouraged a British firm of quantity surveyors to set up business in Milan immediately. Italy's high-speed train project was trumpeted as the first to have a cast-iron cost control system, but five years later the original estimated cost had trebled, and the magistrates were investigating alleged improprieties in the tendering and contract-allocation procedures.

Three months into the work on our farmhouse, we were to fly into Italy to meet the team. There were some vital decisions that could only be made on the spot. By then the structural work was finished, new doorways had been punched through forty-centimetre thick walls and the old openings bricked up, windows were stacked ready to go in, the electrician had cut his spider's web of flexible ducting into every wall of the house, Piero and Leonardo were starting on the new *terrazza* and the external boiler room.

I hired a car in Rome and Audrey and I drove north to see our dream taking shape. It was brilliantly fine weather for November, and I began to realise how much the seasons dominate life and activity in this country. If the building start had been delayed another month or two, Piero and Leonardo could have been battling frosts and possibly snow before they finished. We drove up the dusty hill with David Newman and turned to look down from the house. Below us spread a patchwork of fields, lying fallow or just seeming empty after the autumn sowing, with old farmhouses dotted amongst them. The scene could not have changed much from mediaeval times. And stretched out in the distance, rippling in the pale sunlight, was the lake—*Lago Trasimeno!*

I recall turning to David, and saying rather stupidly, 'Where did that come from?'
He looked at me a little oddly. 'It's always been there— I thought that's why you bought the house, for the view.' Then he remembered how we had blundered around in the fog the previous year, and seen nothing beyond a hundred metres. 'Well, you've got yourselves a bonus, haven't you? And I won't charge you a cent more.'

We spent a frenetic fortnight choosing bathroom and lighting fittings and fretting over details. I remember it as a not very refreshing holiday, although we were buoyed up by excitement. We had some delightful moments, such as the time we bought the hand-wrought copper lamp for the stairwell from the blacksmith's workshop at Magione. Metal working is one of the great skills that have lived on in Umbria since the Middle Ages; a *fabbro* can make anything with a piece of iron and a hammer.

The lamp was to hang in the vast airy space where the roof beams are seven metres above the landing, but with my limited Italian, I didn't try to explain this to the artisan. When he offered us half a metre of chain, I asked for more.

'A metre?'

'More!'

'A metre and a half—that's more than you'll need...Still more?!!'

Reluctantly he gave us the two metres we needed, but obviously thought the foreigners were *pazzo*. Only mad people hung their lamps half a metre off the floor!

Another three months and the house was finished. There was a two thousand-litre liquid gas tank to feed a powerful boiler for hot water and the central heating. I did get double-glazing all round, and louvred shutters on all the windows to keep out summer sun and winter snows. And when David handed me a huge bundle of keys, I discovered a curious deficiency in Italian locksmiths. The house has seven external doorways, most with a protective outer door, and glazed French windows (the Italians call them English windows) within. There were separate keys for each door—eleven in all, twenty-two with duplicates.

'Why can't we have the doors keyed alike, or have a master key?' I asked.

'Unheard of', said David, 'they can't do it'.

I still don't believe it, but since I got the keys sorted out I've never bothered to try to do anything about it.

Alfredo Giardini struggled in with the furniture we had chosen in his shop in Castiglione del Lago; the rest would be coming from Australia, later. It was a house—warm, furnished and liveable—but not yet a home. Nothing had been done about landscaping or tree planting—that would have to wait until we arrived.

And no, the *Comune* could not tell us when the road would be moved.

3. PACIANO—FRONTIER TOWN

Sleepy little Paciano doesn't look like a frontier town. Crouching halfway up the slopes of Mount Petrarvella, in a natural amphitheatre of hills that are distant poor relations of the great Apennine ranges, the village today looks out on a peaceful landscape of silvery olives and golden barley. It is still wrapped in its ancient walls, whose stones, as someone wrote, are 'dark with the breath of ages'; but now nobody needs to barricade its three ogival gateways at night.

Yet Paciano can bear witness to the centuries of bloody strife that convulsed Umbria and Tuscany, from the Middle Ages right through the Renaissance. It was sacked twice, occupied by hostile troops at least three times and for three hundred years lived a knife-edge existence between the forces of Florence, Perugia, Siena, Arezzo and the popes. We know there had been an Etruscan settlement on the hill five hundred years before Christ, the proof being a magnificent bronze helmet now in the Archeological Museum of Perugia. And then a Roman encampment, strategically watching over the main north—south route up the valley.

There is no agreement on the origin of Paciano's name. It would be nice to believe it could derive from a reputed temple on the site dedicated to the Romans' two-faced god, hence *Pax Jani* or Peace of Janus. The sole support for this theory is an ancient bas-relief, now worn nearly smooth, set in the wall of the Church of Saints Salvatore and Ceraseto. It is a primitive stylisation of Janus in his two aspects, with the olive branch of peace. But many think it is simply a corruption of the name of the powerful Cortona family—Pacci, Panci, Pangiani, Panzi (spelling was never very accurate a thousand years ago)—who were the first registered owners of the surrounding lands.

The earliest documentary evidence, in the parish records, dates from AD 900 and testifies to the existence of churches—St Sebastian, St Mary of Peretula and St Lucia of Petroalbella—two of which still stand in the town. I looked up the municipal archives and found a reference that in AD 917, the Emperor Berengario of Friuli conceded the castle of Paciano to Uguccione II of Bourbon, the Marquis of Tuscany. Of that site, however, nothing remains but a fragment of the defensive walls, and a huge mediaeval tower, now magnificently restored, the *Torre d'Orlando*. Sometime around 1240, the Hohenstaufen Emperor Frederick II destroyed the castle during his war with the popes.

The survivors rebuilt, as they always did in Italy. But they moved Paciano down the hill to where it stands today. It was a more isolated position, then hidden in a dense forest of oak and chestnut; easier to defend and close to a spring of excellent water. The spring is still the town's main supply, and the water is cool and sweet, especially on a hot summer's day.

It was this isolation that many times saved the village from the awful destruction that befell its neighbouring hilltowns. Nevertheless it was occupied twice in the fifteenth century by mercenary bands, the *condottieri* who ravaged Umbria for booty or ransom. It also got caught up in the internecine feud between the brutal Baglioni and Oddi families of Perugia. The Oddi gang was then on the run, and one night a traitor within Paciano's walls opened the gates (whether out of pity or fear we do not know) to let them take shelter from their enemies. The Baglionis sent stonebreakers to demolish the walls to get at the Oddi, but some smart negotiating by the Pacianese persuaded both sides to withdraw and leave them in peace.

But down in the Val di Chiana, within sight of Paciano, the most fearful atrocities often took place. I found a book with a description by Segni of Cortona, a contemporary historian, of the great struggle between Florence and Siena that devastated the valley in the 1550s:

'Usavansi in questa guerra dall'una parte e dall'altra crudeltà atrocissime in impiccar contadini ed in isforzar le donne, in ammazzare gli innocenti ed in mettere a fuoco e fiamma ogni cosa; di tal maniera che rade volte si manifesta per le storie essere avvenuto un caso nel quale si esercitassero gli odii si acerbamente l'uno contro l'altro.'

'In this war, both sides resorted to the most frightful cruelties—in hanging the peasants, raping the womenfolk, murdering innocent children and putting

everything to the torch; taking turns to raze everything
to the ground came to be the means by which each side
was able to express its bitter hatred for the other.'
Exactly as Tacitus had put it fourteen hundred years earlier:
'...And where they spread desolation and death—that they
called peace.'

Much of the area had been under the regime of the Republic
of Siena, but castle by castle the Florentines won the territory.
When the Medici armies captured a town, the citizens were
given a brutal choice: they could shout *'Duca!'* to declare their
loyalty to Duke Cosimo, or be put to death. Torrita di Siena
is scarcely more than twenty kilometres from Paciano. When
it fell to the Duke's troops in 1553, one old woman refused
the easy option. Unlike General Stonewall Jackson in the
American Civil War ballad of Barbara Frietchie, ('Shoot if you
must this old grey head//But spare your country's flag', she
said) the Florentines did not spare her old grey head. They
nailed her to the gate of the castle, where she continued to shout
defiantly *'Lupa! Lupa!'* until she died. The wolf is still the proud
symbol of Siena.

The last disaster for Paciano came a hundred years later. If
the Pacianese had thought their incorporation into the Papal
States would guarantee them peace, they were in for a shock.
Urban VIII, the same pope who consecrated the new St Peter's
and condemned Galileo, foolishly launched the Barbarina War
against a coalition of forces from Venice, Parma, Modena and
Tuscany. The new cannon of the Tuscan army easily breached
Paciano's walls and the town was sacked; with the firepower

that gunpowder gave, the era of the walled hilltown as a safe haven was over.

The Barbarina war left an odd enduring legacy. Both sides were nearly bankrupt and rushed to impose new taxes on the suffering populace. Florence introduced the first tax on the new consumer product, tobacco. But its real innovation was a stamp duty on the paper used for official dealings. That is the origin of the notorious *carta da bollo*, the ruled paper with a duty stamp we buy at the tobacconist's. Its cost has risen steadily, to thirty thousand lire today. It is essential for writing all official communications to the bureaucracy, and an even greater source of revenue than the Duchy of Florence could ever have imagined.

Further digging in the archives revealed that when the new Paciano was built in the fourteenth century, it was laid out in a geometrical form based on astronomical studies, with three main streets, three gates and seven towers. Visitors familiar with the bigger, wealthier hilltowns of Umbria find few buildings of historic interest. The Renaissance Cennini and Buitoni *palazzi* with their buttressed walls and delightful balconies are the most impressive, standing guard over the *Porta Rastrella*. Just rescued from ruinous collapse in the *Centro Storico* is the *Palazzo Baldeschi*, a huge rambling home built for a Cardinal of that name several hundred years ago. I used to take our visitors to see its 'death door', the walled-up *porta dei morti*. This arch was a feature of many great houses. It was considered unlucky to take a coffin out through the main door, so when someone died, masons would knock the stones out of the arch for removal of the body, and mortar them back again after the funeral. Unfortunately the restoration of the palazzo has buried the death door under a layer of stucco.

Paciano has seven churches, four within its walls, not bad for such a tiny community, but I was disappointed to find no really important works of art in them. There is a fresco of the Crucifixion covering one whole wall of the parish museum, painted in 1452 by one Francesco Nicolo, the first teacher of Piero Vanucci, *Il Perugino*, but this is our only brush with fame. I like it because its allegorical scenes give it something of the flavour of a cartoon strip. For the town, the most treasured item is neither a painting nor a fresco. It is the *gonfalone*, its ancient standard, dating back to 1460. A pupil of Bonfigli painted the Merciful Virgin on the silk banner, to commemorate the passing of the plague.

This modest little conurbation, attractive above all for its peacefulness and the integrity of its mediaeval simplicity, was to be our home town. And Varacca, so Mayor Alfonso del Buono told me proudly when we were restoring, was the oldest habitation outside Paciano's walls, and looks directly onto them across the valley. I never tire of watching the seasons change the colours of its setting.

But after the restoration was complete, the immediate problem was to get ourselves there. Although we had moved several times around the world, we had always been temporary migrants, returning to home base after a few years' foreign posting. This was a permanent move. Everything was to go. Of course it's so easy in this modern world—the household goes into a container and the owners jump on a jumbo.

I thought of the tens of thousands of Italians who had made the trip in the reverse direction. Six weeks of seasickness and apprehension, all their family possessions in a few trunks in the ship's hold…the welcome on the wharf so often a rough quarantine officer rooting through their battered suitcases to seize their precious *salame* and *pecorino*, conserved as much as talismans of their culture as a future food supply.

As a young cadet reporter I had met many of these people— from Calabria, the Abbruzzo and the Veneto—when I boarded their ships to search out personal stories that would put a human face on the great postwar migration wave for ABC listeners. One such day in the early 1950s my 'scoop' was the discovery of the tenor Tito Schipa whom other reporters had missed in the migrant throng. He was to make his first concert tour of Australia, and although he could have afforded to fly, chose to travel by sea, with his people. 'He sang to us every night', they told me. 'We have had a wonderful trip—it was like bringing Italy all the way to Australia with us.'

In some ways it was more difficult for us. Bureaucracy had proliferated over forty years and had to be dealt with. And we just had so many more things. It was eight months before all the strings were untied and we were able to step on the plane. One of the trickiest problems to solve had been the question of a car. Italy had put us in a catch-22 situation that would have impressed Joseph Heller. To buy a car in Italy, one must have residence in the country. A *Certificato di Residenza* will be issued by the local *Comune* only after three months continuous living in the area, and the presentation of the *Permesso di Soggiorno*, the foreigners' 'Permit of Stay' obtained from the *Questura*, the local police headquarters.

But how to live for three months in rural Umbria, miles from public transport, without a car? David Newman offered to buy a car in his name, but the horrendous cost and complexity involved in subsequently transferring it to me quickly ruled that idea out. Finally I hit on a proper Italianate solution—go around the problem instead of confronting it head on. We placed an order for delivery in Paris of a tax-free Peugeot to be built to Italian specifications, and to be ready for us when we arrived in Europe. At the expiry of the red tourist number plates six months down the road, we would register the car in Italy.

We managed to fill a complete container. Into the 'box' went many things we knew we would need and that were not obtainable in Italy, or at least not readily obtainable in our area. These included a solar hot water system that would help reduce the huge gas bills. Italian gas comes by pipeline, either from Siberia or under the Mediterranean from Algeria, and costs multiples of what we were used to paying in Sydney. Australian solar systems are the most efficient in the world, and although they are exported to Europe, they cost twice as much there.

We bought the Solahart in the Australian winter when sales were slack and, as a special incentive to purchase, a free slow combustion heater had come with it. I knew this would solve another problem. Italian *muratori* are among the best stonemasons and bricklayers in the world, but they have never learned to make a chimney that does not smoke. So when I installed our heater we were able to enjoy both radiant heat and a smokeless room.

Taking delivery of the car in Paris gave us the joy of running it in through the French countryside. And since we were heading south into Burgundy, we could take up a long-standing invitation to stay with the Comtesse Michel de Loisy, in her eighteenth century walled family house in the centre of Nuits-Saint-Georges. Such luxury! We slept between linen sheets in a carved oak bed with a sixteenth century Aubusson tapestry on the wall. We sat and talked in a drawing-room papered in red damask with doors and ceiling decorated by Italian painters.

We were at home with an extraordinary woman. She had had an Italian grandmother and an English governess, so she grew up fluent in both languages. As she was an only child, her father determined that she must be the son to succeed him in the management of his estate. So she was given a boy's education, spent a year in an American college and was then sent to study oenology (the science of winemaking) in Dijon. To satisfy her mother, she also had to learn the skills of a well-bred lady—to play the piano, to embroider and to make amusing conversation.

Then well into her seventies, and the first woman to be elected a *Commandeur de la Confrérie des Chevaliers du Tastevin*, we could not have found a better guide in all France to the delights and history of the wines of Burgundy. She had the most original way of describing her wines:

'This is a '59 premier cru, a Beaune Teurons. They say it is pigeon blood in colour...I have never seen pigeon blood, but what I think is quite amusing is that when you go to your jeweller to buy your dear wife a ruby—as I am sure you do often—he will show you his best stone and say: "This is exceptional—it is pigeon blood in colour, or better, it is burgundy!" '

Vital, young in spirit, the Comtesse seemed to have stepped from the early to the late decades of the twentieth century without faltering. She told us that as a child she dressed as a rose for a costume dance in the palace in Monte Carlo. Her five-year-old companion was the Princess—the future mother of Prince Rainier. During the war she helped escaping Allied airmen clamber down the well in her courtyard to hide in the cellars. She still drove an Alfa Romeo quite fast and dealt charmingly with crass American tourists. Warm, open, hospitable, she is probably the most completely civilised person I have ever met.

It was October, and the trees were in autumn leaf—the best time to drive through France and Switzerland. We made a happy and leisurely way home to Varacca.

Immediately I was brought back to earth by the demands of Italian bureaucracy. We ran up an incredible mileage in the first few weeks going back and forth to Perugia, the Regional and Provincial capital. For every new situation I had to swot up a new vocabulary—none of my Italian lessons seemed to have thought of the things I now needed to say. My wife and I went everywhere as a pair. My hearing is a little defective from my days when rifle shooters didn't wear ear muffs, so we worked out a technique. I would do the talking and my wife would listen to make sure I didn't miss anything. The Italians thought it strange that we consulted constantly during a conversation, but it worked well, with very few misunderstandings. And every time, we would burst out laughing as we put ourselves in mind of one of those *carabiniere* jokes Italians love to tell: the reason that *carabiniere* officers always go around in threes, they say, is because one can read, the other can write, and the third goes along for the intellectual stimulus.

There were documents and photographs needed; I made useless hundred-kilometre round trips because our *Permessi di Soggiorno* weren't ready on time. Luigi Pecetti, our Customs agent, wanted proof of property ownership to clear our container through Customs without duty. The detailed inventory of contents had to be re-written, then—horror!—he discovered that we had brought a television set.

'If only you had put it down as a computer screen!' he almost wailed. 'That's what we always advise.'

At the end of the twentieth century, a television set, especially a small, five-year-old portable might be thought to be merely part of a family's normal possessions. But in Italy, importation of televisions is strictly prohibited.

Our television was buried somewhere in the container and could not be located until it was unloaded. The next day a huge semi-trailer truck carrying our container, made its slow way up the Varacca hill. The driver attempted to turn his rig at the little fork in the road and bogged the truck on the soft shoulder. He got down from the cab and walked around uselessly, repeating '*disastro! disastro!*' A fair traffic jam had built up before Sandro, the village blacksmith and plumber, just happened to come by. He quickly uncoupled the trailer, de-bogged the truck and in no time had it all parked neatly outside our front door.

Paolo, our friend in the village, had organised a couple of local farm labourers to help us unload, and the four of us emptied the entire container in two hours. I wondered what the Storemen and Packers Union would have thought of us. The television set was there, and a quick check showed it did work in Italy. If it hadn't, I was going to take it back to the Perugia Customs and donate it to them. (A friend of mine did that once when he was checked driving into Italy over the Brenner Pass with his old television, and it caused a huge commotion.)

So I wrote out the first of our many official supplications to authority on that infamous *carta da bollo*, begging permission to import one second-hand twelve-inch television set:
'*Il sottoscritto*, Geoffrey Colin Luck, *nato* a Warwick Australia, il 7.10.1931, CHIEDE . . .'
Some weeks and several visits and telephone calls later, the Posts and Telecommunications Department in Perugia gave the all clear, not with a permit for importation of the television, but a much more subtle *nulla osta*—no objection.

• • •

The first of November marks the opening of the *cinghiali* season. That year it fell on a Thursday, but being All Souls

Day, all the locals had a holiday and were free to hunt. The first I knew of this great day was being woken in the half dark by a convoy of four-wheel drive vehicles racing up the road and sliding to a gravelly halt beneath our windows. I threw open the shutters to look down on a platoon of men in camouflage combat uniforms, shotguns over shoulders and bowie knives strapped to thighs, surrounded by excited yelping dogs. Their breath steamed in the cold air and there was much stamping of feet to keep warm. It seemed that the road fork outside our house was the traditional bivouac area. They would leave the cars there before plunging into the scrub, returning later with the pig (if they were lucky) or to a commiserative drink around a campfire.

Up went the warning notices on nearby trees—'*Battuto di Caccia al Cinghiale—Zona Occupata*'. And for the rest of the morning the hillsides echoed to the barking of the dogs, the incoherent shouts of the beaters and finally the volleys from the twelve-gauges. It sounded like a re-enactment of the partisan ambushes of German patrols fifty years earlier. The kill was made up on the ridge. A man was sent back for a car, and the first and last I saw of the boar, it was lashed to the vehicle's roof as it led a triumphant procession homewards.

Wild boar hunting is dangerous work anywhere, and *cinghiale* are no friendlier than the pigs I used to hunt in the channel country of Western Queensland. Umbrian hunters use shotguns because a rifle bullet carries too far and could kill someone in the next farmhouse. A bunch of pellets almost certainly would not stop a big boar, so their cartridges carry a single lead shot, a centimetre in diameter—a miniature cannon-ball guaranteed to bring down anything.

Since we have been here, conservationists mounted a campaign to stop hunting, but the question was narrowly defeated when it was put in a national referendum. The government listened though, and acted by imposing swingeing increases in gun and hunting licences. It now costs nearly one million *lire* a year to be a *cinghiale* hunter. The traditional sport of the peasant is being priced out of existence, and increasing populations of wild pigs are trampling the crops.

. . .

One of my priority jobs was to get the solar heater installed. It wasn't going to do anything for us in the middle of the Italian winter, but the boxes were so big I had to get them out of the way. A telephone call, and the importers in Milan sent the regional agent up from Terni, to organise an experienced plumber to do the job. 'And you are so lucky', said the agent. 'The Umbria regional government at this moment is paying a bounty on solar systems to encourage energy conservation.' For a fee of some hundreds of thousands of *lire*, he would supply all the documents needed for the claim, which should get me about two-million *lire* back in refund.

I should have been more suspicious when I saw his huge black BMW. I did get the documents, complete with impressive computer calculations of thermal efficiency and guaranteed savings to the national power grid. But months later, when I chased up the application with the regional administration, I found it had been disallowed because our unit had not been installed within the proclaimed bounty period. The agent knew this—he had simply organised me into a deliberate fraud attempt, to justify padding my bill. If it had come off, both of us would have benefited, a classic sting on the government.

Umbria's energy conservation incentive scheme ended in tears all round. The region received roomfuls of applications, thousands made under false pretences, like mine. There were so many valid claims the budget was over-stretched. Nobody gained much at all, except vendors of solar systems and double glazing, who had boosted sales nicely. It was an interesting close-up view of Italians rorting the system.

By the time we had unpacked two hundred and seventy-seven boxes and settled everything into its place, Christmas was rapidly approaching. We had organised a family reunion as a house-warming holiday—our two sons Antony and Richard coming from London where they worked, our daughter Fiona flying over with her two little boys from Sydney. It would be the first Christmas together for seven years. And everyone would be there for Audrey's birthday on 18 December. The day before that celebration I decided we should take the boys to see the Christmas lights at Gubbio, the beautiful Montefeltro hilltown in northern Umbria.

Every year, they string lights in the pine trees on the steep slopes of 800-metre high Mount Ingino behind the town to form a giant Christmas tree. From twenty kilometres away on the road from Perugia it stands out as if on the side of a skyscraper, and the locals claim it's the biggest Christmas tree in the world. The snows came early that year, and the ploughs had been clearing the roads. On the mountain, the branches of the pines bent almost double under their load made a pretty postcard. We drove to the top to look down on the town that is best known for the Iguvine tablets, the mysterious, two thousand year-old Etruscan writings on bronze; for the mediaeval Race of the Ceri that celebrates Gubbio's defeat of Perugia; and for the delightful legend of St Francis persuading the giant wolf that had been terrorising the people by taking their babies, to mend his ways.

'There's a house with no roof on it—and its full of snow', cried the boys in excitement. It was no house, but the Monastery of Saint Ubaldo, Gubbio's patron saint, and the cloistered courtyard was indeed deep in snow. Then followed a happy half-hour of Andrew and Alexander sliding down the snow-covered steps until they were tired and soaking wet. We wrapped them in rugs and carried them back to the car. Many wheels had packed the snow and nightfall had frozen it hard. With Alexander wriggling in her arms, Audrey slipped on the ice—she fell and he fell on her ankle. We were about to enter into our first horrendous experience of the Italian medical system.

Long afterwards, English friends told me their ski club had one golden rule—if you break anything, get across the border into Switzerland as fast as you can. And when Deborah Campagnola, Italy's crack woman skier tore her knee apart in a dreadful accident, she went to Lyons in France for her successful repairs. We soon found out why.

Gubbio has its hospital, but it's a long way from home. I reckoned that Perugia, which has two hospitals, one of them a university teaching hospital, would be a more sensible choice. It was a long drive back from Gubbio, and quite late at night when we arrived at the Perugia *Policlinico*. A quick inspection at Casualty, then into a little ambulance to be shuttled to the orthopaedic centre for plastering. By now the ankle had swollen considerably, and Audrey had taken off her shoe and stocking. Perugia has a significant drug problem, and more street crime than it would care to admit. The nurse detailed to go with her in the ambulance completely misread the situation.

'You should be ashamed of yourself, out without shoes—you're nothing but a street woman!'

This was scarcely a propitious beginning. A doctor set her ankle and we took her home in the early hours of her birthday morning. It was a bitter present and cast a gloom over the reunion. The family had never known their mother and grand-mother laid low. But it was only the beginning of a terrible week, made worse by our ignorance.

We didn't know it, but in setting the ankle, the doctor had twisted the foot and had applied the plaster too tightly. This cut off the blood supply, and caused a torturing agony that went on night and day. I'd had a fractured ankle, and knew that after the initial discomfort and shock, you should feel nothing. I just couldn't understand why there should be so much pain with what was only a simple fracture of the radial bone. We had followed the hospital's instructions to keep her resting with her foot elevated, and had dosed her with pain-killers, but by Christmas Day she could stand no more. I took her back to the *Policlinico*. It was bad timing. The hospital was virtually deserted for Christmas partying, there was nobody at all in the orthopaedic department. By the time I found a doctor, I was in no mood for polite conversation.

'That plaster must come off', I said. 'It's too tight and the pressure is causing her incredible pain.'

But the doctor had been celebrating, and began arguing that there was nothing wrong with it. The row that followed could easily have landed me in court on an assault charge, but he quickly saw how angry I was and gave in. He cut off the plaster, and applied a new cast. It was looser, and eased the pain, but he never thought to look further. If he had, he might have realised the damage that had been done.

A few weeks later the hospital called her back to add a *tacco* to the foot, a wooden heel on which she was supposed to hobble around. This added several more kilograms of plaster, so that now she could scarcely lift her leg. The situation was obviously absurd, so I took a saw and and cut the *tacco* off. Then with a rasp and a kitchen knife I started removing the excess layers of plaster to lighten the load. In a careless move, the knife slipped and I stabbed my hand. Too deeply for a bandaid, so into the car and off to the *Pronto Soccorso* at the hospital in Castiglione del Lago. A doctor patched the wound and gave me a tetanus shot, but clearly didn't believe my story. I could see him turning over in his mind whether he should call the *Carabinieri* to report a case of suspected domestic violence. A quick exit was indicated.

As soon as the holidays were over, friends arranged an appointment at a private clinic with one of the leading orthopaedic specialists in Perugia. He thought both the plasters had been too tight, and put on a third, but he too failed to recognise the problem that had been caused. Audrey was still in pain and by this time I was desperate to find what could have gone wrong. I took the latest X-ray, put it up against the window, and traced it as best I could onto a sheet of ordinary typing paper. Then I faxed it to Peter Heery, a doctor friend in Sydney. Peter had been a thoracic surgeon but was by then medical director of a leading pharmaceutical company. He knew everybody who was anybody in the profession, and took my faxed tracing to his best orthopaedic colleague.

Instantly came the reply: Sudeck's Syndrome, not uncommon in wrist fractures but rare in ankles. The blood supply had been cut off by the too-tight plaster, causing intense pain and then atrophying of ligaments and muscles. An Australian hospital would have used a light fibreglass splint for such a break, never a heavy plaster, said Peter. He advised me to get Audrey to an expert as quickly as possible.

I called the Australian Embassy in Rome, and followed its trail of advice to Dr Billi in the Quisisana private hospital. He took X-rays of both ankles for comparison. When he put them up on the screen, we were ready to prompt him, but he took one glance and turned to the young doctor with him. 'Here's a Sudeck's Syndrome', he said in Italian. We heard, and started to breathe easier. At last we had found someone who knew what he was doing. But there was another shock to come.

'The initial plastering caused an embolism in the leg', he said gently to my wife. 'You're lucky to be alive!'

By then it was July, seven months after the accident. We tried a lighter splint, many follow-up trips to Rome in the sweltering heat of August, and then a long course of magneto-therapy to try to get strength back into the ankle. It will never be right. As soon as I could get a moment, I sat down and wrote a brief note in my poor Italian to that doctor in Perugia masquerading as an orthopaedic specialist:

'On each of the four occasions you saw my wife', I said, 'you failed to detect the *atrofia sudeck* or the osteoporosis it caused. Your last advice that her problems were all in her mind and that she should go for long walks on the beach was therefore ludicrous. After seven months and much unnecessary suffering, she must now begin a new course of treatment. I am disappointed to have found such amateurism and incompet-ence in our first contact with Italian medicine.'

What gave me the greatest satisfaction was the certainty that with the Italians' exaggerated respect for authority, nobody had dared say anything like that to him before. And I thought of the piece of Roman graffiti scratched into stone at Ostia Antica, the old port of Rome at the mouth of the Tiber: '*Caca et declina medicus*'—'Shit well and avoid the doctors.' Maybe nothing much had changed in two thousand years.

Our misfortune had been to encounter the lowest level of medical practice, all too common in the provinces and light years away from the best Italian medical and surgical skills which are often world class. The gulf between the two was dramatically illustrated by the brush with death of our first friend in Paciano, Paolo Ascanio. We had come back to Italy to find him convalescing from an incredible operation in which surgeons had removed a tumour from his larynx that had been slowly choking him. This had involved cutting out a whole section of the trachea and lifting his lungs in the chest cavity by the same amount. For more than three months local doctors had insisted that his increasing difficulty in breathing was merely asthma. It was only a chance contact that led to his referral to a leading throat surgeon in Vittoria Veneto, six hundred kilometres to the north, who saved his life.

...

Paolo was born in Paciano and returned to live here when he retired from his business in the north. Handsome, with silver hair and perfect Italian olive skin, he and his wife Angela have done everything they could to make us welcome since we first met them on a walk in the Monte Pausillo National Park above our house. His mother, a little old lady who was remarkably unwrinkled but rather forgetful, still insisted on living on her own in the village centre. For a long time, she continued to make her special *alcoolico* liqueur of a hundred herbs. Paolo fortunately still has a stock of it, and it is just the thing to sip at bedtime after a heavy meal.

Paolo and Angela rented out half a dozen houses and apartments on the hillsides, part of the agritourism that has become so important to the economy of Umbria. They built a huge swimming pool on their hill, and we are always included in the family parties. In the long summer evenings we sit there and chat, enjoying the commanding view of the valley and watching the sun go down behind Montepulciano. Surely one of the best poolside outlooks in Italy.

It was Angela who asked me what we were going to do with our land. I really didn't know, except that I had ruled out vines. Our hillside faces north, with too little sun. In any case, grapes mean too much work and it seemed Italy already had more than enough wine. 'In that case', she said, 'I'll get *Zio* Carlo to help you'. Angela's uncle Carlo, then in his late seventies, had been an estate manager for some of the great *padroni* of the area. Although strictly not an Umbrian—he was born in Arezzo in Tuscany—there was nothing he didn't know about the district, its climate, soils, crops and practices. And he had a great fund of stories and local sayings to spice his advice.

Carlo is now very much the *padrone* himself, still planting olives on his own lands although he knows he may never see their oil. A sprightly little man with a great grin and his white hair still peppered with black, he'd been a tank commander in the war, fighting the Australians and British in the Libyan desert until captured at Tobruk. After the real war he returned home to Italy's civil war. It was the terrible interregnum between the Allied Military Government and the re-establishment of civil authority, he told me, that nobody wants to talk about today. The former communist partisans used the weapons they had been given by the Allies not only to take revenge on fascists but also to settle scores with the managerial classes. Between thirty and one hundred thousand people were killed in this time—nobody knows exactly how many. One day they came for Carlo. He wasn't home, so they shot his sister instead. When he did return, they said to him, 'You ought to thank God we killed your sister—or you wouldn't be alive today'.

Carlo warmed to me when he learned that I had ruled out vines; that was the right decision, he said. So it was to be olives. Perhaps he was a little flattered that Angela had given him the opportunity to demonstrate his knowledge to the *Australiani*, who knew nothing about local agriculture. I thought he was so polite, and too modest. 'If you would you be happy to put yourself in my hands', he said 'I will organise it all for you'. And that is how I came to have the best expert in the district teach me about *olivicoltura*.

4. Pigs and porcupines

That conversation with Carlo took place not long after we had arrived, before plaster and crutches became such an important part of our lives. First, Carlo ordered Ivo Santeroni, the *benzinaio* who ran the local garage and leased agricultural equipment to send up a heavy tractor with a ripper to plough up the *campo*. This, he explained, was necessary to break up the heavy clay, allowing the winter rains to penetrate deep into the soil. All through that winter the land lay in the rough. So rough that it was almost impossible to clamber over the huge clods of earth. Our little grandsons, who had been sent outside to play, disappeared like boats in the troughs of waves.

Late in February the following year, Carlo telephoned to say the time had come to plan the *oliveto*. He would come up in two days' time. It had been a bitter month. There were heavy snowfalls everywhere and much of Italy was stopped in its tracks. Lake Trasimeno froze over. Our hill was snowbound for two days, and we looked out over a biblical scene where only the farmhouses had any shape, and nothing moved.

A clean, sharp beauty. Suddenly the pristine silence was shattered as Francesco Montioni, our neighbour from Pietreto, revved his Fiat like a snowplough through the deep drifts, up to the front door. He was not concerned for our safety but for the stocks in our larder.

'Have you got pasta, wine and bread?' he called up.

I noted the order of the items as I responded, '*Si, tutti* OK!'.

Francesco was then a *Carabinieri* officer. He is the nearest thing to an Australian larrikin it would be possible to find in Italy, and apparently his commanding officers thought so too. He told me he had always been 'a bit of a problem' for the force, and when he over-stepped the mark once too often had been sent to Sardinia. That was proof enough—Sardinia is a hardship posting. Policemen spend dangerous weeks hunting bandits and kidnappers in the impossible jagged interior, where the islanders still refer to Italy as 'the mainland'.

I say he was then in the *Carabinieri*, but he was already preparing for his early retirement. Every year he had himself admitted to a clinic for 'de-stressing'; eventually the weight of medical evidence was so great he was declared unfit. Francesco joined the growing ranks of the so-called 'baby pensioners', Italians who wangle early retirement on a reduced pension to do something else more profitable.

Francesco is also that very un-Italian identity—a handyman. He has a magnificent workshop equipped with professional cabinet-makers' machinery he bought for a song at a bankrupt's sale. He re-built his own house, and excavated a huge underground cellar where he makes his own wine. He

helped his wife Giuseppina operate the little *ristorante/pensione*
the *Comune* established; he is gregarious, hospitable and loyal;
and, a relic of his *Carabinieri* days, he is the fastest, most dangerous driver in the district.

Because nearly everything on our property is on a slope, the
one thing I had known would be useful was some sort of sur-
veying instrument, to check levels and measure the falls. I
couldn't afford a theodolite or even a builder's dumpy level,
but a Sydney company which supplies surveyors came to my
rescue. They recommended, and sold me quite cheaply, a simple
levelling device. In essence, it is a small brass telescope, with
a split field and a bubble to make sure it is set perfectly
horizontal. It is accurate to plus or minus seventy-five millimetres (three inches) over distances up to one hundred
metres, enough for my purposes. I mounted it on my camera
tripod at the top corner of the *campo* and sent Audrey off with
a home-made surveyor's staff improvised from two lengths
of aluminium lashed together, and marked every seventy-five
millimetres with white tape.

While I sighted through my little telescope, she worked her
way across the *campo*, stopping every few metres to move
towards me or to back away until I established places that were
all pretty well on the same level. Marking each spot with a twig,
we succeeded in this way in defining a key contour line across
the property. I had arranged the measurements so that this line
ran through the one remaining old olive tree in the field.

All this was done the day before *Zio* Carlo was due to set
out the *oliveto*, and I have to admit I was very pleased with

myself. But when I explained my idea to plant the olive rows along the contour lines, Carlo's face darkened and he seemed to become much less friendly.

'No! The olives must be planted in rows at right angles to the back boundary.'

There was no fence, but an ancient *fosso*, a ditch that drained flood runoff from the road above, marked the limit to our property.

'No', I retorted in return, really fearful that he would get back in his little truck and go home, but deciding to stand firm. 'I want the lines angled across the *campo* to avoid erosion.'

'Pfuff' came back in reply. It's not in the Italian dictionary, but I recognised the tone. 'Nonsense—the hillside isn't steep enough to need terracing!'

'Anyway', I hurried on, 'we want it angled so we don't have to look straight up the spaces between the olive rows from the house...for aesthetic reasons'.

At the Italian word *estetica*, Carlo threw up his hands. As we were to learn, nobody, but nobody in this part of Italy would think of doing anything on a farm for *ragione d'estetica*. In any case, Italians are all about style and fashion, which they can display. Aesthetics and taste are mere heady abstractions for philosophers, of no relevance.

'*Allora!*...Well', said *Zio* Carlo, waving his walking stick at me, but with a twinkle in his eye and a kindly expression to indicate he was humouring an idiot. 'We will do it your way.' And from his repertoire of proverbs he plucked this bon mot:

'*Legarsi l'asino dove sempre vuole padrone!*'—'The ass is bound to follow the wishes of his master!'

And so we set off to design the grid. Much later, I learned the reason for *Zio* Carlo's opposition. Everyone in the district would know he had laid out the *oliveto*. As ignorant foreigners we couldn't be blamed, but they would laugh at him if it wasn't done right. And right, in this district at least, meant a neat rigid order, with rows at right angles to the boundary.

Compared with my little theodolite, Carlo's instruments could only be described as primitive. He had brought two of the big old hand-made Italian bricks, each thirty centimetres long, a builder's measuring tape, and a bundle of olive branches. Stripped of their leaves, these had been gathered from his annual pruning, just completed. He looked at the field and decided that the trees should be planted on a five-metre square grid.

Obediently starting from my contour line in the middle of the field, he put the two bricks on the ground, one on top of the other, but at right angles to each other. Then as he carefully sighted along one of the bricks, he had me run the measuring tape out to twenty-five metres. At that spot I was instructed to put a branch in the ground. Next, working back towards him, I marked each five-metre interval with a branch. The same operation was repeated on the other arm of the right angle, Carlo sighting along the second brick while I ran out the tape. This time, before we put in the intermediate markers, he checked the squareness by measuring the hypotenuse of the triangle. His eye, of course, was dead true.

From there it was a simple matter to fill in the square, which gave us the positions for the first thirty-six trees. We had space for more, so the horizontal and vertical rows were extended, leaving an adequate clearance between the last tree in a row and the boundary. When we finished, there were fifty markers in the ground, in seven rows. Carlo was not really happy that some rows had more than others, but this was unavoidable, because of my perverse insistence on angling the whole layout to conform to the contours. As an engineer friend later observed, it was like a computer spreadsheet, in columns and rows. In fact I had already decided to identify each tree in just this way—as B4, D6, and so on—so I could log its progress, and later, I hoped, record its yield.

Below the *oliveto*, I had kept space for a small orchard, and we then laid out another twenty spaces for the fruit trees. That was all for the first stage. Carlo went off to organise Santeroni's excavator, and to order a load of chestnut *pali* to stake the trees—jobs for the next month.

March is the pivotal month of the farming year in Umbria. The pithy sayings of the *contadino*, more potted wisdom than proverb, emphasise that just how the countryside comes out of its winter sleep in March determines the success of the agricultural year. It's an unpredictable month, not yet spring:

Marzo pazzarello
Guarda il sole e prendi l'ombrello

which I translate as:

March is a giddy fella
Look for the sun but take an umbrella.

In fact the district hopes for a dry month to develop the roots of fruit trees, olives and the autumn-sown grain. Too much rain in March sends growth into the stems and stalks; when it's needed is in April.

It's the season when the migratory birds may start to make their re-appearance. Our English proverb, 'One swallow doesn't make a summer', runs right through Italian folklore. It appears even in Dante, who himself took it from Aristotle. Do the English still write to *The Times* to boast of the first cuckoo of Spring? I've never seen it reported in Italian newspapers, but I do know that my neighbours listen keenly for the distinctive *'cu-cu'* of the male, and the answering *'cucucuc'* of his mate. They say that if the cuckoo arrives as early as March it is a sure sign of a bounteous season. In the past, this meant the *padrone* would need every man for the harvest, so what better time to negotiate a new contract?

Canta il cuculo sulla quercia nera
ricordati padrone che è primavera.
The cuckoo is singing in the black oak tree
Springtime, Master—what's in it for me?

Santeroni's chief tractor operator is Celestino. I have never learned his first name, but his *cognome*, meaning 'sky blue', perfectly fits his cheerful disposition. He's also one of the best plant operators in the district, handling everything from crawler tractors to harvesters with the dexterity of a Rome *scooterista*.

Celestino, with his *scavatore* (which we would call a backhoe), was to dig the holes for the trees. As he positioned the machine on its hydraulic feet, I removed the marker twig and he then dug a hole about a metre in diameter and a metre-and-a-half deep. The heavy excavated soil was turned over and broken up, and the bucket swept it back into the hole. Seventy holes took seven hours. Carlo said not many people bothered to do this, but assured me that at a cost of about three hundred dollars, I had made the best possible preparation for the roots of the little olives.

The next day he took me shopping for our trees. Where could you find nurserymen more appropriately named than the Margheritis, Enzo and Mario—the Daisy brothers! Everyone in the district knows the Margheritis, but most new-comers like us know only their sprawling retail nursery not far from Lake Chiusi, exactly on the border of Umbria and Tuscany. Seven hundred years ago warring Perugia and Siena confronted each other at this very spot. The Sienese built a watchtower which they named, provocatively, 'Beccati Questo' ('Look at this one!'). On their side of the line the Perugians built a bigger and higher one. From its battlements they called down 'Beccati Quest'altro' ('Get a load of this one then!'). The towers stand there today. Quest'altro is cracked from top to bottom, and notices warn visitors of the danger of falling masonry; Questo is intact but has sunk so far into the clay of the plain that it looks ridiculously puny.

In his managerial days Carlo had bought thousands of trees from the Margheritis, so we headed straight for their wholesale nursery at Monte S. Paolo. We had a good bargainer. For once I was the padrone with nothing to do but watch. Carlo buying the olives was a piece of rural theatre I would not have missed. First there was a long discussion with Enzo about the best age. He decided on three-year-old trees which cost a little more than younger plants, but were advanced enough to start producing in a few years. And at that size, about a metre-and-a-half high, he could better spot any weaklings. I nodded approval, not from any knowledge but because I was paying. Then the varieties. Of course these must be equally divided between the three main types in Umbria—*Frantoio*, *Leccino* and *Moraiolo*, with one *Pendolino* for cross-fertilising. He carefully vetted every plant that was offered.

We moved on to choose for the orchard—apricot, apple, fig, plum, cherry, hazelnut, pear, walnut. As Enzo pulled the pathetic nude-rooted sticks from the loose soil then cut them back savagely with his secateurs, I wondered how they would ever grow into fruit trees. All this time, the first skirmishings on price were under way. There was Carlo's past business to take into account, he reminded Margheriti, and then the honour due to the adventurous Australian who had come all this way to buy his plants. The bargaining went on and on, most of it unintelligible to me, but by the time all the plants were securely lashed down in Carlo's little truck, agreement had been reached. Fourteen thousand lire each for the olives, seven for the fruits. These were good prices, I learned later, and more importantly, they were quality trees.

After all this build-up, the planting was almost anticlimactic. Carlo arrived a few days later with two of the *operai* who tended his olives. Quintilio Truccolo (whom everyone calls Aldo) worked for the *Comune* in the mornings but his afternoons were free to do casual farming work at ten thousand lire an hour. He was in such demand that a few years later he took the pension to work solely for local landowners.

Aldo and his brother Ivo rammed the stakes into the softened earth by hand, scratched a small hole and tamped each slim olive tree into place. It took them only two hours. I had thought I was smart to have bought a bundle of the green plastic *macaroni* I had seen in the hardware shops to tie the trees, but Aldo would have none of it. He had come with the genuine article—thin branches of weeping willow, still green and supple. Twice around the stake and tree, then tied off with a half bow. It might have been authentically traditional, but after two years the willow ties dried, rotted and fell off. I had to replace them with the plastic. It's elastic, kinder to the tree and lasts much longer. Sometimes, I reflected, as I laboriously worked my way around the fifty trees, cutting and tying, industrial society can offer advantages.

My instructions were to give each tree two buckets of water the next morning, and then leave them to fend for themselves. *Zio* Carlo had given us a hefty push-start, but I didn't want to have to rely on him. Being thrown in at the deep end, as it were, makes one even more determined to swim. I thought we might just be able to dog paddle. I remembered gardening programmes on Australian radio saying that whatever care you give to a tree in the first three years will determine its success in life. We had brought up children—it made sense. All I had to do was understand the climate.

Lake Trasimeno is the largest lake on the Italian peninsula, about fifty kilometres around. Being shut in by hills up to five hundred metres high on three sides produces a large number of microclimates, and at Varacca we had drawn one with the lowest rainfall. I can always stand and watch it raining somewhere else. Three hundred and fifty to four hundred millimetres (fourteen to sixteen inches) a year is merino sheep country to an Australian. Now factor in that most of it falls in autumn and winter, and that summer temperatures can easily be in the mid to high thirties. I might be living in Umbria, 'the Green Heart of Italy' as the tourist brochures boast, but it was clear we had bought a damned dry patch of it.

The obvious conclusion to be drawn from this brief meteorological analysis was that a lot of watering would be necessary to nurse those trees. We had put down a well when the house was restored, because the *Comune* was running about three years late with its promise to connect a town supply. It had served all our household purposes adequately, but I didn't know how much would be left over for the garden. The *pozzo* wasn't really a well, but a bore tapping an underground acquifer. Italian has only one word for both well and bore, so I have become lazy. There is a submersible pump at the bottom and a pressure switch turns it on when someone opens a tap. Exactly as in many parts of rural Australia.

The drilling of the well had seen a clash of technologies. The law required a geologist's report to back up the application for permission to drill. This was an impressive, costly and useless document, like so many demanded by the Italian bureaucracy.

It described in textbook detail the underlying formations of shaly marl dating from the Oligocene/Miocene epoch, and buttressed this with geological and section maps, indicating where water was to be found. The driller David Newman hired, Alberto Barbanera (Blackbeard) took one look at it and spat. Then he took out his olive twig and chose his own spot. When he cased and perforated the well at a depth of thirty metres he had a fourteen-metre column of water in it.

For those first few years, this was just enough. But a couple of dry winters, and the extra load of another two hundred hedging trees and shrubs we planted brought the well to its knees. When the communal water became available, I decided it would be foolish not to connect to it to guarantee the house supply. All the well water could be kept for the garden.

All through the summer months, my wife and I carried buckets to the trees, or stood with a hose measuring two precious minutes of water to each. They thrived. But much else was happening. With Audrey still on crutches, we together levelled and gravelled the rear terrace of one hundred square metres by hand; carted disused railway sleepers to make steps and borders; dug out blackberry infestations and erected the rotary clothes line. A Hill's Hoist in Umbria? The neighbours hang their washing on the fence, and had never seen anything like it. When we folded it down, a jangle of green tubes and yellow lines, I teased them that it doubled as a plastic Christmas tree, but I don't think they really believed me.

The biggest job was clearing thousands of stones from the *campo*. The largest rocks the plough had turned up had to be levered out, so I went to buy a crowbar at the hardware store. Language problem! I had forgotten to look up the dictionary before heading for the *ferramenta*. I knew the word for crow was *cornacchia*, but trying *'barre di cornacchia'* produced blank looks, and then embarrassed giggles. Had I inadvertently hit on a risque phrase? Could a crow be idiomatically erotic? We solved the problem with a tour of the tool racks. A crowbar is a *'piede di porco'* or pig's foot. Not so silly—one end of an Italian crowbar has two toes and a heel, to give more purchase.

Like me, farmers used to wonder why stones kept coming to the surface in their fields. I remember reading somewhere that Australian scientists who studied this trivial mystery found that they didn't—soil and smaller stones in fact worked their way down. But after centuries of watching stones come to the surface, and with piles of rocks at the edges of their fields to prove it, nobody around here is going to believe it happens any other way. There's an ancient proverb that says Italy is sixty per cent clay and forty per cent misery. After labouring for weeks to clean up the land, I told our village friends that our land was forty per cent clay, twenty per cent stones and sixty per cent misery.

'But that's more than 100%!' they exclaimed.

'You're right—that's Varacca' I replied.

Zio Carlo had arranged that Celestino would come with his crawler tractor and disc harrow twice a year to keep the *oliveto* tilled. Even so, the area around each tree had to be kept clean, and that, in local practice, has always been a job for the *zappa*. The word has passed into English slang, I suspect after the comic strip sci-fi writers discovered its power and economy to shoot down space ships. Now with our remote controls we can even zap a television program we don't like. And to complete the circle of linguistic borrowing, one Italian magazine calls its TV program guide *Zapping*.

The *zappa* is nothing more than a hoe. In mediaeval times it was the *contadino's* only defensive weapon; razor sharp, it could slice off an arm or even a head, if he could get close enough. Besides the plough, the cart and the hay fork, it was virtually his only agricultural implement. It could be square, long and thin, fan-shaped, heart-shaped, pointed, two-pronged, four-pronged or double-ended. In Tuscany it was known as a *zappone* or *zappetta*; in Sicily it's a *zappudda*; in other regions a *zappino* or *zappello*. The handles too had different names in dialect, their length ranging from nearly two metres in the north to seventy centimetres in the south.

Carmela and Zeno are weekend neighbours. He has his glazier's workshop in one of the historic back streets of Florence, but escapes the oppressive climate of that city to till his vegetables and olives in our clear air. Carmela grew up in Puglia, where the *zappa* handles are very short. One summer evening when we were enjoying a bottle of Trasimeno white in the garden, she explained why:

'*Lo zappatore che ha il naso sulla terra non ha tempo di guardar intorno e lavora di più.*'

Nose to the grindstone! With a short handle and bent back the *contadino* couldn't look around, so more work got done for the *padrone*.

I started with the standard local *zappa*, its blade longer than it is wide, but later bought a four-pronged implement because it was better for weeding around trees without damaging their surface roots. I then found a lighter type for Audrey, ideal for cultivating around her shrubs. In the fancy gardening sections of the big supermarkets, there are now designer models. Don't be fooled—they are all hard work.

With the *Campo* tamed and the olives settled in, there was time now to think about establishing a garden. I had learned very early on that of the two possible planting seasons, autumn is much to be preferred to early spring for planting trees and shrubs. The root systems are kept moist through the cool wet winter, allowing the plant to adjust comfortably to its new environment, and ready itself for spring growth. However we could not really afford to wait six months for the perfect season. It would mean much more careful nurturing. The local practice is to sell trees 'in zolla'. It's a clay ball around the roots, which have been cut back severely. The root ball is then enclosed in a netting bag, retaining the clay soil for the move but easily cut away when planting.

For bushes and young trees the ball is normally about twenty centimetres in diameter. When we came to plant our *Magnolia Grandiflora*, however, it was already three metres tall and its roots were in a half-metre sphere of heavy clay. It was so heavy it had to be unloaded by crane, but the truck couldn't get within twenty metres of the hole we had dug. The ball was like a big wheel, so the nurseryman and I rolled it to the hole and just plopped it in.

We had set ourselves a hectic planting program. From the beginning we had decided we needed to hedge our long frontage to the communal road, for privacy and to control the dust which boiled up from every passing car. I calculated we needed one hundred trees. This was going to be expensive, until we learned that the *Comunità Montana* in Perugia had tree nurseries that sold seedlings cheaply to encourage mass planting. At four hundred lire (forty cents) a tree, the hundred cost us only forty Australian dollars. Most locals plant the hardy blue-green Arizona cypress, but we chose *Cupressus Macrocarpa*, the Monterey cypress. We liked its dark green foliage and needed the benefit of its quicker growth.

I had brought a post-hole digger which made planting easier in some places, but in others there was so much rock that the crowbar was the only suitable tool. In the back corner, beyond the orchard went a *Cedrus Deodara* (the Indian cedar with the floppy top that is so popular in Umbria), some golden Leyland cypresses and a couple of willows to soak up the excess water when it rained. In all, more than three hundred trees, and as each fragile plant was staked and tied, the watering commitment grew.

Jasmines are of the same family as olives, so they stand up well to our climatic extremes. We had also noted that oleanders grew well in the district; they went into the north-facing bed at the end of the house, while the jasmine was a perfect climber for the posts of the *terrazza*. Over time the three plants have taken over the huge beams, and developed into a perfumed frieze the entire length of the house.

For the sloping bank between the house and the garage, we had decided on junipers, because they are so hardy. I didn't know just how hardy they had to be until we came to plant them. Each of the fourteen holes took two hours or more to dig with crowbar, hammer and rock chisel. There was no top-soil, so I had to excavate a virtual pot in the rock big enough to sustain them until their roots would be strong enough to prise their own way through the strata.

Immediately in front of the house, but on the other side of the road, we owned a small strip of land. There we wanted to plant thirty golden Leyland cypresses, but the rock shelf was too much for my muscles. It was time to call for Celestino with his excavator to dig a trench. It turned out to be a little larger than I had envisaged, half-a-metre wide and a metre deep, so I needed a fifteen-tonne load of so-called *buon terreno* to fill it. The 'good earth' is really only a lighter style of clayey loam, but it's the nearest thing to topsoil available. The contractor delivered it in the morning and promised to return with his mechanical loader to fill the trench in the afternoon. He failed to appear. The trees had already been waiting for several days and had to be planted. There was nothing else for it but to dump the soil ourselves. It took all afternoon and all the next morning—more than four-hundred wheelbarrow loads.

As in all country areas, every family in Paciano must grow its own vegetables and everyone was waiting to see what our *orto* could produce. That first year we had planted *pomodori* (tomatoes), with basil plants at the end of the row to deter insects, zucchini, spinach, *melanzane* (aubergines) and *peperoni* (capsicum); we already had a number of *carciofi* (artichokes), and we had brought some 'Baby Sweet' watermelon seeds with us. In virgin soil, with our inexperience but much tender loving care, they all thrived. The first problem as the fruit began to ripen was midnight attacks by the *istrici*, the giant porcupines—they just loved the tomatoes. In the past, a *contadino* would have killed them, plucked their quills, cooked and eaten them, but now they are a protected species. I defeated them by flattening the cardboard packing boxes saved from our move and stacking them around the plants every night.

With all the weeding, fertilising and quantities of precious well water, the *orto* could hardly have failed. The return, in produce, was overwhelming. There was ten times as much as we could eat, but everyone else had a glut too, and I couldn't give the stuff away. But the real test would be the watermelons. It seemed that Pacianese buy watermelons, never attempting to grow them, so it was going to be a matter of pride to show them how to do it.

Our nearest neighbour Cerimonia (who never failed to proffer advice, even if he had no experience) told me that *cocomeri* must not be picked before August 15, the Feast of the Assumption. That coincides with *Ferragosto*, the public holiday marking the mid-point of August. That year, the sun over Italy was blood-red from the dust of the Mount Pinatubo eruption in the Philippines—was it an omen? The morning of the 16th I went out to discover that the biggest and best watermelon was gone. Thirty metres away, amongst the fruit trees, I found its remains. In the night, wild pigs had torn it from the vine, wrestled it into the *campo*, smashed it open with tusk and hoof—and devoured the beautiful cool fruit. It was impressive that Paciano pigs knew their calendar of feast days, but little consolation. A dozen other watermelons were ripe, so to frustrate the pigs I picked and stacked them like cannonballs for photographic proof, and gave most of them away.

It is not always apparent to city people like us who are attracted to the country that they may find themselves living close to parts of nature that are not so agreeable. For example, we had been warned about rats and mice. David Newman had some horror stories of huge field rats coming down chimneys and eating half a house's furnishings in the months the owners were away. As soon as we arrived I had bought wire mesh and closed off our chimneys, but I had not reckoned on dealing with pigs and porcupines.

The following year, I bought a hundred metres of plastic fencing and enclosed the entire vegetable garden. By this time we were also growing beans, carrots and beetroot. I also installed a miniature spray irrigation system controlled at the tap by a timer, so we didn't have to water by hand, and could ration supplies precisely. It was becoming obvious, however, that for the longer term, the property would have to be fenced. The land was, of course, all properly defined and described in the land registry in Perugia but, in line with common practice, we had bought without a ground survey being done or the boundaries being pegged. Outside the town itself, few people fenced. But I discovered that since Italy had no trespass laws, people as well as pigs were free to wander all over our land.

I turned to Gabriele Tomassoni, the Comune's *geometra*, who had handled all our plans and submissions. Tomassoni was employed there as technical officer only a few days a week; the rest of the time he was free for private practice. The two roles frequently overlapped, however, and this could cause some difficulties. He was constantly behind with his official work, and had the most inventive mind for excuses I have ever encountered. Short bald and rotund, Tomassoni didn't talk, he gabbled, and I was constantly asking him to slow down. '*Piano! piano!*' I would interrupt every time we had a conversation, but he never learned to accommodate himself to my slow ears. As well as being the only professional employee, he was an oddity in being the only Christian Democrat supporter employed by a completely Communist council. I never detected any overt signs of friction, but have always had an uneasy feeling that the political differences may have contributed to the delays we experienced.

The very function of *geometra* is a postwar invention and, as Tomassoni explained it to me, came about in a typically Italian way. By the early 1970s the extent of illegal building throughout the country had reached crisis proportions. '*Abusivo*' development began immediately after the war, taking advantage of the destruction of many land registers and the blurring of property boundaries in the rubble left by bombing. But over time it became just another evasion, a way of life so entrenched, so widespread, that local authorities were powerless to combat it. The government of the day hit on a way to simultaneously regularise the situation and garner more revenue. The solution was borrowed straight from the Church of Rome—confession, a penalty for expiation of the sin, then absolution. It was a formula everyone could understand, and it was called 'il condono'.

It was one thing to grant forgiveness, but the land registers still had to be put in order. A new professional role, the 'geometra' was created to carry out the hundreds of thousands of surveys needed. Part-surveyor, part-engineer, part-architect, part-lawyer, the geometra spans all these disciplines though he is not any one of them. He is permitted to design domestic buildings up to a certain size, but is more a draftsman than an architect. And every council must have one—a sort of down-market shire or borough engineer. For the first condono, the government granted an amnesty period of twelve months to have surveys done and submit applications. The inevitable Italian result? Frantic building activity to get as much abusivo development as possible done before the deadline.

Tomassoni undertook to do my survey, but it was some two months before he started. I had imagined he was qualified and equipped to do it himself, but no. On my behalf he engaged Adriano Lucarelli, a professional surveyor who was employed by the Trasimeno Co-operative Society. His work in the afternoons was 'moonlighting', using the Society's instrument. It was amusing to find that Tomassoni was only his assistant and had to do all the running around with the measuring staff. Lucarelli brought the very latest technology to the job. His laser theodolite flashed a pulse of light that was reflected back from a small mirror on the staff. A computer in the instrument instantly timed the bounce, calculated angle, elevation and distance, and displayed them on a little screen. All Lucarelli had to do was jot down the readings in his field book.

Watching him work, I suddenly realised that in this district I had never seen a 'trig point'—those fixed markers on hill-tops which our surveyors use as reference points to work out just where they are on the map.

'We don't need them', Lucarelli explained. 'See that steeple at Sanfatuccio over there? That's the parish church of San Felice Papa…It's been there for a few hundred years, and we know exactly where it is on the Italian grid. All I have to do is to measure the distance and the angle from the cross, and I have my precise position. By pressing this button, and in less than a second.' Laser beams, computers and Renaissance steeples— a powerful combination! What if Michelangelo had had Lucarelli's little box to help him, I wondered. But then would the dome of St Peter's be any more perfect?

The laser theodolite might be quick, but it was another three months before Lucarelli and Tomassoni returned to drive the pegs. I paid the fee, but never did get the plan of the survey.

. . .

I was still finding my way with the local Pacianese, friendly enough but reticent with strangers, as country folk usually are. About this time, we were driving out of town when Audrey spotted a woman's handbag in the middle of the road. It was easy to guess what had happened—she had driven out with the bag on the roof and it had been flung off at the first bend.

We identified Anna Guazzeroni from her driving licence. She had obviously been on her way to pay some accounts; in her purse were about seven hundred thousand lire in cash, and bills for the electricity and telephone. We didn't know the name, but traced her to the hamlet of Mazzarelli not a kilometre away. Anna had missed her handbag at the post office, and returned home in a panic, hoping to find it there. She might have found it on the road herself, but we had come along in the meantime.

After those heart-stopping moments, there were effusive thanks; the neighbours joining in the congratulations and the relief. We thought no more of it. But later that day we had a visit from the Guazzeronis. Anna and her husband came with two bottles of their own wine and a plastic bag containing a live cockerel. No matter that with no fowlyard we had to give the cockerel away, and that the home-made wine was undrinkable and went down the sink. The gesture was the important thing, and we learned that at least in this area, no good turn must go unrequited.

After much prodding, the *Comune* was moving the road. The rough track was cut on the Biavati's hillside with a bulldozer, then trucks began dumping demolition rubble for the roadbase. When the time came to spread and roll it, an expert came from Perugia to define the new line. No survey, no pegs. Just two sweeps of his arm—one vertically to show the direction, then one horizontally to indicate the finished level. Which is how the new road came to be two metres on our land, an error never officially admitted.

It would be an enormous relief not to have the traffic passing within a metre or two of the house. We had never got used to the truck drivers pausing outside to stare down from their cabs into the dining room. We had got tired of picking up their discarded cigarette packets. The dust their vehicles stirred up penetrated everywhere, making housekeeping a misery.

However, it was taking some time for drivers to learn to use the new road because the *Comune* failed to put up any direction signs. For about two hundred metres, there were now two parallel roads ten to fifteen metres apart. We found ourselves on a sort of railway loop line, with traffic passing on either track according to whim. We had to put a stop to it. After all, under our purchase agreement, the area was to revert to us when the new road was made. I called Santeroni to send up Celestino with his excavator. Directly in front of the house, where the old road had sloped downhill, he cut a level terrace. Any car now coming up past the house found itself facing a bank about half a metre high. There was nothing to do but curse and reverse. Simple, but effective. The traffic stopped immediately.

One night many weeks later, we jumped up from the dinner table at the sound of an almighty crash outside. Our neighbour up the hill, Maria Novella Boccioli had forgotten about the new road and our terracing of the old one, and had driven into space over our embankment. She was surprised but unhurt, which was fortunate, since she never used a seat belt. Her little four-wheel-drive Panda was unbroken, a credit to Fiat car building.

On the subject of cars, it was time to register ours. First, back to Luigi Pecetti to handle the delicate matter of paying the IVA. This was a Customs responsibility, so off to the *Dogana* we went. Luigi wanted a quick word with me as to what the car was worth. He looked at the leather seats, the air-conditioning, the radio and raised his eyebrows. I tried to explain honestly what it had cost, but he waved me to silence. 'Leave all this to me', he said. 'Whatever happens, don't say a word!'

He marched into the office of the *Capo* and stood over him.

'This man is a foreigner, an Australian', he announced. 'Unlike some people, he has come here voluntarily, honestly, to offer to pay his tax on his car, not just drive it around until he is caught. Now this is what I propose we do.'

Shamelessly, Luigi then put forward a preposterously low figure. I had to look out the window not to give it all away. The *Capo* knew he was being sandbagged, but what the hell! Nobody would criticise him for collecting three or four million lire!

I was turned over to the second in command. I said *'buon giorno'* politely and waited while he applied nine(!) stamps to the document Luigi had prepared. He took it ten paces to his colleague at the other end of the room, who added another five, before it was handed back to me. I said *'buon giorno'* again, got up and left. They were the only four words uttered in the room in the ten minutes.

The actual registration of the car took another six months to accomplish, but that saga is far too long, too complicated, and too painful to recount.

5. Whales come to Umbria

Whales are probably the last thing one would expect to find in a hilltown in Umbria, one of the only two landlocked regions of Italy. But soon after we arrived, I found that whales were big news in Paciano. The little town had been promised a whale museum and, as a result, there is a now a link, through the early whalers, with a community on the other side of the world. To explain such unlikely events involves going back several steps.

Everyone knows David McTaggart as the founder of Greenpeace International. Many might not know that the 'hard-drinking workaholic', as *Time* magazine once described him, had semi-retired to Paciano, where he is now a neighbour of ours, also living in a restored farmhouse, a stone's throw away across the gully. In a continuous strip around the walls of his lounge room hang a series of enlarged photographs. They are action photos, many of them blurred in their haste and the excitement of danger. The French commandos are there jumping aboard his yacht, the *Vega*, wrestling with crew members in the cockpit, punching, bludgeoning, arresting. It was the bloody outcome to his first attempt, in the early 1970s, to protest against French nuclear tests on Mururoa Atoll in the South Pacific. 'Those photos shouldn't exist', he told me one night at a party in his house. Outside it was freezing, but deep in the soft sofas in front of the big log fire it was cozy. McTaggart is a taciturn man—either shy or canny, I've never been sure which—so it came as quite a surprise when he confided:

'The commandos thought they had thrown every camera overboard, but one crew member in the bow filmed the whole thing, and hid the cassette. The film proved the official French version of events was a lie.'

More than twenty years later, the resumption of French tests took him away from his olives, back to the Pacific, back into the news with an identical protest and an identical outcome. He was bashed again.

'This time they really would have liked to have killed me.'

In the years between his Pacific nuclear protests, he had led the international campaign against whaling. One of the experts he used for scientific backup was Giorgio Pilleri, a zoologist in Berne University in Switzerland. Giorgio's work on marine mammals had, as he puts it, 'dropped the bomb' on porpoise pools, by proving that dolphins' brains atrophied while in captivity. When Giorgio decided to retire, David McTaggart persuaded him to come to live in Paciano too, and to bring his entire collection of research material and specimens, gathered over thirty years, with him. The Umbria regional administration agreed to buy the empty and derelict *Palazzo Baldeschi* for conversion into a natural history museum. Giorgio's whales and dolphins would be the centrepiece. Everyone was enthusiastic—Italy has three thousand five hundred museums, with the concentration on art and archeology, but the country is woefully deficient in natural history collections.

My wife and I had lived for ten years and more in Mosman, the beautiful Sydney harbourside suburb that had been founded by Archibald Mosman in the early 1830s as the site of his whaling station. Whales harpooned as they made their seasonal journey along the Australian east coast were towed into Mosman Bay and rendered down. The infant industry collapsed after eighteen years, and today nothing remains of Mosman's whaling station but some iron ringbolts set in rocks around the shoreline of the bay—once used in hauling his ships over for careening—and his flagpole, high above the modern ferry wharf. If Paciano were going to have this improbable interest in whales, I reasoned, why not go further, and link it with a municipality which proudly proclaims its origins through the display of a whale symbol on its coat of arms? Other towns and villages in the area had sister cities around the world—why not Paciano?

Il Sindaco, Alfonso del Buono, was immediately enthusiastic, and so was the then Mayor of Mosman, Domenico (Dom) Lopez, when I took the proposal back on my next trip to Australia. As his first name suggests, Dom is a second generation Italo–Australian; his family village is in the Aolian islands, off Sicily.

The connection between the two municipalities is a modest one. I carry presentations of books and historic photographs back and forth, the link persuades tourists to visit a pretty little town off the beaten track, and we have now established a cultural exchange between schools. Neither council can afford to send a goodwill delegation halfway around the world, so I have to remain the *Ambasciatore Onorario* for both.

The natural history museum, alas, fell into the same bureaucratic black hole as our road. After spending an initial grant of nearly two hundred million lire to repair the roof of the *Palazzo Baldeschi*, official enthusiasm evaporated, and the politicking began. The Umbrian administrators jibbed at finding more money to finish the building; both Perugia and Florence tried to capture the Pilleri collection for their own museums. Giorgio would come and sit on our terrace, sip a whisky and take a pinch of snuff while he poured out his troubles. With his white hair and bristly white beard, he looked every inch the scientist. He's a stocky northerner, originally from Trieste, and can't understand the lax ways of this area.

'Giorgio', I would say to him, 'your problem is you spent too long in efficient Switzerland'.

But after ten years pleading and waiting, he became so furious and frustrated he gave the entire collection away to museums in Germany and Switzerland. No whales for Paciano—the *Palazzo Baldeschi* is a now a white elephant.

Giorgio had a head full of dreams—of extending the collection to the flora and fauna of Umbria. He envisaged children coming from all over the country to see, feel and learn.

He would have liked to extend its appeal by including Australian marsupials and I had made contact for him with appropriate zoos and museums. But like so many good ideas in Italy, it turned to dust between the fingers of politicians.

It was Giorgio and his Swiss wife Rosa who introduced us to the venerable Roman practice of thermal bathing. As it lies in a volcanic zone, Italy is dotted with thermal springs, mud pools and mineralised water sources, but I had never thought of trying them. I wouldn't have had to go far. Chianciano Terme, one of the most popular spa towns in Italy, is so close we can see the lights twinkling along the skyline at night. It has two hundred and fifty hotels, and draws bathers from all over Europe to take the liver cure. Just outside the town, archeologists have unearthed the cold-water baths they believe the Emperor Augustus used.

To drive into Chianciano is a startling contrast—boulevards with luxury boutique shopping on the hills only a stone's throw from peasant farms below. But Giorgio doesn't go to Chianciano. He discovered a hot spring bath that was once the private preserve of a Roman villa, and he let us into the secret. It's out in the open air, in a little grove of pines and acacias, and it's absolutely free.

Just outside the walls of San Casciano dei Bagni (its mediaeval name defines its therapeutic reputation) a narrow dirt track plunges steeply into the valley. Farming land flanks it on either side, an up-coming tractor may well threaten the car around the next bend. Almost at the bottom a sulphur spring gushes from a mud pond and feeds a group of three shallow pools before coursing downhill to find the River Paglia.

Giorgio and Rosa first took us there in the autumn. The steam was rising into the morning air, and we shivered as we slipped out of our bath robes. The main bath is about seven metres by three, with the outlet level set to keep the water about knee deep. I found I could lie in steaming water at forty-one degrees Celsius, my head resting on the marble edge which the Romans had thoughtfully chamfered, probably for just such comfort, and look up to the towers and ramparts of the town above. There seemed no better way to spend a morning.

The ferric-sulphurous waters are definitely beneficial. They gave ease to our joint and muscular pains that lasted for days and they softened our skin. It was surprising that an hour in the water left no wrinkling of the fingertips.

On one of the huge blocks along the edge there was some incision—an inscription, or more accurately, a hieroglyph. I splashed water on it to see it better in the oblique light. It wasn't Etruscan, it certainly wasn't Roman script, perhaps it was the symbol of the Roman noble whose villa it had served. Who and what was he? Soldier, pioneer settler, administrator? In a farmer's field fifty metres away a few scattered blocks of travertine are all that remains of that villa. Perhaps in another century or two, the inscription will have worn off the bath. It is just one of thousands of fragments of that civilisation scattered across the country, tantalising but quite unimportant. We will never know its story.

. . .

I don't suppose anything has given me the same sense of power and importance as being the *padrone* of a bitumen-laying road plant for three hours. It all came as something of a surprise, both for me and for the *Comune*. As the traffic increased on the new road, the dust problem had worsened. When a south-westerly wind was blowing, clouds of fine white powder billowed over the house, penetrating everywhere. It was a housewife's nightmare, and it seemed there would be no end to it.

Then one day, I came across a team of contractors resurfacing one of our district roads. An inspiration struck me. I asked the supervisor if he could he lay a strip of bitumen on the road outside my house. '*Certo!*' he replied. It would cost thirteen thousand lire per square metre, he said, but I would have to make up my mind in a hurry because the road plant was going to be in the district for only a few more days.

I made an urgent telephone call to Alfonso. Would the *Comune* permit me to seal the road around our boundary, at my expense? '*Non è un problema*' was his response. I would have to submit a request in writing and it could be formally approved by the *giunta*, the management committee of the *Comune*, due to meet in a few days' time.

Then, because he was always canny with the council's *lire*, he thought it would be a good idea if the other residents would contribute, so the bitumen could be extended. Would I contact them? In the event, none of my neighbours, either the Italians or the wealthy absentee English owners, would come to the party, so I booked the road plant for the following Monday morning, on my account alone.

I had calculated that we could afford to seal one hundred and five metres of the road bounding our property. This would cost around five million lire. The strip in front of the house would be four metres wide, the smaller road from the fork leading to Giuseppina's restaurant three metres. I was a little surprised, but rather relieved, that the *Comune* left me to determine these widths. Why, emerged later.

Sharp at half past seven, the gang arrived. Two trucks full of steaming asphalt, seven men and a contraption that looked like a cross between a fairground ride and the surrey with the fringe on top. We decided to start at the top and work downhill. The first truck filled the hopper of the bitumen-laying machine (for that is what the contraption was), the engine roared, wheels turned and in a cloud of steam, rollers extruded it out the back. Slowly the black carpet unrolled. I stood to one side, arms folded, trying to look the part expected of me, as the engineer in charge shuttled back and forth, converting my instructions into adjustments of the width controls.

We had almost finished when Alfonso arrived with the Perugia Province engineer responsible for road works. By then, I was primed for praise and ready to graciously accept their gratitude and admiration for my generous contribution to the civic weal. The road would solve our dust problem, but it also would be to everybody's benefit. However, they had not come to offer congratulations. The Province was miffed that Paciano had not informed it of this maverick's idea of laying his own road. Alfonso confessed to a great embarrassment. The meeting of the *giunta*, set for the previous Friday had been abandoned for lack of a quorum. Our bitumen strip was technically *abusivo*! I thought how fortunate it was that he had not bothered to tell me.

Audrey and I went inside laughing quietly to ourselves. We were confident that they would solve the legal technicalities and find a way to back-date the permission. After all, they could hardly roll up the road and take it away.

. . .

At first, I thought I was imagining things when the roof of the big terrace all along the back of the house seemed to be subsiding. The builders had supported the inner side on foot-thick logs bound to the house wall with hoops of iron; the outside edge rested on five great posts. It was supposed to be earthquake-proof, how could it give way? I drove nails into the posts a few inches above the surface of the terrace, then jammed small pieces of thin glass between the nails and the stone. After about a week, when the glass tell-tales began to shatter, I knew the posts were sinking and we had a serious problem. I calculated that at the eaves, the roof was by then about ten centimetres lower that it should have been.

I made an urgent telephone call to Piero Passaglia for help while we turned to our photographs of the construction work to try to solve the puzzle. We knew that enough concrete had gone into the foundations of the terrace to support an average-sized skyscraper, so what was giving way? It turned out that Piero had never built a large terrace roof like ours, so sensibly he had asked Tomassoni how to go about it. The instructions he followed called for the five posts to be set in concrete tubes, embedded in the terrace foundations. This was the explanation, a recipe for disaster. Water running off the terrace had collected in the tubes, and the posts had begun rotting from the bottom up. Piero brought steel props to prevent a complete collapse of the roof, and I went for my sketch pad to design a proper support system.

Part of the great heritage of Umbria is the skill of ironworkers and blacksmiths. Today their ability in *ferro battuto*, literally, beaten (wrought) iron, is directed to making lamps, bedsteads and elaborate gates and fencing panels, rather than halberds and crossbows. Caviglioli, my *fabbro* in Castiglione del Lago could do anything with a piece of iron. I had given him our designs and he had fabricated garden arches, farm gates and a superbly wrought decorative wellhead. Now I turned to him to make the supports. Each was a stirrup, simply a big steel 'U' to carry the post, welded to a short length of stout tubing, and in turn supported by a thick steel baseplate. When this was bolted to the concrete terrace foundations, it would hold the post well clear of any water. Then, the expensive part—I had to buy five new posts in solid and expensive chestnut timber.

It took Piero and his team only a morning to chop out the rotten posts, anchor-bolt my steelwork, jack the roof back to its proper height and hoist the new posts into position. *Ecco fatto!* But the experience had taught me never to trust a *geometra*, and especially Tomassoni, again.

Our roof was not the only thing collapsing. The indefensible lire fell thirty per cent when Italy was forced to withdraw it from the European Exchange Rate Mechanism. The successes of the tax evaders and the failures of various governments to control wasteful public spending combined to produce a massive budget deficit and a national debt one and a quarter times the Gross Domestic Product. To finance the shortfalls, governments had kept selling more bonds, which simply increased the interest burden, and the repayments.

The effect for us was serious. Prices rose sharply, particularly for imported goods, and the government turned its inventive mind to new ways of raising money. About this time a semi-official organisation calculated that Italy had nearly one hundred different taxes. As might be expected, ninety per cent of the revenue came from a mere handful of them. Small business, which has been the backbone of Italy's economic revival, suffers most. Giuseppina in her little restaurant has to pay a *camino* tax on the fireplace in the corner. Because she could not afford to install one large cold room, which would have attracted a single *motore elettrico* tax, she had to pay the same tax on each of her five small refrigerators.

Italy has not had a system of property rates as we know them. Local government is centrally funded, except for service charges for water and garbage collection. Rome saw its opening and hit us all with ISI, *l'imposta straordinario sulla casa italiana*. We noted the 'extraordinary' nature of the new tax on the home, as the government promised it was a once-off measure to help the exchequer tackle the deficit.

Well, they kept their promise. No more ISI. The following year they simply changed its name, to *l'imposta comunale sugli immobili,* or the communal tax on property, ICI for short. The only other difference was that this would go directly to the local *Comune.* Local government was no better off however, because the central grant was reduced commensurately. It was all part of the legerdemain that passes for financial responsibility, seemingly irrespective of who is in power. The new tax, pronounced 'ee-chee', has already passed into the language as a word in its own right. Nowhere does the government brochure explaining the measure mention what the letters stand for. I pun that it's not so much an itch as a saddle sore on the back of the poor over-taxed Italian.

This penchant for acronyms can be quite confusing for a stranger. At the beginning, the widespread use of this organisational shorthand in the newspapers gave me enormous difficulty in understanding who was doing what to whom. The only way I could cope was by constructing my own glossary, pouncing on every parenthetical definition of the letters. Things are made worse when the contraction is then pronounced as a word in its own right. I puzzled for weeks over what seemed to sound like 'Chisel, Chiggle and Wheel' on the nightly TV news. This turned out to be CISL, CGIL and UIL, the three main Italian trade unions.

Some organisations seem to have gone to extraordinary lengths to invent names for themselves just so they could be contracted into catchy acronyms. The Health Department's methadone clinics for drug addicts are *Nuclei Operativi*

Tossicodipendenza, or NOT. The *Centrale Operativa Polizia* yields COP, while Italy's gay rights group constructed the mouthful *Fronte Unitario Omosessuale Rivoluzionario Italiano* so that it could be known as FUORI, Italian for 'out'.

I now have a collection of hundreds of such acronyms, an essential little lexicon of words that you will never find in any Italian dictionary. The problem, of course, is the circumlocution of the language, locked in the grammatical straitjacket of its Greco-Roman origins. Unlike Germany, there is no sign that anyone here has thought of simplifying it since Mussolini failed in his attempt to make '*voi*' the universal pronoun for 'you'.

Italians are not as xenophobic as the French about the importation of English words; in fact, they rather fancy using them, no matter how inappropriately, on their cars as well as on their clothing. Shoes and jackets sell at a premium if they carry obviously English brand names, even if they are made in Italy. I often wonder whether, with the spread of English as the global language, Italian will die in a couple of hundred years time, as Latin did before it, and for the same reasons.

· · ·

One should never miss an opportunity to re-visit Florence. The old city always has something new to offer, and there is always something old to be discovered, overlooked on previous visits. So when I got wind of a huge row blowing up in the heart of the city that would make a good feature story, it was the perfect excuse to jump in the car and head north.

I discovered that for nearly four hundred years the gold-smiths of Florence had plied their trade on the Ponte Vecchio—and done their other business straight into the River Arno. Suddenly, the city council had issued an edict—install a proper sewerage system within a month, or put the lid down on the loo. Permanently.

The forty-four shops on perhaps the most famous and best-loved bridge in the world have enjoyed a privileged position since the end of the sixteenth century. Grand Duke Ferdinand I established the goldsmiths' monopoly there when he banished the butchers, tanners and pursemakers whose stalls made up an untidy bazaar in the 1500s. It was said that their noise, as well as their smells, disturbed him as he passed overhead in the private corridor Vasari built for the Medici so they could move between the Palazzo Vecchio and the Pitti Palace, unseen by their enemies, or the common populace.

Four hundred years later, it was the smells of the discharge from the goldsmiths' toilets, bidets and handbasins that aroused the ire of the city fathers. With a detailed report from the local health department on the unsanitary conditions, they served 'show cause' notices on the proprietors. What intrigued me most was what could have triggered the flurry of bureau-cratic activity after four centuries of indifference.

A few discreet enquiries and I found the answer, just a short distance upstream. The Florence rowers have their boatshed on the *Lungarno Anna Maria Louisa de' Medici*, just below the Uffizi. They had complained that it was difficult enough to train on the fast-flowing Arno, but impossible if they had to listen for the roar of the cisterns and dodge the cascades of water! The summonses put the goldsmiths in another of those catch-22 situations. Under city ordinances, they were not permitted to employ staff on premises where toilet and washing facilities were not provided. What particularly enraged them was the fact that they had already commissioned an engineer's report to find ways of sewering the Ponte Vecchio acceptably.

That was some years ago. The old bridge, which has stood since 1345, and the only one on the Arno Hitler spared from demolition in 1944 because he thought it cute, got its sewerage system a year later. I followed up the story to find out what had happened. The system cost each of the goldsmiths twelve million lire, half a million Australian dollars in total, more than the bridge cost to build. Uniquely, each toilet is equipped with a little red light. 'Why?' I asked Piero Fallaci, our favourite goldsmith on the bridge.

'The system is so unreliable and prone to blockage that we're not supposed to use the toilet when the red warning light is on', he replied. 'Sometimes it takes the council days to fix. It's all worse than before.'

But the million tourists a year who queue for Florence's museums and galleries and dream of history as they gaze down the Arno don't notice a thing. The rowers are better off, though.

This experience helped me retain my equanimity when Domenico, the Paciano *Vigile* arrived with an ultimatum from the *Comune* to me and the other seven home owners of Varacca. Construct a treatment plant for our septic tank effluents within thirty days, or face a fine. This proved to me that it never pays to put ideas into the heads of Italian officialdom. Two years earlier, one of our neighbours, Lorenzo Melani, a *Fiorentino* and a friend of Zeno's, had bought one of the little Varacca houses as a weekend escape. He had been troubled by a bad odour from his toilet, so he got up a petition, asking the *Comune* to build a filtration/dispersion trench for the combined effluent of all the houses. There was, naturally, no response at the time.

I need to break off to explain an unsavoury detail of life in Umbria. In this area at least, nobody knows how to make a working septic tank or *fossa biologica*, as it is called. A septic tank needs oxygen to effect the biological degradation, so an air vent somewhere between the toilet and the tank is essential. But here there are no air vents, they are all closed systems. The *fossa biologica* is nothing more than a cesspit. Then, if the water trap in the line dries out, as happened in Lorenzo's case, the smell comes straight back into the house.

Long after we had forgotten about the petition, Domenico had found it somewhere in the archives. Without saying anything to the Varaccans, he brought up an inspector from the Health Department who as he expected and hoped, promptly condemned the existing arrangements.

This struck us all as *ingiusto*—unfair. We had all complied scrupulously with the *Comune*'s directions at the time of building, piping the effluent (known as 'black water') to drain away on neighbouring farmland, but now, like the Ponte Vecchio, it seemed this was not enough. Lorenzo was particularly upset that his request had been ignored for two years, and then turned against him.

Two months after the first warning, we responded with a petition asking the *Comune* to plan and manage the project, and demanding that it make a contribution. Again, no response. Seven months later, the mayor convened a meeting of house-holders to discuss plans and estimates. The system proposed would cost eight million lire, to be shared equally, one million per property. By the time the contractor arrived to excavate the trench and lay the filter bed, winter had arrived and the ground was too boggy for the workmen and machines to move. And the costs had gone up. So almost another year went by before the little Umbrian hamlet of Varacca got its sewerage system, which is more than can be said for one of the great cities of Europe, Milan. All that city's wastes were still going, untreated, into the appropriately-named River Po.

. . .

Hundreds of summer music festivals flourish throughout Italy, from the great operatic performances in La Scala to Umbria Jazz, which now brings the best bands and soloists from all over the world. We could hear Rostropovich in Città di Castello, Sviatoslav Richter and Viktoria Mullova in Perugia, and in nearby Città della Pieve, sacred and profane mediaeval music played on hurdy-gurdys, double flutes, rebecks and portable organs. Early music on instruments of the era is all the rage in Italy today.

On the 250th anniversary of Vivaldi's death, we went to an open-air concert in the pocket-handkerchief *piazza* of Corciano, a model hilltown beautifully restored, not far from

Perugia. It faced all the hazards of a performance *a fuori*. The harpsichord arrived in the back of a little Fiat. We sat licking a *gelato* in the warm evening air, watching the harpsichordist screw its legs back on and then balance them on concrete blocks to compensate for the uneven ancient flagstones. A hundred people filled the seats, the latecomers propped themselves against the walls, neighbours leaned out of their upstairs windows.

The concert started well enough with Scarlatti, Vivaldi and Lotti, a composer I had never heard of. Then as the star of the evening, soprano Kate Gamberucci, launched into Pergolesi's '*Ah Serpina, penserete*', an Alsatian at one side of the *piazza* and a Pomeranian at the other joined her in a duet.

The audience tried at first to cover their giggles with their programs, and Kate pretended not to hear the dogs. But as the three-way competition hotted up, and the concert became a Spike Jones spoof, none of us could hold back our laughter any longer. Suddenly the soprano stopped in mid-phrase. The audience hushed, the dogs fell silent, obviously puzzled at the loss of their accompanist. Into the stillness, Kate sang a plaintive 'miaow'. A brief pause, and she picked up Pergolesi where she had left him. The dogs retired, defeated.

But the excitement was not over. The Italian Air Force chose just that night for two of its Tornado fighter-bombers to beat up the town with some low-level passes. Then the wind got up and blew music everywhere. The cellist, caught turning the page at that moment, had his instrument and bow in one hand and the music sheet in the other. He struggled against the breeze but he needed another hand...his ten-bar rest was nearly up!...there was nothing else for it...he lunged—and replaced the clothes-peg music clips with his teeth! Which brought the biggest cheer of the night.

It was a memorable experience, if not the greatest of concerts. I suppose nobody there that night will ever forget it. For me, it underlined the wonderful phlegmatic aspect of the Italian character that refuses to allow the soul of an event to be destroyed by incident.

In the long summer evenings our greatest musical pleasure has always come from the little cycle called simply 'Incontri in Terra di Siena'—Meetings in Siena Country—dedicated to the memory of Iris Origo. Apart from the quality of the music and the splendour of the venues, for me it closes the circle of admiration for a woman of great courage and achievement—an Irish–American–Italian woman and the author of a dozen books, who has been described as 'the best writer in English about things Italian'.

I had never heard of Iris Origo until I happened upon a reprint of her War in Val d'Orcia in a remainder bookshop in Sydney. When we came to live here, one of the first things we did was to drive to her house, 'La Foce', not far away across the hills in south-east Tuscany, in the hope of meeting her. We were two years too late. She lies beside her husband Antonio, to whom she was married for fifty-two years, at the top of the little family graveyard they laid out themselves. On her grave beside the chapel amongst the cypresses, there are just two lines from St Catherine of Siena:

Chi più conosce più ama

E più amando più giusta

The more one knows, the more one loves.

And loving more, one is more righteous for it.

Iris Origo wrote a dozen books about Italy, her adopted country, but *War in Val d'Orcia* is for me the most moving. It is her diary, written furtively and kept hidden from the enemy in the time when she found her farm, her family and all their dependents in the front line of the battle for Italy between 1943 and 1944. It is a true and truly remarkable story of the ordinary people of a peasant society caught up in war.

Her story's climax is the flight of the entire *La Foce* community—farmers and their families together with a clutch of evacuee children she had been sheltering, as the Allied advance reached their valley. Eight miles along the dusty road to Montepulciano, under shellfire, past corpses and German soldiers laying mines, Iris and Antonio led the party to safety. What better way to keep alive the memory of this brave and talented woman than through concerts of fine music, performed in palaces, castles and farmhouses of her own district?

We go often to the concert in Pienza, the impressive little Renaissance town that was known as Corsignano when it was a collection of hovels, a nest of brigands and prostitutes. Then in the late fourteenth century, the city of Siena drove out the noble Piccolomini family after a dispute with the *signorie*. They settled in Corsignano and cleaned it up. Enea Silvio Piccolomini was born there in 1405, and fifty-three years later became Pope Pius II. These are the bare bones of Pienza's history. The new pope, a distinguished humanist, diplomat, orator and writer, set out to make his home town a model city. In part I think this must have stemmed from a determination to shame Siena for his family's unjust expulsion. A popular couplet that embodies local Tuscan enmity towards Siena dates from that period:

'*Siena, Siena, di tre cose tu sei piena*
di torri di campana e di figli di puttane'

which translates loosely as:

'Siena, Siena, count three things as your riches
Your towers, your bells, and your sons of bitches'

Enea hired distinguished architects and artists and set them on one of the world's first town-planning exercises. In less than four years the den of thieves, *Corsignan de' Ladri*, was transformed; then the pope died while trying unsuccessfully to inspire a crusade against the Turks in pursuit of his utopian vision of a united Christian Europe. Work stopped at what we have today—an elegant Renaissance square surrounded by the cathedral, the papal palace, the town hall, and the Palazzo Piccolomini. It is the central courtyard of this great house that becomes the auditorium for our concert.

Imagine a chamber music group on a small staging set up between the pillars of a grand cloister, the audience seated in the open space in front. Closed off from the world, all distracting sounds are shut out. The setting is intimate, the acoustics perfect for the two or three hundred privileged people. I look up, past architect Rossellino's severe windows of the two upper floors, to the square of enclosed sky; as darkness falls, it turns a deeper and deeper blue, but never becomes black. A single star appears. The music begins.

The program is Mozart's Quartet K493 with Jeremy Menuhin at the piano; a modern Trio for Strings by Alfred Schnittke, and the Brahms Quintet in F Minor Op. 34 for piano and strings. For a brief few hours, we are part of a magic combination of great music and ideal space; it evaporates all too soon. I look for the star—it has tracked across the dark blue square and is about to disappear. Alas, it is time to go home.

6. SPRING—WEEDS!

'Wildflowers are only weeds in someone else's garden' (Anon)

Springtime in Umbria, and the life force emerges dramatically. From ancient times Umbrians have celebrated the return of the songbirds, the screech of the insects and the perfumes of the invisible pollens with the coming of this season. Three centuries before Christ, the Romans brought the *ludi floreales*, spring games in honour of the goddess Flora; from the Middle Ages down to the present, Umbrians have observed May Day—*Calendimaggio*. But survival has always depended on the success of the crops, so the weather is more critical than the season:

> *aprile piovoso*
> *maggio ventoso*
> *anno fruttuoso*
> rain in April
> wind in May
> an abundant year
> in every way

Unfortunately, this abundance manifested very early, in the worst possible way for me, in the fecundity of the soil. I should have known that weeding could become addictive, even obsessive. It runs in the family. Every Sunday afternoon my mother would take a long nap after lunch, then launch herself into the garden around five o'clock to 'do a spot of weeding before it gets too dark'. Two hours later, in the winter dusk, she would still be battling the oxalis, the dandelions and the persistent runners of the buffalo grass, spiking herself on bougainvillea thorns and inevitably ripping out little daisies and marigolds, by then anonymous in the gloom. My younger brothers would call plaintively to her to come in to get dinner, but by then she was hooked. For when you get your face close to the ground, you see weeds that were quite invisible when standing, and the weeding challenge stretches to infinity. Only total darkness drove her indoors, her week always ending in frustration. Not only had she not finished all the beds, she knew that by next Sunday the offspring of this day's weeds would have re-populated the tilled soil, knew with a terrible certainty that the task could never be finished.

My mother would have been in her element at Varacca. When we bought it, the three-quarters of an acre behind the house had not been cultivated for thirty-five years. The land was mostly rich heavy clay, shading to poorer gravelly soil in the top corner. Perhaps a century ago it had been an *oliveto*, but now only three ancient trees were left. In more recent times it had grown the grain crops to feed the cattle of the estate, cattle that spent their entire lives in the *stalla* that is now our kitchen/dining room.

When we first saw it, an enormous scrub of secondary growth, in places five metres high, had taken over. Thickets of oak, elm and elder saplings were congested with blackberry, broom and dog rose, impenetrable to all but the wild pigs and the snakes they hunted. Hidden in the tangle around the house itself were nettles—Audrey brushed against one and the poison stung for three days.

The builders refused to start work on the reconstruction until it was all removed, so two men worked for three weeks to slash the confusion down. Then, after deep ripping of the roots with a crawler tractor and a massive burnoff, the land was ready, enriched by its long rest, to produce superb crops of weeds.

Local Umbrians control weeds around their olives by disc harrowing twice a year. Once started, however, this process becomes a treadmill. The discs turn the seeds back into the ground, but what is worse, they slice up the plants instead of digging them out. Each piece of thistle or sorrel root grows again—an agricultural version of the Sorcerer's Apprentice.

Knowing nothing about agriculture, and so following *Zio Carlo's* instructions carefully, we disc harrowed for the first year. Ivo Santoroni was only too pleased to have another customer. Celestino would wheel his machine around the tiny new olive trees with the skill and daring of a *Formula Uno* driver, the trailing gangs of shining disks missing their stems by inches. It was thrilling to watch, if a little scary. In an hour he would turn up the whole field, in a continuous slalom around the fifty olive and twenty fruit trees.

What made me decide to cancel Celestino, thereby condemning myself to manual weed control, was the simple observation that every ploughing moved more and more of the soil downhill. Afterwards, there would be no ground cover to catch morning dews and slow down evaporation. Also, without any growth to bind it, the open soil was vulnerable to erosion in heavy rain. In one big storm, water carved a channel diagonally across the *campo*, flooded the rear terrace of the house, and caused a minor landslide as it coursed down the steep bank at the northern edge of the property.

By now, I had also noticed that the smart Pacianese didn't break their backs with the manual *zappa*; they could indulge their love of machinery by using a motorised version. A *moto-zappa* could keep a circle around each of our trees clean too. I managed to buy a second-hand one quite cheaply from an agricultural machinery firm at Chiusi. The machine is similar to the rotary hoes that market gardeners use, but without their wheels. Instead, the engine is mounted directly over the tines, its weight helping them bite into heavy soil and— very important for us—cope with stones and rocks. Smaller stones close to the surface it could dig out, but I found that if it hit a large buried stone, the whole machine would leap into the air. Clinging desperately to the huge handlebars, I had no option but to leap with it. Audrey had some moments of mixed amusement and apprehension watching our antics, and decided to re-name it the '*kanga-zappa*'.

As for the rest of the property, I would encourage the growth of the wild couch grass the locals called *gramigna*. Farmers hate the *gramigna* for its strong persistent roots which run rapidly in summer, robbing their crops of nourishment. In winter it lies dormant, apparently killed off by the frosts, but it reappears stronger than ever the following season. Just what I needed, but first I had to eliminate the weeds.

It was easy enough to decide what to tackle first. Sour dock or garden sorrel infests any cleared field left idle here for very long. It puts down a strong radish-like root that can grow to an incredible size; the hundreds of reddish-green seeds in its tall stalks quickly sow and re-sow the whole area. Dock was the prime target that first year; I dug out thousands of plants. It was back-breaking work—work for a *contadino*, certainly not for someone the locals thought should have been acting the *padrone*. Hour after hour in the baking sun, the sweat running in little streams down my forehead until it stung my eyes, I began to experience the raptures of the long-distance runner. As with jogging, weeding becomes obsessive, and it seems to detach the mind. As the muscles tire and tighten, the brain seems to relax. Thoughts and ideas come easily. The fork goes in under the boot, levers, lifts and threshes. Automatically. And when my back could stand no more, I would straighten up, lean on the fork and look across the fields of sunflowers through the heat haze to one of the most beautiful views in Italy—to the island of Polvese seemingly floating on the waters of Lake Trasimeno.

But the frustration! As fast as I cleared a patch, the dock seemed to spring up again. Perhaps the Etruscans had put a spell on the place. Horace, two-thousand years ago, seemed to have encountered the same problem: *'naturam expelles furca, tamen usque recurret'*—'If you drive nature out with a pitchfork, she will soon find a way back.' It was then that I discovered that even a small piece of root, broken off, would grow again. And as the horrible clay soil dried and hardened towards summer it became more and more difficult to get the roots out whole. I broke three forks. The digging had to be abandoned until after autumn rain could soften the ground again.

In the beginning, as a botanical and horticultural illiterate, I knew nothing about the weeds I was digging out. English friends said they were horseradishes, but others disagreed. It was time for some research. Just at the right moment, the popular magazines came out with rave reviews of a new botanical guide for gardeners. *Erbe di Campi e Prati*—*Plants of Fields and Meadows*, quickly became my bible. Not only did its hundreds of colour illustrations enable me to identify our weeds, its text described their origins and listed their medicinal properties as Italian peasants had applied them over the centuries. Botany, which I had always avoided, could become interesting!

For example, the edible leaves of our dock, (*rumex acetosa* to the botanists) yielded a yellow dye—and the roots a red one. The leaves contain oxalic acid, and were believed good treatment for loss of appetite. A concoction of its extract, in combination with those from St John's Wort and walnut leaves was prescribed for *enuresi notturna*—bed wetting! I don't know whether anyone around here still cooks up dock as a cure for the children's nightly incontinence, but even the casual traveller can see that the past is not so far away in Umbria. All along the road verges, old women are out with their knives and sickles, searching for *finocchio*, the wild fennel, and filling their plastic bags with leaves of *cicoria*.

Once, at a summer lunch under our neighbour Zeno's olive trees, we were served a salad of seven different types of these greens, all gathered free in the fields. But I can't enthuse—I find them all too bitter for my taste. Wild chicory (*cichorum intybus*)—known as 'cats' eyes' because that's what its flowers look like—is often substituted for spinach, but the favourite Umbrian way to use it is as filling in a *torta*. The plant will grow up to a metre high with a bright blue flower, but the old women want to get it young and tender, so they have to search hard for it in the confusion of other weeds.

With Italy's prosperity, chicory's value as a wartime coffee substitute has passed into history. Italian ladies can now afford to buy their cosmetics—though only a couple of generations ago a *contadina* would apply a facemask of freshly-ground chicory roots to prevent reddening of her skin, while her husband used it to expel the afterbirth when his cows calved.

Then there's pigweed. One of our builders became quite excited when he found a big patch of *portulaca oleracea* in a damp corner. It was a luxurious delicacy during the war, he remembered. We must take it inside and dry it, he insisted, or if we liked, preserve it in vinegar. Apparently it made a great broth that we would find delectable. We invited him to help himself, but he declined. He ran a little *trattoria* on the side, but obviously preferred to serve *insalata* that came from the supermarket.

Identifying our weeds was only momentarily satisfying. Shock took over when I found we had at least fifty of these unwanted plant varieties. Each year different species and families of plants seemed to take centre stage and assume plague proportions. Removing one pest clearly made room for another. Since our hillside *campo* faces north, it is particularly exposed to the airborne seeds carried on the prevailing winds. I would watch in impotent dismay as the puffballs floated in to thousands of happy landings.

No sooner had I subdued the dock, than I was confronted by an outbreak of thistles. *Cardi* in ten different varieties suddenly appeared, all with the same subversive habit of growing zig-zag roots which cannot be pulled without breaking and leaving bits behind that would before long replicate the plant. From stinging childhood encounters, thistles had always been kept at a distance. I had no idea they could have been so valuable to societies without a pharmaceutical industry. Checking with *Erbe di Campi e Prati*, it seemed that each one of our thistles had a story to tell, and in times past had been put to good use.

The roots of horribly prickly *cirsium vulgare* were used to cure varicose veins. The Romans borrowed the idea from the Greeks whose word *kirsos* apparently means varicose. The huge seed-head of *carlina acaulis*, up to twelve centimetres in diameter, was a mediaeval fast food. Cooked before the flowering, it was carried as lunch to the fields, and in alpine areas was known as 'hunter's bread'.

The name itself, *carlina*, identifies Charlemagne, King of the Franks. Legend has it that when he invaded Italy in the eighth century, plague broke out amongst his soldiers. In response to his prayers, an angel appeared and shot an arrow from his bow, saying that where it landed the king would find a plant to cure his men. He did, it did, and Charlemagne reached Rome to be crowned Emperor by the Pope.

But the most popular and useful of all the thistles, the Blessed Mary thistle (*silybum marianum*), was our biggest problem. Its dark green leaves have white veinings, said to originate from drops of the Virgin's milk. Horticultural liebfraumilch! In earlier times, every spring, after carefully drying out its edible roots and young leaves for salad vegetables, the seeds were shaken out and ground up for prescription medicines. These included a diuretic, an aperitif and a fever-reducing tonic. Italians are paranoid about possible problems with their livers, and the *cardomariano* was highly esteemed for treating all problems of the *fegato*.

Most thistles also made good animal fodder, but some had undesirable side effects. My Scots forebears would have been mortified to learn that the proud emblem of Scotland, *onopordum acanthium*, takes part of its Greek name from a word meaning ass's fart (our ancestors had vehicle emission problems too!). Tacking on acanthus leaves, architecturally immortalised on Corinthian columns, scarcely makes up for that.

The only sure cure for thistles is a herbicide, and careful spotting directly on the leaves has all but eliminated them. But then the accident happened. All I could think of was Italo Calvino's folktale of the girl who talked to flowers, but hated weeds. To her, they were treacherous creatures of the dark netherworld beneath the soil. The fruit trees were in blossom and it was time to spray for the fly. I mistook the pre-mixed herbicide for the insecticide and killed three of our best trees—two apricots and a nectarine. It seemed like the evil empire striking back. Now I mix things only as I use them.

After the thistles, there was the plague of *xanthium spinosum*; I dubbed it the Crown of Thorns. It dries brittle and a nearly invisible brown in the summer heat and its spines can poison, but it does pull out easily. Far worse was the knotgrass, a type of fast-running five-leaf clover, with a pretty little yellow flower. We traced its sudden spread to the great increase in the bird population, the result of the shooting bans which had so enraged the local hunters.

We don't discourage the Flanders poppies that paint the fields crimson. They are the delight of our visitors, but the farmers detest them because they contaminate grain crops, reducing their value. These poor, weak cousins of the heroin-producing poppies of the Golden Triangle are strong enough to have sedative properties. In mediaeval times, they were used to put babies to sleep, and the rhoedina extracted from seeds was administered to Italian soldiers in World War I to cushion battle shock. The Italian government has now banned the cultivation of poppies, but why bother when so many can be gathered in the wild? I once suggested to a neighbour that if he cultivated wheat and poppies together, he could market poppy seed hallucinogenic bread and make a small fortune. He didn't see the joke, but then leg pulling isn't part of the Italians' sense of humour.

Seven hundred years ago, all over Europe, the monasteries ran the pharmaceutical research laboratories of the age. The monks developed skills in extracting herbal cures from common plants, as well as designing some very pleasant alcoholic elixirs. The Benedictines were the most accomplished, and since they were the missionary force in this area of Umbria, it probably explains the strong tradition of herbal remedies here. Unfortunately not one of their Umbrian monasteries survived Napoleon's suppression in 1810.

An hour's drive away in Tuscany however, the Abbey of Monte Oliveto Maggiore, founded in the fourteenth century by a Sienese lawyer, Bernard Tolomei, survives. We often take visiting friends there to see the inlay work in the choir stalls, among the best in Europe, but it is the frescoes that Signorelli and Sodoma painted all around the great cloister to depict events in the life of St Benedict that give Monte Oliveto its special appeal. At Mount Olivet I found the Benedictines still at their ancient craft, distilling cures from plants. Their little shop sells a range of extracts, some in powder form, some in a syrup, some as oil. Every one of them comes from a weed that I can find somewhere on our *campo.*

Prince of them all is *melissa*, the lemon balm that is the principal ingredient of Chartreuse, concocted by their French Benedictine cousins. Disappointingly, the French kept the recipe to themselves, so Mount Olivet is only a pharmacy, not a bar. Its *melissa* extract is recommended for poor appetite, for vertigo and neuralgia and is said to be especially good for migraines. The ancients thought it stimulated the memory—

Greek and Roman students drank lemon balm tea before their exams and wore wreaths of *melissa* to get higher marks. I wish I had known this earlier.

The common German chamomile (*matricaria chamomilla*) yields an oil that is recommended for stomach cramps. There's no sign of it today, but as recently as the 1920s men smoked dried chamomile flowers in their pipes because in their peasant poverty they couldn't afford tobacco.

For gastric and duodenal ulcers, the monks sell extracts of the wild cabbage, *brassica oleracea*. The prescription says drink one glass of the juice daily for fifteen days. If that works, it would be much cheaper than Tagomet or Zantac.

Don't think that ends the treatments available. Here's a quick rundown on others from the Benedictine medicine kit:

• Common yarrrow (*acchilea millefolium*), is nicknamed angel flower, bunch of daisies and soldier's wound-wort. Achilles is supposed to have discovered its medical properties as the first clotting agent, although it didn't save him at the end. Prescribed for menstruation problems, haemorrhoids, and blood loss from wounds and other injuries, it also makes marvellous dried arrangements—Audrey gathers armfuls in the summer to dry and spray red and gold for Christmas decorations.

• Common celery (*apium graveolens*), was valued by the Romans as an aphrodisiac; they also used it to decorate the tombs of their dear departed, perhaps for a more exciting afterlife. In later centuries, however, it had more prosaic uses—as a cure for dropsy, rheumatism, gout, obesity and gingivitis.

• Bugloss, or borage (*borago officinalis*) has a fascinating provenance. Its name comes from the arabic 'abou rach' meaning 'the father of all sweats', and this is apparently exactly what it produces. Hence it has been used through history as a decongestant, prescribed for colds, bronchitis and pleurisy. Its ancient reputation for promoting and sustaining good temper, the reference books sadly admit, is not proven.

• *Convolvulus arvensis*, with its pretty rosy-white flowers, was known as 'old man's nightcap'. Why, I don't understand—it keeps me awake worrying about the speed with which it infests the lawns and the garden beds.

• Blue mallow (*malva silvestris*), was held in such respect by the ancients that it was nicknamed 'old man's bread and cheese'. The queen of all medicinal plants, it was an emollient for toothache, stomach pains and urinary infections; as an expectorant in cases of gingivitis, coughs and conjunctivitis; and as a laxative. The leaves made poultices, the flowers inhalants—an all-purpose medicine to put drug companies out of business.

• Plantain (*plantago major*), or *piantaggine* in Italian, is common enough around the world. Here in Italy it was used for many ailments, from diarrhoea to insect bites. The crushed roots were inserted into the ear for toothache. Monte Oliveto's extract today is recommended for the fegato and ulcers.

- Vervain (*verbena officinalis*) has the most interesting pedigree of all. Its name derives from one of the few Celtic words to migrate to Italy, *ferfaen*. Its aromatic, astringent, fever-reducing properties were highly regarded by the Romans. Its reputation spread—early settlers in Australia used it to treat wounds and fevers. But in the Australian bush, they may not have been aware of its magical properties. For (my books assure me) if you pick it in the night of the feast of S.Giovanni Battista (June 24), it can make you lucky in love. My only explanation for this untried proposition is that in the melding of pagan and Christian rites, the feast of St John the Baptist was substituted for the celebration of the summer solstice, which everyone knows to be the moment of high suggestion.

Finally, to the common dandelion family. As I write, the *campo* is a carpet of yellow, for this year the dandelions are in control. Tarassaco, (*taraxacum officinale*), was probably the most widely used plant in rural Italy three generations ago—as a bitter vegetable and as a detoxicant for those omnipresent liver problems. At Monte Oliveto, the monks mix it with the wild chicory and prescribe it as a digestive aid, and for constipation. The dandelion's origins are obscure. Its botanical name suggests Persia, where it means 'bitter herb'. To the Greeks, it was a 'cure for anxiety'.

I can't make up my mind which of the two terms for the pesky little *dente di leone* is most apt for my situation. It's been a bitter lesson, my battle with nature. But after five years of digging and swearing, the war is over. They have won, and my surrender is perhaps the cure for my anxiety. Now we can look forward to the blue of the malva, the white umbrellas of hogweed, the pale pinks of wild convolvulus and vervain, interspersed with the crimson of the poppies. They share space with the grape hyacinth, the scotch crocus, 'Lords and Ladies' lilies, and the 'Star of Bethlehem', all of which I have tried to preserve. They re-appear, indomitably, year after year.

Every spring, I still have to mow the *campo*, but it's some compensation to know that no longer do I have a field of weeds—I have wildflowers. And if we should ever need it, a complete pharmacopoeia.

7. MIRACLES, FOOD AND A MAD DENTIST

The idea of leaving Australia to live permanently in Italy seemed so exotic to many of our friends that they had to hurry over to assure themselves of our mental state. This led to a spate of visits which were very welcome, and not just because visitors could be pressed to carry items unobtainable here—from 'soakit' hoses for the hedges to gelatine, golden syrup and deodorants with anti-perspirant. I'm told that one Australian pharmacist thought anyone buying six cans of deodorant must have a serious hygiene problem, but when the buyer confided that it was for a friend in Italy (where deodorants do not contain anti-perspirant) it seemed to explain everything.

We were delighted to have the stimulus of their company, the relaxation from the strain of always thinking and speaking Italian, and the pleasure of taking them tripping off to out-of-the-way places, many of which we had not had time to explore for ourselves. Inevitably, on one of these little journeys, we would come across a checkpoint—at a road junction or a lay-by—manned by *Carabinieri*. We were rarely stopped, because just which car was to be pulled over seemed to be a little roadside lottery. But the sight of the uniform, the flak jacket and the loaded submachine gun at the ready was often disconcerting for our visitors.

I have developed a certain technique for dealing with the situation if we are ever waved to the side of the road by the officer with the lollipop stick. I am extremely polite, I always speak English, and when '*Documenti!*' are demanded, I produce the International Driving Permit which I obtain in Australia every year. This has a photograph and lots of red stamps which Italians respect, and so is guaranteed to confuse the patrol, and assure us safe passage. 'Good afternoon' or 'Have a nice trip' to proudly demonstrate his English, and the officer waves us on our way.

I have to confess that I have never obtained a *patente*, the Italian driving licence, because of the huge trouble and cost involved. An agent to negotiate the paperwork is essential, so even the application costs a lot of money. Then it has to go to the Ministry of Transport in Rome for a check for a criminal record, a requirement which does not seem to hinder *mafiosi* or other undesirable elements. Even Britons have difficulties— the Italian motoring press regularly points out that despite the so-called European Union, it is five times more complex for an Englishman to re-validate his British licence in Italy than for an Italian to do the reverse in Britain.

Since I drive an Italian-registered car, I should have a *patente*, and so I am technically illegal. However—and I have not yet had to put this advice to the test—since I leave the country for three or four months each year, and have twelve months from the date of arrival to apply for a licence, I am always in a state of grace, so to speak, with time to go and apply if challenged. 'Good grief', my wife said to me after I had explained this rationalisation, 'you're starting to think like an Italian'.

One time with visitors we were stopped, and I went through my routine. The *Carabiniere* took the driving permit back to his car and spread it out on the bonnet to puzzle over it. Our friend sitting beside me began to laugh. The more I tried to stop him, the more he guffawed, and to make it worse, he was pointing at the man with the machine-gun. 'Roger!' I hissed 'These guys are serious—if they realise you're laughing at them, anything could happen. Shut up!'

The road blocks do sometimes apprehend wrongdoers, but they are mostly an inefficient and costly way of ensuring that Italian motorists have paid their registration and compulsory insurance. Other countries have better ways of doing it, but they don't have to cope with the Italian evasion mentality.

There is another equally powerful Italian reason for the *Carabinieri* to stand by the roads for hours every day—tradition. They have been doing it for nearly two hundred years. The *Arma*, as it likes to be known (motto: Faithful through the Centuries), was founded by Victor Emmanuel I, King of Sardinia as *Il Corpo de' Carabinieri Reali* in 1814. When he was able to return from exile after the defeat of Napoleon, King Victor decided he needed a military force loyal only to him. It could keep watch on all the roads leading to Turin, to guard against any nascent aspirations of the populace that might lead to a march on his capital.

Thoughout the years, the *Carabinieri* have been both police force and a part of the army. Its members are drilled and trained as a military force, and can in theory be called on to fight anywhere, even abroad. Although this happens rarely, any proposal to de-militarise it is strongly resisted and seen as doing violence to its traditions, yet its civil policing functions frequently cause competition and friction with the *Polizia*. The *Arma* may be a little schizophrenic about its role today, but is infinitely more professional and better to deal with than the regular police force, whose members seem ruder and sometimes loutish.

One of the visitors' trips usually ends in the hilltown of Montepulciano, less than an hour's drive away in Tuscany. It's still a mediaeval and Renaissance walled town, sliding steeply up a hill and full of beautiful buildings in stone and brick, a junior version of Florence and Siena. From the tower of the fifteenth century *Palazzo Comunale* the view on a clear day extends from the peaks of the *Gran Sasso* to the *torri* of Siena.

There are good restaurants in Montepulciano (and thousands of litres of the excellent *Vino Nobile* in cellars under the main square), but we sometimes take our friends for a picnic in the little park below the walls. I rearrange the park benches, and spread a rug, Australian-style, laying out the bread, cheese, prosciutto and wine. The locals, short-cutting through the park on their way home to *pranzo* seem surprised at this improvisation (Italians are not picnickers), but they're always charming, and offer us a '*buon appetito*' as they pass.

On one of these trips, we were admiring the golden altar in the *duomo* when a young priest drew us aside into a side chapel. There, easy to overlook, is one of the town's treasures—the Madonna of San Martino. Four hundred years ago, he explained, it was in a roadside shrine outside the town. A young man playing *pallamaglio*, an antique forerunner of croquet, was so enraged when he lost the game that he smashed his mallet into the face of the Madonna. The painting suffered no damage, not a chip. But the Madonna's temple erupted in a livid wound as if it were live flesh. Many years later, the painting was moved into the cathedral for safekeeping and in 1707 a gold crown set the Vatican's seal of approval on the miracle. 'And the sportsman?', I asked.

'They say he was struck with apoplexy and remained an invalid for the rest of his life.'

The age of miracles is not dead, however. There have been so many apparitions of the Virgin in the last few years that a book, *When the Madonna Weeps*, published a map of 55 locations of the marvels and accounts of each. Many of the weeping statues were made at Medjugorje in the former Yugoslavia; some were found to have been constructed with secret internal ducts that would dispense a liquid under certain conditions. A cartoon in the left-leaning newspaper, *La Repubblica* poked fun at this, showing half the Madonnas in Italy weeping and the other half unemployed.

The most famous of these statuettes, the *Maddonina* of Civitavecchia, the dormitory town just north of Rome, was 'arrested' by the authorities on suspicion of this type of fraud.

Huge crowds had besieged the house where the little statuette had been set up in the garden crypt of a man who had been a Jehovah's Witness, but had recanted. The magistrates responded to an allegation that the 'miracle' had been staged to boost the flagging faith of the citizens of Civitavecchia and the income of the parish church.

X-rays revealed no fraudulent piping, and laboratory tests confirmed the 'tears' were human blood. However, the home-owner declined to give samples for DNA comparisons to be made, and the Constitutional Court upheld his right of refusal. Thus the matter, like so many in Italy, was unresolved. The pious and the suspicious remained entrenched in their opposing camps, never to agree.

Perhaps this era of the construction of the new Europe is the second age of the mystics. Historians have noted that the triumph of the humanist culture of the Renaissance was accompanied by a religious revival. Some of those manifestations would have impressed David Copperfield. In 1540, Caterina de' Ricci, a Domenican nun of the Convent of San Vincenzo of Prato, was said to have passed thirty-two kidney stones without any pain, by the intervention of Savonarola; the first prelates of Florence reported watching her body float-ing up from the floor of the chapel to be embraced by Christ as He leapt from the Crucifix.

There are, and have always been sceptics—even in Italy. For example, a research chemist in the University of Pavia, Luigi Garlaschelli, has shown that a solution of carbonate of calcium, chloride of iron and a little common salt will solidify, dark red in colour, but will re-liquify at the first vigorous shaking. This simple chemistry he says, was well known to the ancients, and easily explains the so-called miracle of the blood of Saint Gennaro of Naples. Every year since 1389 it has liquified on 19 September, seemingly in response to hours of prayer.

I watch in wry amusement as the battles rage back and forth in the newspapers. Such passionate controversies are one of the surprising but redeeming features of a country that I had always believed highly conformist. With no Inquisition, the sceptics can be assured of a wide press coverage.

It's not always architecture and miracles for our guests. One year, visiting friends arrived just in time for us to take them to the great festival of kites held every two years in Castiglione del Lago. It's called 'Colour the Skies' and that is exactly what they do. Hundreds of kite makers from all over the world bring their beautiful craft. The jumbos of the event are the giant box kites like the ones Lawrence Hargraves flew in his historic aviation experiments on the clifftops of Stanwell Park, just south of Sydney. There are duelling competitions for the Chinese killer kites, there are birds and butterflies of every shape and size. On the last day of the festival, they launch them all together, and the sky over Lake Trasimeno becomes a gigantic fluid patchwork of shape and colour against the azure Italian heavens.

The kites fly from an old wartime airstrip on the shores of the lake. Trasimeno has had its share of historic battles, from the defeat by Hannibal of Caius Flaminius in 217BC to the rout of the Germans by New Zealanders of the British Eighth

Army in 1944; but the battle of Trasimeno airstrip lasted longer than any other. After more than thirty years, it has only just been resolved. Fortunately, it was bloodless, although at times it is said to have been a near thing.

A Sardinian *pastore*, a sheep farmer from Nuoro, brought his flock to the mainland and squatted on the unused hundred hectares. Local authorities wanted the magnificent lakeside site for tourist development and tried to evict him. Stories that councillors were threatened with guns and even the favoured Sardinian response of kidnap if they pressed too hard have passed into the local mythology of the dispute. Twenty years after the war, the land was still a military establishment, however, and the Air Force had no interest in driving off Sardinian sheep. When the Castiglione council at last succeeded in having the land transferred to civil authority in 1974, it thought the battle was won. Then the Sardo shepherd played his trump card. He cited a traditional rural right that a flock could not be moved if the ewes were pregnant. For years the various competing plans—for a tourist light airstrip, an agricultural experimental station, a lakeside park with holiday apartments—remained in their pigeonholes. Nobody could find a time when at least some of the flock were not expecting.

. . .

Dinners on the terrace, in the cool evening air were opportunities for our guests to experience Audrey's skill in the kitchen. She was interested and accomplished in Italian cooking long before we came to Italy, but found the transition was not easy. Cooking in Umbria can be tedious and is often frustrating.

The great writers on Italian cookery for non-Italians, Elizabeth David, Marcella Hazan and Lorenza de' Medici, had been her guides. Their recipes were authentic, painstakingly collected and researched, and then adapted if necessary, for other countries. Their books extol the seasonal freshness of produce in Italy, and the wide range and variety of regional foods. They point out, correctly, that there is no such thing as 'Italian cooking'. After all, Italy was only a 'geographical expression', in Metternich's dismissive phrase, until unity was achieved in 1861. Since then, it has often seemed that except for World Cup fevers, most Italians are more interested in their village, their province or their region—in that order—than their nation. So it is with their cooking, which remains strictly regional, and to which they remain fiercely loyal.

What the cookery writers don't emphasise is the rigidity of the seasonality of the produce. For a cook used to being able to find the whole range of high quality fresh produce virtually all year round in Australia, Britain or the United States, this imposes great constraints. Umbrians seem to have elevated the difficulty into a virtue—Francesco Montioni once asked Audrey why she was preparing tomatoes in December, when it wasn't their season. She should simply have switched to broccoli!

When it came to finding ingredients for our own recipes, the difficulty was even greater. Audrey is used to buying almonds whole, slivered, flaked, or ground, ready for use. Here almonds, walnuts and hazelnuts were in the shell, adding considerable time to preparation. There is no allspice, there are no currants, raisins or dried peel, and icing sugar comes in two-ounce sachets that cost a fortune. Sour cream and heavy creams are unobtainable, and the UHT alternatives whip only one time out of three.

The rice is the *arborio* short-grain variety essential for *risotto milanese*, but there is no brown or wild rice. Gelatine has to be brought from Sydney or London, because the local product is only a *torta gel* for setting fruit on a tart. There are no brown sugars, treacle or golden syrup (only imported demerara) because Italian sugar comes from beet, not cane. Self-raising flour does not seem to exist and we have been unable to find wholemeal flour, although *integrale* bread is baked. Many Italians who had it imposed on them during the war, still believe it is fit only for the dogs.

The ordinary flour is totally baffling. It comes in two grades, '0' and '00' but both are heavy, by our standards. We are told that the '*zero*' is for bread and pizzas, while the '*doppio zero*' is supposedly lighter, for making pasta and baking cakes. The difference is only marginal. Finally there is a *levito* in the shops, for rising, but it's nowhere near as good or reliable as baking powder. Whenever we carry in a couple of tins of Aunt Mary's, we are always nervous that Customs will find it and suspect the white powder is something else. Then there are the cultural differences. It is impossible to relate Italian cuts of meat to the butchering patterns of Australia, Britain or the United States; Garlic grown in Australia is much stronger than *aglio*; Italian *prezzemolo* is less pungent than English parsley;

Italian onions are sweeter; and salted butter has until recently been unobtainable, but now comes in from Denmark.

It is a little difficult to follow a local cookbook when quantities are described as 'a handful' or not given at all. Australian and English cooks use teaspoons and tablespoons as standard measures; Italian recipes seem to recommend *cucchiaio*, *cucchiaia*, *cucchiaino* and *cucchiaione*, indiscriminately and inconsistently. Conversion was necessary—a *cucchiaino* = one of our teaspoons; a *cucchiaione tavola* = a dessert spoon, not a tablespoon. Elizabeth David quotes a French chef as saying the dangerous person in the kitchen is the one who goes rigidly by weights, measures, thermometers and scales. Yes, my wife says somewhat testily, but one does need to know how much is a 'cupful' and what a 'ladle' holds.

The cultural differences are most marked in the format of the meal. We are used to eating several vegetables with our meat course. Italian restaurant menus rarely offer a choice of more than two vegetables with the second course (and they are extras); if a diner opts for only the first course, he or she will not be offered any *contorni* at all. (The first course may be called the *primo piatto* but is properly known as the *minestra* or soup course, because even if it is pasta, it is served in a deep bowl.)

If the hostess decides to end her dinner party with a dessert, it will almost certainly be rich, expensive and from the *pasticceria*. We have never found anyone who cooks pastry at home, only *torte*—cakes and tarts. Our rich range of sweets is beyond the average Italian hostess' experience. It is far more usual, at least in this area, for a meal in the home to end with fruit, and perhaps with cheese also. Audrey created a sensation by presenting the guest of honour at a birthday dinner with a Bombe Alaska, complete with sparklers!

Now to commit the ultimate heresy—for a foreigner living in Italy, the Italian diet is basically boring!

'How can you say that,' I can hear the reader shouting, 'with the immense range of local dishes from one end of the country to the other, the variety of styles and ingredients; given the eulogies heaped on it by every cookery expert, and its success and popularity when it has been exported around the world?'

My response is simple, and contradicts none of that. It is fine for tourists on a short visit to travel through Italy, the home of *prosciutto* and *parmesan*, white truffles and pizzas. In Bologna, they can savour *tagliatelle* with a proper *ragu* (our Emilian friends insist there is no such thing as spaghetti bolognese in Bologna), and experience real *Genovese pesto* made with local basil and *Sardo* cheese. It is stimulating for food writers and restaurateurs who can fly in for a week, sample some of the really excellent dishes in first-class restaurants and then fly home with the recipes they came to collect.

But for a family from any of the great cities of the world where tastes and kitchens have now been opened to embrace dozens of national cuisines, eating Italian permanently is quite another matter. To put it more simply, few people living in London, Sydney or New York, would think of eating only Greek, Lebanese, Japanese, Indian—or Italian—food every day. At first, it was a puzzle to me why Italy, which was the most innovative gastronomic country in Europe two or three hundred years ago, has remained traditional while others have experimented and developed. Even the experts on Italian cooking defer to the superiority of French cuisine. And while the French may not like to admit it, the foundations of their culinary art were laid by Italian cooks.

Charles VIII was the first to take home Italian recipes after his expedition to Naples in 1494; and the two Medici princesses Catherine and Maria whose marriages made them queens of France the following century, consolidated the Italian influence. Once, in Vienna's Schönbrunn Palace, a tour guide told me *sotto voce* that Wiener Schnitzel originated in Florence, where the Austrian court had been amazed to see veal cooked wrapped in gold leaf.

I believe it was all the invasions, the foreign tyrannies, the incessant subjugations that turned Italians in on themselves and made the family table the one central constant of their lives. If French cuisine challenges nature, Italian simply tries to present nature at its best. This is why there is no *haute cuisine* in Italy, just *buona cucina*.

The epithets Umbrians most frequently apply to their cooking—*semplice, genuina, simpatico*—simple, genuine and pleasant, underline its peasant origins and traditions. Early on, someone gave my wife a little local cookbook, *Umbria in Bocca—The Taste of Umbria*. It is printed on brown recycled paper, set between corrugated cardboard covers, and serves up its recipes in English, Italian and local dialect. In his preface, Enrico Vaime makes it clear that Umbrian cooking is 'poor cooking'. He recalls the bladder of lard that always hung by the stove and was the basis of so many dishes; the spelt (an antique wheat) cooked up with hambones; the long evenings around the fire, throwing in grains of *granturco* maize and watching them explode into white flowers long before he heard the word popcorn.

'Eating as we did, and in some ways as we still do, was more than mere nutrition; it was a moment of friendship and conviviality, a way of letting fantasy take over and disguise a relative poverty of ingredients.'

Umbrian food is still based on what can be grown or raised in the farmyard, and what can be foraged for or shot in the bush. So we have superb pork and pigmeat products, Norcia sausages, rabbits, chicken, turkey and pheasant, some of the best you could taste anywhere. The lamb, however, is pathetically young, small and flavourless, kept mainly for the ritual *Pasqua* dinner; and dairy products are strictly limited, mostly coming from other regions of Italy. For us, the high points of *cucina umbra* are the black truffles, with their distinctive earthy flavour, and the *porcini* we gather in the chestnut woods in October and November.

We cannot eat the Italian staples of pasta or rice every day. We needed to bring our culinary habits with us, and we believe we have the best of both worlds. Our friends here still cannot understand why we have not adopted Italian food one hundred per cent, but they now accept it.

When the Ascanios and our mutual friends from Bologna, the Finottis, first came to dinner, my wife served a basil and tomato risotto; turkey breasts stuffed with Umbrian sausage, parmesan, juniper, sage and mozarella; mixed vegetables (carrots, beans, peas, cauliflower and potato sliced and seasoned, then baked to a crisp); pears poached in red wine and arranged around a centre mould of cinnamon cream; and a fruit cake baked in honour of my approaching birthday. We had a very nice Chardonnay from the Trentino to accompany it. In the beginning, our guests were puzzled to put a name to it. It was definitely not Italian, although it had Italian elements. Then they decided it was *cucina internazionale* and felt happier.

If they come for summer lunch under the big umbrella on the terrace, they are likely to find a cold tomato and orange soup; a tuna and salmon *tagliatelle* with lots of cream; a mixed salad; gingered rockmelon and a rum cake. For our anniversary dinner, Audrey prepared salmon and caviar crepes; a meat loaf with pumpkin, sweet corn, beans, and potatoes rolled in oil and salt, then baked; and an Irish cream mousse. And a Cartizze, the prince of Proseccos from Valdobbiadene, because we were celebrating.

...

It was only a matter of time before one of us would break a tooth on the crust of hard Umbrian bread. A local saying is:
'*Chi ha denti non ha pane; e chi ha pane non ha denti.*'
'Those with teeth have no bread, those with bread have no teeth.'
This was coined as a barbed peasant jibe at the rich *padroni*, but it described perfectly our experience of the saltless taste-less cowpats labelled '*pane comune*'. The little crisis however

introduced us to Mario, the dentist in Castiglione del Lago, one of the more surreal characters in our orbit.

Mario had an English mother and Italian father (or the other way around, I can't remember which) and was constantly and schizophrenically emphasising either one cultural inheritance or the other. The first time he had me captive in the chair, he hit me with the question that had been worrying him for some time: 'How can I register my armoured car here?' My initial concern was that he was going single-handed to help the Americans in the Gulf War. But no, Mario had bought the ten-tonne vehicle for a song from Russian military disposals with the idea of using it, he said, as a mobile dental laboratory. He had already registered it for road use in Britain. The *Carabinieri* in quiet downtown Castiglione del Lago would have none of it, however, and I couldn't suggest a solution, so we never did see it in Italy.

It would be a slight understatement to say that Mario was preoccupied with sex. As soon as my mouth was wide open, he would begin his lament about Italian women as lovers.
'Keep away from them', he advised me needlessly, 'they're all mad. They can't make up their minds—one day they're climbing all over you, the next they don't want you to touch them'. And he would add, slightly tangentially, 'I'm half Italian myself, you know.'
One never knows what constitutes attractiveness; but Mario did not immediately commend himself as the Umbrian Casanova. About five feet tall, his white dental gown swept the floor like a cassock, and it seemed he was always about to

trip on its hem. With piercing black eyes and a sharp face, it was difficult to decide whether he looked more like Savonarola or a television comic.

His other passion was gadgetry. He had bought an obsolete sixty-thousand volt de-fibrillator from a London hospital for the surgery—he thought it might come in handy if a patient's heart should stop. Luckily none of his Italian patients knew what the box was, or their hearts might have stopped.

One day he was able to combine his two interests—sex and electronics—to advantage. When he had set up the surgery, he had installed all the wiring himself. Before he could be licensed, the electrical installation had to be passed by the electricity authority, ENEL. The inspector, who didn't seem to like the idea of a do-it-yourself job, was being very critical of what he was finding. One of the devices Mario had bought was an imaging scanner, which enabled him to project his dental X-rays onto a large TV screen. Waiting until the inspector's back was turned, Mario slipped a pornographic slide into the scanner; when the ENEL man switched on the set to test it, he could not take his eyes off the screen. And when he found Mario had a collection of these slides, he was hooked; it was the end of his tests and Mario's wiring got a clean bill of health.

8. JUSTICE, FASCISM AND WINE

'Justice is my being allowed to do whatever I like.
Injustice is whatever prevents my doing so.'
Samuel Butler

'More law, less justice.'
Cicero

In every courtroom in Italy, on the wall behind the bench, there is a large lettered sign where we have the national coat of arms. It reads: 'LA LEGGE È UGUALE PER TUTTI'—The Law is the Same For Everybody.

'Ah yes', said a friend (who had better remain unidentified), 'but what does it say about Justice?'

That little piece of quiet cynicism just about sums up the average Italian's confidence in his chances under the Civil and Criminal Codes. I have sensed a quiet envy of those of us privileged to have grown up under the British system of justice. It could be argued that of all the invaders who have left their mark on the country, Napoleon did the most lasting damage in his nine short years as King of Italy. By introducing the French codes he brought order to the chaotic and fragmented legal situation that existed between various states one hundred and ninety years ago (commerce, nationally and internationally, had become all but impossible). But ever since, Italians have been denied *habeas corpus*, refused the right to remain silent, and been stuck with the burden of proving their innocence.

The postman, Gian-Carlo arrived one morning with a registered letter to sign for and, I thought, a smirk on his face. 'You have been naughty haven't you?'

I looked blankly at the envelope, marked COMUNE DI ROMA, but he had seen many of them before, and he knew it contained a *multa*, a fine. I wasn't going to disappoint him, so I opened it there and then. Sure enough, a traffic violation notice. For having operated a motor scooter in a pedestrian precinct, to wit, the *Piazza di Spagna*, some three months earlier. The document generously offered me the opportunity to pay a concessional fine of fifty thousand *lire* immediately. If I delayed, it would be doubled, and interest would begin to mount. Gian-Carlo was watching my face.

'But this is absurd! I haven't been to Rome this year, and my scooter hasn't been out of this area. How would I ride it a hundred and fifty kilometres to Rome?'

He leaned over my shoulder to inspect the summons. 'Is that your *targa*?'

'Yes that's my number plate, but they've obviously made a mistake somehow.'

Number plates and registrations had only just been introduced for scooters and *motorini*. Ever since the first scooter was cobbled together by Lambretta from war disposal materials—the wheels from bomb trolleys and the engines from aircraft starter motors—all these vehicles with tiny 50cc engines had travelled free on the roads. They had got a war-ravaged country mobile again, but had also been a boon for the bag snatchers who could operate *incognito* in Rome. Licensing them ended that advantage and provided a nice fiscal windfall for the government—there were nine million of these machines. The imposition was accepted surprisingly calmly, except for the protest that the number plate, rectangular with its two top corners clipped, was identical to that on wartime vehicles of the hated German SS.

Gian-Carlo wagged his finger at me. Poor silly *straniero*! 'If it's your targa, you'll just have to pay it. It's no use arguing, it will only cost you more in the end, you can't win.' He felt sorry for me, and obviously I needed good advice.

'I can't win? Do you want to bet?'

I felt the Ned Kelly syndrome taking over, the rush of blood to the Australian head at injustice that led to the Eureka Stockade (and much more besides), but Gian-Carlo went off shaking his head. The next day I was up at the post office when it opened, to register a letter to the *Comune di Roma*. A letter of outrage in English and Italian, pointing out that this time they had picked the wrong man, giving the reasons why, declaring the availability of supporting witnesses and demanding a withdrawal of the notice and the fine forthwith. Gian-Carlo commended me on my translation but said, rather hopelessly I thought, 'Buona fortuna!'

I had long since learned that Italian officialdom never answers letters—it's the first rule of self-preservation—so as the months went by I wasn't surprised at the lack of response. Gian-Carlo was worried that the fine was mounting up, but eventually he tired of asking me if there'd been any news. Six months later came a pro-forma letter from Rome, asking me to return the original notice. Nothing more. No acknowledgement, no explanation, no admission, no apology. Perhaps the magistrates who were investigating corruption involving some hundreds of Rome *vigili* had had something to do with it, but I will never know. I was in the post office when the letter arrived, and I was pleased to see there were a few locals at the counter. It was a brief opportunity to get a message to these unfortunate law-trodden people to stick up for themselves. 'Gian-Carlo' I said, loudly enough for the audience to take it in, 'this proves that you Italians must learn to fight bureaucracy. *Combattere!* You can win if it is unjust.'
It was a stirring moment I thought, but he just looked at me kindly over his glasses, smiled and said nothing. Poor silly *straniero!*

. . .

As a boy growing up during the war years, all I knew of Benito Mussolini was the propaganda caricature of the newspapers. The puffed up strutting figure in comic opera uniform, pudding-basin helmet on head, jaw out-thrust and right arm raised in the salute he invented to avoid the English custom of shaking hands, was such a tempting target for the newspaper cartoonists.

During the siege of Tobruk and the battle for El Alamein not a week went by without a sneering reference to 'Musso', as we knew him. After the battle for Sidi Barrani, we laughed when the battalion headquarters of the Coldstream Guards reported the capture of 'about five acres of officers and two hundred acres of other ranks'. The photographs of columns of Italian soldiers marching into captivity, guarded by a single Digger or Tommy, confirmed our contemptuous view of the Italian fighting spirit, despite the *braggadocio* of their leader.

What I didn't know then, was that long before that time, most ordinary Italians held Mussolini in the same contempt. That wasn't cowardice in the desert, but blessed release from an unwanted war. I didn't know that while we were shocked by that terrible image of the dictator strung up by his heels in a Milan square, most ordinary Italians felt relief, if not outright satisfaction.

Italians are attracted to symbolism. Of all the squares in Milan, the Piazza Loreto was chosen specially as the place of public humiliation after his execution. Eight months earlier, fifteen partisans had been executed there by the Fascists. I was fascinated to discover that the infamous manner of his disgrace which so horrified the world was probably also specially chosen, if not consciously, then at least subliminally, from a page in Italian history.

Almost five hundred years before, Cola di Rienza, son of a washerwoman, rose from obscurity to displace the ruling nobility of Rome—the Colonna, the Orsini, the Caetani—and proclaim himself Tribune of a new republic. Like Mussolini, he had visions of unifying Italy, of recapturing the grandeur and power of ancient Rome. But he too fell victim to his own megalomania and suffered a similar dramatic reversal of popularity. Like Mussolini, he attempted to escape *incognito* at the end. But he was recognised by his rings and gold bracelets, hacked to death and hanged by the feet outside the church of San Marcello. His rule lasted seven months; Mussolini's lasted twenty-one years.

I have often wondered if the gruesome spectacle of Piazza Loreto was a sort of national expiation of Italy's crime of once having loved the man and supported his regime. Unlike Britain and France, Italy had never killed a king; perhaps the cleansing and healing power of the scaffold was needed.

It is difficult for an Australian to fully understand the extent to which the war scarred the Italian national psyche. It was not so much losing the war, as ending it held in contempt both by Germany, the ally they betrayed with their separate armistice, and by the ultimate victors, whose liberation effort they so badly impeded with their incompetence at the surrender and afterwards.

Richard Lamb, the English historian who fought as an infantry officer in the Italian campaign, has written a definitive account of those events in his *War in Italy—a Brutal Story*. He documents the dithering of the Italian War Office, and of Marshall Badoglio in particular. Badoglio had been appointed

Prime Minister by King Victor Emmanuel III after he had dismissed Mussolini and had him arrested. Hitler immediately suspected the Italians of treachery. By failing to block the alpine passes, Badoglio allowed him to pour eight German divisions into Italy and occupy the entire north and centre of the country in the forty-five fateful days before the unconditional surrender was finally signed.

To coincide with the armistice, General Eisenhower had planned 'Operation Giant Two' in which the US 82nd Airborne Division would capture the Rome airfields, followed by seaborne landings at the mouth of the Tiber twenty-four hours later. At the very last minute, when the paratroopers were already in the air, their planes had to be turned back to Sicily. It was discovered that the Italian command had not even bothered to translate the plans for the landing, and had been lying when they gave the excuse that petrol and ammunition were not available for their forces to support the air-drop. The opportunity to outflank the Germans was lost and they massed a heavy and costly opposition to the Salerno landing. Monte Cassino was destroyed and Rome remained in enemy hands for another nine months.

It was even worse for the Italians. Badoglio's broadcast on the armistice was vague and confusing. He merely ordered Italian troops not to fight the Anglo-Americans and 'to resist attacks from wherever they come'. The whole Badoglio government and the King then fled Rome. The Italian army, which could have given such great support to the Allies, disintegrated. Lamb writes, 'Many Italian soldiers were shot, or sent to

Germany in cattle wagons; most took the announcement of the Armistice as a signal to go to their homes as quickly as possible, by bicycle, train or on foot.'

The collapse of Mussolini's regime left the country confused and demoralised. It is only since coming to live in Italy that it has been possible for me to comprehend the extraordinary impact *Il Duce* had in only two decades. But it was a surprise to realise how he continues to divide the country. There is an undying hatred of the leader who wanted peace but led the country into a disastrous war. There is contempt for the man who founded an empire but ended up head of a puny republic. Mussolini was the demagogue who promised to remake Italy, but instead destroyed it. And yet a macabre fascination surrounding him has never been exorcised. How many people have their own posthumous official site on the Internet? (http://www.mussolini.it).

Until recently, only foreign historians had attempted an objective evaluation of the Fascist phenomenon. It was taboo to Italians. The so-called 'Values of the Resistance' had become so embedded in postwar mythology as to be sacrosant. To point out that Italy was liberated by the American and British armies, not the partisans; that much of *'La Resistenza'* was under central communist control, acting with an opportunistic eye to postwar political gain, and under Moscow's direction; that Mussolini's execution itself was carried out to further that aim—all this was not merely heretical, it could be illegal. A 1975 law laid down severe penalties for any group that dared criticise those undefined Resistance values.

One of the problems Italians have in understanding their recent past became clear to me when RAI, the national television service, broadcast a documentary series titled *Combat Film*. It used graphic wartime footage shot by cameramen attached to the American forces, freshly discovered in the National Archives in Washington. In a studio discussion audience including students from Milan University, only one girl knew who Marshall Badoglio was. It emerged that in Italian schools, history teaching stopped at 1918. One history professor even went so far as to say that in European history, nothing after Cardinal Richelieu was of importance! As we watched in disbelief, we realised that Italy's education system had completely ducked the problem of putting the Fascist era, World War II and the last fifty years into perspective. The nerves were still too raw; the deep political divisions made it impossible to write a universally acceptable account.

But as the fiftieth anniversary of the end of World War II approached, an avalanche of books and articles on the Fascist era descended on Italy. The role of the Resistance came under real scrutiny by Italian historians for the first time. 'It has been over-valued', some concluded. 'Anti-Fascism has sustained us for fifty years', said others, 'now Italians must decide what they are <u>for</u>!' The leading historian of that period, Renzo De Felice, had researched Mussolini and his Fascism for thirty years. He concluded that relatively few were involved in the Resistance; the vast majority of Italians wanted nothing to do with them or the Fascists. Richard Lamb agrees, quoting Mussolini's letter to Hitler:

'The great majority of the population are still stunned by the events...and swing from a desire for revenge to a state of resignation.'

How to explain the renewed fascination with Mussolini? It could have been the swing to the right in European politics in the mid-1990s, and of course he is central to the explanation of Fascism. But perhaps it is because there is a little bit of him in every Italian; Mussolini represents the bad conscience of Italy. On Liberation Day, Indro Montanelli, the grand old man of Italian journalism, was asked if he could give a balanced view of Mussolini, fifty years on. He wrote:

'Mussolini represents the worst of the best in Italians, and the best of our worst. He was above all an Italian, with faults and virtues. His illusions, weaknesses and the disastrous errors that derived from them are illusions and errors that appear to us part of our mentality and our collective imagination. This is why his name so divides us. In essence, he was tuned in to the country. A frightful tragedy that has scored the destiny of our nation.'

All through the 1920s and into the 1930s, Mussolini was undoubtedly more popular than any man since the Caesars. The country revelled in his theatricality, and rose to the passion of his powerful if empty oratory, the hysterical crowds in front of the Palazzo Venezia in Rome shouting *'Duce! Duce!'* and that meaningless war cry dreamed up by the flamboyant poet, Gabriele D'Annunzio, *'eia! eia! alala!'* For a time the fascist slogan—*Credere! Obbedire! Combattere!*—Believe! Obey! Fight!—convinced sheeplike Italians that they could become lions, recapturing the power and the glory of ancient Rome. But as events in the Western Desert proved, they were much less willing to respond to his melodramatic call to arms: 'If I advance, follow me; if I retreat, kill me; if I die, avenge me!'. They did not need long memories. In the fascists' loudly-trumpeted 'March on Rome' to seize power in 1922, Mussolini travelled by train.

Mussolini was essentially a showman, 'a flamboyant actor of heroic roles in the style of nineteenth-century tragedians or operatic baritones', as Luigi Barzini once described him. He was openly contemptuous of his fellow Italians, but he believed he could change them. He wrote:

'Le tare del carattere italiano sono il semplicissimo, la facíloneria, il credere che tutto andrà bene.'

'The hereditary defects of the Italian character are the superficiality, the easy-goingness, the belief that everything will turn out OK.'

Do I hear echoes of the Australian 'She'll be right, mate'?

The Germans have made a determined effort to put Hitler and Nazism behind them. Of the Reich Chancellery in Berlin nothing remains but an air vent to the bunkers. No tomb, no memorial, no focus for a revival. But there is a Mussolini tomb and shrine, and every year more and more Italians are drawn to it. It's on the outskirts of the prosperous little Romagnolo town of Predappio where the son of a blacksmith was born under a propitious sign. 'The sun had entered the constellation of Leo eight days before', he wrote in his autobiography. The fiftieth anniversary of his execution seemed a good time to see just who these pilgrims were, and to try to understand the dictator's continuing magnetism.

It's a delightful if tiring drive from Umbria to the Romagna. Along the valley of the Upper Tiber into Tuscany; past the walls of Sansepolcro, birthplace of Piero della Francesca, with the forbidding Mountains of the Moon looming behind; then climbing over the Serra Alps of the Apennines, part of the Gothic Line where the Allied advance was halted in the winter of 1943; then down into Romagna and along the Savio River to Cesena. Predappio is just a short distance away, at the foot of the vine-covered hills.

In Cesena we picked up Vittorio Pezzi, a retired Air Force avionics engineer and local history enthusiast, who was to be our guide. We were fortunate to know him. A Romagnolo born and bred, he has tramped all over his province. He is proud of its culture and, a big plus for us, also knows its best wineries. Vittorio was charmingly tolerant of the Australians who wanted to delve into the Fascist past, but he made it perfectly clear where he stood.

'I am on the other side of the fence', he announced. 'For me and my country, Mussolini with his Fascism was a disaster. I have no time for those who want to revere him.'

Vittorio didn't take us directly to Predappio. First he wanted to show us a much more impressive relic of the Mussolini years, one probably unknown to the Fascist neophytes we were to meet later. So we took a back road, and wound our way up through vineyards to the top of a hill, four hundred metres high. There was too much smog for us to see far, but before industry came, there was a commanding view of the country—west to the Apennines, and east over a hundred kilometres of the coastal plain, from Ravenna to Pesaro. Which is why the Sforza chose the hill to build their feudal castle, *Fortezza Ravaldino*.

Five hundred years ago, this *condottieri* family from the Abruzzo was among the upwardly mobile of Italy. They swung their little army of mercenaries in support of the Malatestas of Rimini against the Venetians and won. As a reward—whether given or merely taken is not clear from the histories—they carved out this piece of territory in the Romagna for themselves. Francesco Sforza went on to become Duke of Milan. He forged documents to bolster his shaky claim to the seat through marriage to the illegitimate daughter of the last Visconti. In the guide books, the Sforza are remembered as a Milan family, but the Romagna was their launching pad.

The *Fortezza Ravaldino* became the *Rocca delle Caminate*, fell into ruins, and passed to the care of the Province of Forli. It was perhaps as much to avoid the ruinous cost of restoration as to honour a famous son of the district that the Province decided to present the *Rocca* to Mussolini as his country home. The Fascist government of the 1930s spent an enormous sum to restore it. I wished I could have seen it then. *Il Duce* loved to relax there, looking out over the countryside of his boyhood. He filled it with treasures of the Roman Empire, and the gifts that flooded in from all around the world. His study walls were papered with photographs of himself—as statesman, soldier, family man, pilot, or shirtless in the fields leading the 'Battle for Wheat'.

When Otto Skorzeny daringly rescued him from imprisonment at Gran Sasso after his overthrow in September 1943, Mussolini regrouped his fascist hierarchy at the *Rocca*. There they planned the Socialist Republic of Italy to be set up at Salo on Lake Garda as a puppet government for the Germans. He was, however, virtually a prisoner on his favourite hill. Sick and pessimistic, he is reported to have said to his secretary: 'You haven't had the courage to tell me that today I am the most hated man in Italy.' Despite his dislike of Quisling and the term taken from his name, Mussolini knew that ironically, he had become Italy's equivalent. De Felice in the last volume of his enormous history of Fascism gives him credit for doing it to save his country from an even worse fate—an Italy destroyed like Poland.

During the grand days Mussolini had made one big addition to the hilltop—a lighthouse. On a square tower seventy-five metres high he had mounted a revolving light that could be seen by ships out in the Adriatic, forty kilometres away. And from all the towns around. Like the Queen's standard flown at Windsor, Balmoral or Sandringham, Mussolini's flashing beacon signalled that he was in residence. The tower is still a landmark. Vittorio told us nobody could remember when the light last flashed. He explained that at the end of the war, *Rocca delle Caminate* was the only property the Mussolini family owned. His widow, Rachele, lived there almost until her death in 1979, after which it was returned to the Province of Forli. Today it stands locked, empty and deteriorating because nobody can agree on what to do with it, or how to fund its repair.

All down the road, opposite the massive wall around the grounds, there is a series of small stone buildings, now crumbling into decay. I would have driven past with hardly a glance, but Vittorio stopped me.

'Those were the guardhouses', he explained. 'Every fifty metres, manned with fully armed troops when Mussolini was here.'

We snaked slowly down through the tight hairpins on the road to Predappio and a big surprise. We expected a nondescript village living off the surrounding agriculture like hundreds of others in Emilia-Romagna. But the main street was almost a boulevard, wide enough for a military parade. None of the usual huddle of shops and houses; rows of grand *palazzi* in the classic style faced each other across the space.

At the end of the street, a vast *piazza* opened out. And on the corner stood the most improbable building imaginable in such a country township—a multi-storey block with a huge tower in the *razionalismo* style, the brutish Fascist version of vertical modernism. That austere, deliberately awe-inspiring architecture remains in every Italian city today in its law court building, the *Palazzo di Iustitzia*. In Predappio, however, this was the *Casa del Fascio*, the local Fascist Party headquarters. For some years after World War II it was occupied by a clothing factory, but today it stands empty and rusting. In its setting in the Romagna countryside, it looked an architectural dinosaur.

Just as he had 'improved' Rome by demolishing whole districts to create triumphal avenues—the *Via della Conciliazione* leading to St Peter's and the *Via dei Fori Imperiali*—Mussolini had set about improving his home town. In the work-starved depression years the Mussolini connection gave Predappio a construction boom. As well as the buildings in the town centre, he designed an imposing semicircular colonnade. It looks as if it belongs in a Roman forum, but leads nowhere and served no purpose except to symbolise the birth of the glorious new empire. The plaster is now peeling, and the walls have become a canvas for the *graffitisti*. Predappio's mayor talks about turning the *Casa del Fascio* into a museum displaying all the projects and technical inventions of the 1920s, but the funds would have to come from the central government in Rome, and that's hardly likely.

Vittorio took us on a little excursion to find the poor house where Mussolini was born, on a small hill above the town. It's a typical peasant cottage with rubble walls and an outside stair-case, built onto the side of a much bigger house. His mother Rosa ran a small school there—the family had to go through the classroom to reach their bedroom. Someone had nailed a crudely-lettered sign on plywood over the door: '*Casa natale di Benito Mussolini*'.

I thought it rather surprising that the Mayor should suggest turning the house into a reference library devoted to Fascism—with books both pro and con. After all, he is a former communist, now a member of the sanitised Democratic Left. He doesn't seem to have his heart in it, however, and has devoted his energies to prosecuting street pedlars of Fascist souvenirs. I came to the conclusion that Predappio would like to forget its most famous son, but in typically Italian fashion will do nothing, just waiting for time to erase his traces.

We drove up the road to Predappio Alto, with its mediaeval fortress high up in the Apennine foothills. Before Mussolini's time it was bigger and more important than the Predappio of today. As a boy, Vittorio had been sent there for the clear fresh air, to cure his chest problems. He recalled that the old priest used to make his own wine and sell it to the villagers, but always took care to water it down first.

Around a turn in that road, we came on a huge ochre-coloured building, another Mussolini white elephant. It had been a wartime aircraft factory, relocated to Predappio to create more jobs. The obsolescent Falcon fighters that were so easily outclassed by British Spitfires and American Mustangs were built in huge underground workshops there, dug back into the hillside as protection against air raids. A sign on the fading facade made me think of swords into ploughshares. Sixty years later, it's a mushroom factory.

All this patronage brought *Il Duce* local affection, and his home town may be the better for it. But (there is always a 'but' in the Mussolini saga) his greatest architectural contribution was entirely egocentric. At Dovia, a couple of kilometres outside Predappio, the Romanesque basilica of San Cassiano in Appennino has stood for more than a thousand years. Its golden walls of the local tufa-like stone glow in the afternoon sunlight. High above the portal, the work of the ancient stone masons—representations of animals of the countryside as well as saints—nestle, sheltered from the weather in hooded niches, almost perfectly preserved.

Inside, the massive simple pillars flanking the nave lead the eye directly to a broad flight of steps and up to the altar on a mezzanine level, with the crypt below. In the early 1930s, the church was in ruins; Mussolini had it restored at state expense. I was about to remark that it was a tribute to him when I noticed the reconstructed stone balustrading of the stairs was incised with *fasci*, the bundle of lictor's rods and axe that was the Fascist logo. Alongside, carved in a roundel was 'EF XII', meaning the twelfth year of the Fascist era, 1934. It was a vulgar political touch, which cheapened the contribution. But the man who had scandalised the *Curia* twenty-five years earlier with his trashy novel, *The Cardinal's Mistress*, had by then reached his Concordat with the Vatican, so no doubt felt free to claim public credit for his good works.

The restoration of San Cassiano may have been intended only as a diplomatic sop to the *Curia*, to gain permission for his great design. In the same year, Mussolini ordered the construction behind the church of a semicircular cloister for the tombs of important locals and members of the Fascist hierarchy. At the centre was a chapel, and beneath that a crypt for his parents, and ultimately for himself. He was preparing his place in history. We went down into the crypt, a tiny mausoleum. At the turn of the steps he had so placed a wall plaque that it was impossible to miss. It carried a quotation from the book he had written two years earlier to honour his dead brother Arnaldo, the only confidant in his life:

'*Sarei grandemente ingenuo se chiedessi di essere lasciato in pace dopo morto. Attorno alle tombe dei capi di quelle grandi trasformazione, che si chiamono rivoluzioni, non ci puo essere*

pace; ma tutto quello che fu fatto non potra essere cancellato.
Mentre il mio spirito, ormai liberato dalla materia, vivra, dopo
la piccola vita terrena, la vita immortale e universale di Dio. Non
ho che un desiderio, quello di essere sepolto accanto ai miei nel
cimitero di S.Cassiano.'

'It would be highly ingenuous of me to ask to be left in
peace when I am dead. There can never be peace around
the tombs of the leaders of those great transformations
that men call revolutions; but the achievements will
never be erased. Whereas my spirit, by now freed from
the body after its brief stay on earth, will live God's
immortal and universal life. I have only one wish—to
be buried alongside my family in the cemetery of San
Cassiano.'

The crypt itself seemed crowded—filled with tombs and
with blackshirts. The lights were dim. In the cramped space,
the air was charged, not with violence, but with the reverence
I have seen at war cemeteries. There were a few old men of
World War II, who said nothing, betrayed no emotion.

The huge stone sarcophagi carried the names in large
brass letters: parents Alessandro and Rosa; wife, Rachele;
sister, Anna Maria; son Bruno (killed in an air crash at Pisa);
daughter-in-law Gina Ruberti. Photographs and busts lined
the walls. But the pilgrims hardly glanced at them. All eyes
were turned to the brightly-lit alcove where a white marble
bust of the dictator, three times life size, glared arrogantly
over his tomb. Sheaves of flowers—roses, carnations and
gladioli—covered the stone, and spilled onto the floor.

The blackshirts were almost all young, in their twenties or thirties. They had known nothing of Fascism; the man they now idolised had been blown away on the winds of history twenty years before they were born. But they were there, one told me, to honour a strong leader. Italy today was just a mess of gutless politicians. They shuffled in quietly and stood staring at the tomb. Some laid more flowers. Every few minutes one would stride forward, click heels and snap out the Roman salute. Some had themselves photographed in that pose, to prove they had made their obeisance at the shrine. The calm was reassuring; I had been half-expecting an aggressive reaction to the intrusion of curious foreigners.

On the wall on either side of the great marble bust, glass-fronted display cases held memorabilia of *Il Duce*. In one, the plumed hat of his dress *Bersaglieri* uniform (he fought in World War I, was wounded, and it was said that he got around Milan on crutches somewhat longer than necessary). In others, his black shirt and the boots he was wearing at the end. On the wall was the boldly stylised 'M' of his signature; in the 1930s it had been as well known as his face.

Outside, in the bright sunlight of a spring afternoon, we found a dozen of the young faithful gathered around an old woman. She had been a *fascista*, she said, and was proud of it. The group listened in awe.

'Do you know', she told them, 'the body of *Il Duce* had been buried anonymously in the Musocco Cemetery in Milan, so that nobody could come to pay homage. But our people found the grave. One night in 1946, Domenico Leccisi, a man who later became a member of parliament, stole the body and hid it in the Convent of the Minor Friars of Sant'Angelo. Much later they brought it here from Milan, in a fruit case!' (Official photographs of the 1957 transfer show this was something of an exaggeration).

The pilgrims came and went quietly, and the *carabinieri* squads rostered to cope with any trouble looked bored. A year earlier the day had been much more dramatic. Mussolini's grand-daughter Alessandra and other neo-Fascist members of parliament had been heckled as they arrived for a commemorative mass. Neo-Fascists had tried to drape their banner on the altar and had to be restrained by the police. The old priest, Don Giuseppe Piscitelli, instead of delivering the usual homily, had read what he said was Mussolini's last letter, written the night before he was shot:

> '*Perdono a quanti non mi perdonano e mi condannano condannando se stessi...penso a coloro cui sarà negato per anni di amare la patria, vorrei che si sentissero non solo testimoni di una disfatta, ma alfieri della rivincità.*'

> 'I forgive all those who do not forgive me; condemning me, they condemn themselves...I think of those who for years will be denied the right to love their country, I would like them to feel themselves not merely witnesses of a defeat, but standard bearers of the revenge.'

On our way out of Predappio, we stopped at the Patriot Shop. It is devoted to memorabilia of Mussolini. Now that the 1983 decree prohibiting the sale of souvenirs of Fascism has been withdrawn, you can buy watches, keyrings, tiepins, inkstands and cigarette lighters, all bearing the Fascist insignia. There are Roman eagles and busts of Mussolini in every attitude, in every size, and tape recordings of all his speeches. The proprietor told me he does a brisk trade from the one hundred thousand pilgrims to Predappio every year; in death, Mussolini's fascination continues to sell. Outside the shop, a young blackshirt posed for my camera in a truculent stance typical of *Il Duce*, then got into his Mercedes to drive home to Bologna. There was no sign of 'the revenge'. For all but the fanatics, in his home town Mussolini has been reduced to a tourist gimmick.

...

Then it was off to the hills. Fifteen hundred years ago, Galla Placidia, whose mausoleum in Ravenna still sparkles with the gold and lapis mosaic stars of its vault and is one of the wonders of Italy, was Empress of the Visigoth Empire. There's a legend that the local *Albana* wine so captivated her that she raised her terracotta cup and exclaimed: 'You should not be drunk in such a humble way. *Berti in oro!*—I will drink you in gold.' And that, the story goes, is how the hilltown of Bertinoro, centre of the Romagna wine trade got its name. It's now the home base of the *Ente Tutela Vini Romagnoli*, the consortium which pulled off a coup some years ago in winning the coveted DOCG (*Denominazione di Origine Controllata e Garantita*) appellation for *Albana*. There was a furious reaction from its competitors in other wine areas but, on paper at least, this elevated it to the status of Italy's premier white wine. The symbol of the consortium is the *passatore*, a bearded nineteenth century brigand in cocked hat, a legend for his defiance of authority. Now he's the embodiment of local success in battling Italy's wine legislators for recognition.

If Bertinoro is the balcony of the Romagna, with a huge view of its hills and valleys, the Ente's headquarters is the box seat. We sipped *Albana Secco* and enjoyed the magnificent vista through the huge plate-glass windows. The modern building, in mediaeval style, is part wine museum, part tasting and selling centre, and part guildhall for the district's winemakers.

Vittorio was anxious to take us to meet the best of them, Mario Pezzi at Fattoria Paradiso. The estate has been growing vines since the fifteenth century, but in the last thirty years has been at the forefront in lifting the quality of Romagnolo wines to world class. Mario led us into the tasting room to try the *Albana* first. The *Dolce* is a golden straw-coloured dessert wine, not too sweet. It's undoubtedly the most subtle wine I have tasted in Italy. The *Secco*, also with a DOCG classification, was the real discovery. It is pale, straw-coloured also but, unusually for Italian whites, has a delicate bouquet.

If you want to pick a fight, tell a Tuscan winemaker that the *Sangiovese* grape (*sanguis Jovis*—the blood of Jupiter), one of Italy's noble red-wine grapes, originates in the Romagna. On the other hand, it's wise not to mention *Chianti Classico* or *Brunello* around Bertinoro. Fattoria Paradiso makes two fabulous *Sangiovese* DOC wines, both of which hold their own with the best of *Montalcino*, *Montepulciano* or *Chianti Classico*, in my view. Pezzi's *Superiore Riserva* from his *Vigna delle Lepri* vineyard is a magnificently understated wine, soft, with a bouquet of cherries.

The deep cellars are full of his other wines too—*Barbarossa*, *Cagnina*, *Garibaldino*, *Trebbiano* and *Jacopo*. Few of them would be known outside Italy, although Mario told me the *Barbarossa* has been a hit in the White House. But the fun wine for me—because it has a catchy story behind it too—was another white, his *Pagadebit*. The name says it all. The grape, known in other regions as *Bombino Bianco*, makes into a very ordinary wine, but gives such consistent yields it enables farmers to pay off their debts when other crops fail.

When we got back to Cesena at the end of a long day, we found Vittorio's wife, Adriana, had prepared a simple Romagnola meal for us. Plates of cold meat—*prosciutto, coppa, salame* and *mortadella*—creamy *squaquerone,* the local milk cheese, and a salad of tomatoes and field greens. Hot from the stone came a stack of her own *piadine,* the thin flat griddlecake, once the daily bread of Romagna's peasants. And a *Paradiso rosso.* Then home, the car heavy with *Albana, Sangiovese* and *Pagadebit.*

9. SUMMER—FIREFLIES, FESTIVALS AND FIRES

Summer in sunny Italy is what brings the tourists—as many as forty million come every year—but it's hell for the natives. For a frantic two months in July and August the *autostrade* and the streets of historic cities and picturesque hilltowns are jammed with cars, tourist coaches and campervans, disrupting local lives and poisoning the air.

In inferno-like temperatures, chefs in *ristoranti* and *pizzerie* up and down the country sweat to cook for the hungry northern hordes. The tourists come, as their forefathers did centuries ago, for the local food, but now they pay for it. Economic success for the Italians still depends on decisions made far away, but now the determining factors are global exchange rates rather than the ambitions of Austrian and French emperors. The season is a short one, and at the end everyone is exhausted.

Those who can, that is the ones who don't have to serve the tourists, escape to the sea. Twelve million cars will be on the roads the day the summer exodus begins. At every available unpolluted stretch along Italy's littoral of eight thousand kilometres, Italians will pay to sit shoulder to shoulder in the phalanxes of deck chairs hired out by local *imprenditori* who have gained monopoly rights to the beach. They will splash themselves in the tepid water, few will swim (they can't or they dare not for fear of *inquinamento*), but they will return home proudly with the obligatory *abbronzatura*. Tanning is the whole purpose of the holiday. A pale skin at the end of summer is a fashion failure. Zeno's wife Carmela was so distressed at Audrey's pale skin that she pressed on her a bottle of '*huile de Tahiti*'. The label promised a 'gilded tan' from the powerful tanning agent it contained; fortunately Audrey tried it first on only a small sample of skin. It turned yellow.

In Paciano all of this frenetic activity passes us by. Life slows as the temperature climbs into the high thirties, but doesn't stop. Ivo Santeroni's tractor drivers are hard at work with their giant rippers, hurrying to turn the fields into rows of huge grey clods after the harvest. Ivo swaps his trademark greasy blue overalls for shorts and singlet and sits panting near his petrol pumps. We're off the beaten track, so he's only bothered by the few English tourists and muscular Germans who come with their mountain bikes on top of their cars to ride in our hills.

This is the season of *afa*, the sweltering combination of high temperature and high humidity without wind. The relentless sun sucks every drop of moisture from the ground, producing a blue-white haze that spoils the tourists' photos. There will be no relief before September. At Boldrini's Bar on the corner, all the chairs and tables are moved outside under the lime trees, and are more or less permanently occupied by the old men of the village. Old Remo Boldrini himself, now in his eighties, returns from his early morning *zapping* of his olives to join them. He was mayor for twenty-eight years, and saw through much of the beautification of the town. Across the road, on the terraced gardens and playground cascading down the slope outside the town walls that will be his memorial, the sprinklers battle the sun's heat. In the town centre the *Comune* hangs notices on all the public taps, limiting water use to ten litres a family.

The teenage boys show off, buzzing up and down the *Viale Roma* on their new mopeds, then park and talk to the girls as they do everywhere in Italy. They're at a loose end. Summer school holidays last three months, an outdated relic of the time when the whole family was needed to help bring in the harvest. While they all wear the latest gear, none of them would think of taking a holiday job; we calculate summer holidays cost parents more than the whole of the school year. The spoilt youth of the modern prosperous Italy is better able than ever to follow the famous advice of a dying Roman father: 'My sons, you must all try to have an occupation in life. Life without an occupation is contemptible and meaningless. But always remember this: you must never allow your occupation to degenerate into work.'

Every summer the countryside below us looks different as the cropping pattern changes. This is partly the result of normal rotation, but the Common Agricultural Policy of the

European Union has a big influence. The *Confederazione Italiana Agricoltori* keeps its farmers aware of what attracts the best subsidies; this year, for example, it's oilseeds, so the country is ablaze with sunflowers. (We felt quite cheated by the Italians calling them *girasole*. They may turn their faces to the morning sun, but they don't follow it round all day.) In our first year, grain crops and corn were all the go. As the summer began, our nights were shattered by deafening reports of a howitzer every three or four minutes till dawn. When this had gone on for several days and our sleep was suffering, I asked *Zio* Carlo what all the bangs were for.

'It's for the mice', he replied.

'The mice!? Is there a plague of mice?'

'No, no! it's the mice...in the *campo*', he looked a little exasperated, 'because of the pigs!'

So the pigs were chasing the mice...it didn't make sense.

'Carlo, where are the mice?'

'Why, in the field below you', he replied, 'at the bottom of the hill'.

I mentally ticked off the paddocks down the road until I came to the one above the dam . . . down by the lake yes, but never up here had I seen farmers grow corn before...ah...corn! maize!—not mice, but *mais*. I was reacting like Mark Twain, an innocent abroad: 'They spell it *Vinci* and pronounce it Vin-chy; foreigners always spell better than they pronounce.'

I found the howitzers. They were big gas guns. They had a short, wide steel barrel like a mediaeval mortar. A propane bottle was set to leak its gas steadily into the barrel where a piezo-electric spark triggered by a timer exploded it. The booms echoing up the valley would keep any wild pig out of the corn—as well as any mice that might be thinking of a snack.

If it's a year for barley or wheat, the locals aren't worrying too much about the pigs. They may do some damage trampling the crop, but even their tough snouts can't cope with the sharp spikes that protect the grain within the ear. No, the farmers will be more interested in the fireflies.

Well into July, the warm still nights are perforated by the magical winking lights of the *lucciole*. By then, they seem to like the cool of the gullies and the roadside banks and at times they almost swarm through our fruit trees. In the spring and early summer they mate, helicoptering, in the warm air above the sweeping expanse of the fields of grain, flashing their coded signals in an aerial love dance. In their hordes they seem to light up the fields. Rural tradition has it that by turning night into day for the grain, the *lucciole* encourage the crop to grow. The old *contadini* say '*Bel lucciolaio, bel granaio*'.

But summertime in the hilltowns of Umbria is above all festival time. Each centre has its own *sagra*, its popular celebration that once commemorated the consecration of its church or the day of its patron saint. Now it is likely to be named after the distinctive local product—*funghi, carciofi, aglio, uva, cinghiale, pesce, meloni, tulipani*—and almost everything else that is grown, raised or shot. However, each of these has its own season, and that doesn't always coincide with midsummer. Paciano's is the *Festa dell' Olio*, in December, after the oil is made. After World War II, the Communist Party very smartly captured the high ground of provincial culture by re-establishing the ancient rural tradition of summer communal festivity. It launched the *Festa dell'Unità* to an immediate success. Every town and village in Umbria has its Unity Festival.

For days before the festive week begins, little vans with loud-speakers wobbling precariously on top tour the district, and the metallic recorded voice lists the attractions for the year. There is great competition to secure the top pop group and people travel miles out of their own territory to hear the brilliant boy piano accordionist, who performs in Tyrolese garb. During the week, there may be a gymkhana, a classic car competition and games for the children. But whatever the variations in the enter-tainment programme, it all comes down to the core activities of eating and dancing. An old Umbrian proverb has it: *'Chi non vuol ballare, non vada alla festa'*—'If you don't want to dance, don't go to the party' which has some overtones of 'If you can't stand the heat, keep out of the kitchen'.

Here in Paciano, a camp kitchen is set up behind the Church of Our Lady of the Assumption to prepare the *bruschetta*, the inevitable *pasta*, and the *bistecc'alla maiale* or *salsicce*; trestle tables set up under the stars (it's too hot to eat before eight or nine o'clock in the evening); up in the *piazza*, there's a stage for the performers overlooking the dancing area. But at this point, the community divides.

Even though the Communist Party has now transmogrified into the PDS—the Democratic Party of the Left—the ten to fifteen per cent of the village who don't vote for it won't hear of their support or their money going to the Party, and so stay away. This has given an opportunity for voluntary organisations to stage their own dinner party, which everyone can attend. Paciano's is run by AVIS (not rental cars but *Associazione Voluntari Italiani Sangue*), the blood donors' society. Since the Ascanios and their friends support AVIS but not left-wing political parties, we always end up there. It's a very pleasant way to pass a couple of hours, yarning with friends over a simple meal and a few glasses of the bulk red wine that comes from the bowser at the Trasimeno Co-operative winery at not much more than a dollar a litre.

We wander up to the brick-paved *piazza* where a highly amplified band is interspersing American songs from the 1970s with last year's mooning numbers from the San Remo Festival. The Italian tunes all sound the same to us. Dozens of chairs are brought out of storage for the old ladies of Paciano to sit around the edge and fan themselves while they watch the dancing. They show absolutely no reaction to anything that is going on, but they don't miss a thing.

Gradually all the able-bodied Pacianese join in; when there's a suitably lively piece from the band, we try a little chicken-scratching from the fifties, but I quickly get puffed. The locals have never seen anything like it, and some even applaud; Paolo Serafini, the *anagrafe* clerk from the *Comune*, who keeps all the demographic records and is an expert old-time ballroom dancer, comes over and congratulates us. We think it is time to merge with the onlookers, then go home with Angela and Paolo for iced tea before bed.

. . .

Summertime is also, alas, danger time. In August, Italy burns. The statistics are frightening: in 1993, the country's blackest year, there were more than twenty thousand separate outbreaks. Twelve people lost their lives, one hundred thousand hectares of woodland and Mediterranean scrub were destroyed, and the country spent eighty billion lire on water-bombing from planes and helicopters. Most of the fires are deliberately lit; in Sardinia and Sicily, some begin from firing the stubble, but many are started by those who seek to create employment for themselves as auxiliary firefighters for the season.

Paciano sits below a girdle of pine and chestnut forest in the Monte Pausillo Nature Reserve, and every year the residents become nervous. Not long ago one hundred hectares were burned out when winds swept a fire through the Reserve. My first experience of the danger had been a few months earlier in the spring, the season when local farmers safely burn off their olive prunings. A fire started somehow down in the gully opposite our house in a long pile of overgrown bush that had been cleared for new plantings. At first it didn't look too serious. The local *Carabinieri* had turned out, the mayor came, Cerimonia our neighbour sent his wife down to see if she could help. But then the wind funnelled up the gully and it took off. I ran down to find the policemen trying to fight the flames by throwing shovelfuls of dirt on them. I grabbed a shovel from one as he was retreating, blinded by the smoke, and with Francesco Montioni, our larrikin friend from Pietreto, succeeded in pulling the pile of bushes apart, creating a break so the fire would burn itself out.

Afterwards I asked Mayor Alfonso del Buono why the *Comune* didn't have a few people with simple equipment ready to deal with a little outbreak like that, before it could get out of control. There are professional fire-fighting units in Perugia, but they could take two hours or more to get to the scene. I suggested that with Australia's experience in fighting bushfires, I might be able to get him some help.

Alfonso is a difficult man to understand. I have never met anyone so hugely and embarrassingly diffident. He is one of those people who never knows what to do with his hands. His eyes always avoid you and his reticence makes conversation difficult. The nickname locals give him is '*ninnananna*' (lullaby), but his dreamy demeanour masks a sharp mind. Fascists put his father against a wall of the family house and shot him; perhaps that affected him more than his younger brother Piergiorgio. Alfonso studied for the priesthood but dropped out to become an architect, a profession he practices with his brother from a little studio in the village. When it came to ideas to improve his town, nobody could be more encouraging.

So I wrote to the Department of Bushfire Services in Sydney. Back came a boxful of training material, guidelines for setting up a volunteer brigade, technical brochures and recommendations on equipment. There was even a clever little rotary calculator for predicting high fire risk periods, according to temperature, humidity, wind strength and days since rain. Alfonso called a meeting and we set up the Paciano *Squadra Anti-Incendio*. The idea was well received, but we were soon bogged down in a dispute between the *carabiniere* sergeant,

Paladina, and the *Vigile,* Domenico Verga, as to who was to hold the key to the equipment store. This seemed to me a little premature, as we had no equipment. After twenty minutes of fruitless argument, it was time to inject a little practicality.

'Excuse me, Mr Mayor', I said. 'What should we do if a fire breaks out this afternoon?'

The argument was abandoned without loss of face on either side. The *Vigile* drew up a list of our telephone numbers, we agreed on a calling system and a rendezvous point to gather for transport to a fire in the *Comune* truck. We had only our bare hands, so I promised to bring back some Australian firefighting tools on my next trip to Sydney.

A month later, we had a visit from Loredana Verdacchi. It was her land where the fire had started; somehow she had heard I was involved and had brought two bottles of wine as a thankyou present. Her husband Cesare came too, and they stayed for a short chat. Cesare, now long retired, had been a lawyer and a general in the Italian Air Force. The next day, he explained, he was off to Orbetello—the old flying boat base on the Tuscan coast—for the annual memorial service to Italo Balbo, with whom he had served.

As it happened, I had just read a book about Balbo, Italy's greatest aviator. He made history by leading a squadron of Italian flying boats across the Atlantic to the Chicago World Fair in 1933. He also ran Italy's unsuccessful challenge for the Schneider Trophy seaplane race. Britain won it outright with the Supermarine S1, the design forerunner of the Spitfire. Italy remembers Balbo's darker side. A huge, swashbuckling bearded man, he had led teams of fascist *squadristi* in brutally suppressing dissent in the Ferrara district. However, his flying exploits made him a national hero. Mussolini feared his popularity and his tongue (Balbo too openly described *Il Duce* as 'a product of syphilis') and exiled him as Governor of Libya.

In June 1940, three British Blenheims bombed the Italian base at Tobruk. The anti-aircraft crews were sleeping and scrambled to their guns only after the Blenheims had gone. Balbo was flying back to his headquarters from Rome that day, and arrived overhead a few minutes later. The gunners, by then alert, shot him down. To this day there are those, including Cesare Verdacchi, who don't believe it was just incompetence.

. . .

Only two years after we established the volunteer brigade, it justified itself. One Sunday morning, someone taking flowers to a family tomb in the Panicale cemetery, the other side of Mount Petrarvella, threw away his cigarette butt. I happened to look up from the garden to see the plume of smoke and telephoned Alfonso; the squad gathered quickly at the end of town and climbed into the *Comune* truck.

Petrarvella is the highest point in our semicircle of hills, six hundred and forty-five metres above sea level. It's top is crowned with an ancient pine wood that sheltered a Benedictine hermitage centuries ago; from the distance it looks like a tonsured head, a thatch of hair after a very severe 'short back and sides'. The fire had raced up the grassy north-eastern slopes and had just reached the pine forest when we arrived. The first trees were exploding, the noise frightening; if the flames got into their tops we would have a 'crown' fire that would be unstoppable and highly dangerous for Paciano.

Alfiero Ricci is the oldest and most experienced of the council workers. Stocky and tough as an olive trunk, he ran forward to the edge of the fire and began felling trees with a chainsaw, dropping them back into the burnt area. Some of the rest of us ran down the hill to start a back-burn to out-flank the fire. Others began beating out the blazing grass and low scrub with shovels and cutting a firebreak with the six McLeod tools I had brought from Sydney. The McLeods, or 'rake-hoes', were instantly recognised by my brigade colleagues as a double-sided Italian *zappa* in hardened steel. One side was a broad sharp blade to cut away branches, the other a row of fingers to rake leaves and other combustible material from the path of the fire and clear a break.

The wind changed, and the fire swept around the flank of the hill towards a number of isolated houses. They were far below us and there was nothing we could do for them; we had to save the *pineta* to prevent the fire crossing the ridge and bearing down on Paciano. At that desperate point, more than two hours after we had begun our slashing and burning, the cavalry arrived: a giant Air Force Chinook helicopter, two light Fire Service helicopters, a twin-engined military transport to act as aerial controller, and then two bright yellow Canadair water bombers, on standby for the summer fire season, all the way from Ciampino airport, Rome.

The military pilot dived to ten metres over the trees, laying down a trail of red dye-smoke to mark the edge of the fire; the helicopters picked up bucketfuls of water from irrigation dams and dumped them on the markers; then came the Canadairs, filling their bellies as they skimmed Lake Trasimeno and loosing tonnes of drenching spray on the hillside. The aerial attack was focussed on saving the houses; we had to win our own battle in the pines. It took all day, with another alarming flare-up late in the afternoon. By then the professional firefighters of the *Comunità Montana*, the *Vigili del Fuoco* and the *Corpo Forestale* were on the job with water tankers and hoses. We went home with blackened faces and sore hands, but thankfully unhurt. That day three firemen were seriously burnt in another fire at Narni in Southern Umbria.

The next morning, our local newspaper, the *Corriere dell' Umbria*, reported the day's drama, and also recorded our modest contribution, to the great satisfaction of Alfonso. '*Cinquanta ettari di bosco in cenere, danni incalcolabile*' ('Fifty hectares of bushland in ashes, inestimable damage') ran the main headline. The story continued: 'To put out the flames, there were also forty volunteers from Paciano. The Mayor himself was in the team.'

10. DON CAMILLO LIVES!

Only ten per cent of Italian holidaymakers choose the mountains, but this is where we head when boredom, bushfires and nursing the garden through summer drought get too much for us. After the big fire, we decided to take a week off in the Alps and explore some of the lesser-known of the many mountain routes out of Italy. But first we were going to make a small detour up the Po Valley, on the trail of Don Camillo, the hero of the first Italian stories I ever read.

Giovanni Guareschi, the author of these stories, grew up in Parma. As he himself explained, his parents decided that he should become a naval engineer, so he ended up studying law, and thus in a short time became famous as a signboard artist and caricaturist. For nineteen months of the war, Lieutenant Guareschi starved in German concentration camps, like six hundred thousand other Italian soldiers rounded up after the 1943 armistice. He sustained his fellow prisoners with his humorous drawings and writings, and kept up his own spirits by repeating, 'I will not die, even if they kill me.'

A year after the peace he was in Milan editing a satirical magazine called *Candido*. One night, an empty space as the deadline approached compelled him to write his first story of Don Camillo, the pugnacious parish priest and a fiery intolerant communist mayor. In those times of the Cold War and the Iron Curtain, the Don Camillo–Peppone confrontation in an obscure and nameless Emilian village caught fire with the ordinary people. Italians recognised it as an allegory of the political turmoil convulsing the country. In the stories, Guareschi represented all the contrasts, the mistakes, the suspicions, and the illusions of postwar Italy.

The intellectual elite sneered and dismissed the tales as of no literary value, but *The Little World of Don Camillo* raced to bestseller status, and then around the world in translation. I still have my 1956 Don Camillo omnibus edition of the stories.

Then the filmmakers took them up, with the leading Italian comic actors Fernandel and Gino Cervi. The living set they chose for the six films was the sleepy agricultural town of Brescello, on the banks of the River Po. There, fiction and reality have become blurred. The Don Camillo Cafe and the Peppone Bar are in a stand-off on opposite corners of the *piazza*. When the 1951 Po River floods devastated the countryside, hundreds of relief parcels of clothing and food addressed to Don Camillo arrived from all over the world.

I wanted to see the museum devoted to Guareschi's characters that the *Pro-loco*, the local tourist committee, had set up. And there seemed to be a good magazine story behind the growing rumours that life was imitating art in Brescello—that

Church and Town Hall were in conflict again. And they were. Supported by the current left-wing council, the tourist committee had gathered the props, posters and clothing used to bring the stories to life on the screen. Well—almost all the props. The most important, the hand-carved figure of the crucified Christ, to whom Don Camillo turned for comfort and advice in times of vexation, had been left by the filmmakers in the parish church. And the parish priest, Don Giuliano Cugini, resolutely refused to give it up. Worse, he had installed it in a side chapel as his own drawcard, with postcards and an offertory dish.

Don Cugini is no Don Camillo. A quiet elderly man with a pale fleshy face and receding white hair, he was courteous but rather suspicious when I called at his presbytery to ask about the statue.

'It's a sacred object, and its place is in the church. The Committee seems to want the crucifix at all costs, probably because they don't have any other interesting objects to show.'

'This sculpture is an important relic, a big tourist attraction, and we must have it', retorted Enzo Brioni, the museum director. 'The producers just left the statue near the altar when they finished filming; the priest has no right to appropriate it. Besides which, there are plenty of other sacred objects in the church.'

Brioni went on to allege that part of the wooden statue had gone missing while in Don Cugini's care. For the films, it had been carved with five detachable heads. Each had a different expression according to the mood Don Camillo encountered when he turned to the Lord for help on how to deal with 'Peppone the Red'. Where the other four heads are today, nobody seems to know. Brioni said he would settle for the heads if he can't get the whole figure, but nobody at the church has made him an offer.

The crucifix would certainly be the *pièce de resistance* for the museum, but it's interesting enough as it is. There are old phonographs and radios from the 1950s, Don Camillo's bicycle and Peppone's motorcycle outfit, as well as hundreds of photographs—stills from the six films, and scenes of the town itself forty-five years ago, including the devastation of the 1951 flood. A feast of nostalgia. On sale are videotapes of the films, all the Guareschi books, postcards, even presentation packs of Don Camillo wine.

We stopped for a coffee at the Peppone Bar. There was an argument over the crucifix going on around the pavement tables; the Italian love–hate relationship between *La Chiesa* and *Comune*, between Church and Town Hall which face each other across the square as they do in every town in Italy, was still alive, it seemed. Or was it just for the benefit of the strangers? Are both sides in the dispute really serious? What better promotion for the town, its museum and its church than the illusion of a brouhaha? We drove out of town and across the wide Po flood plain, still wondering, but suspecting it's all tongue-in-cheek. Guareschi would have chuckled.

Once we had fought our way past Lecco and up the eastern shore of Lake Como, its beauty totally obliterated by the smog caused by the cars and motor boats of wealthy Milanese, we came out into clearer air at Chiavenna. This clean, pretty little market town lies at the foothills of the Alps, where the main red route from Italy to the fashionable ski resorts of St Moritz and Zernez turns north-east. But we were taking the narrow yellow road due north, up the Liro valley. The Liro is not mapped as a *fiume*, a river, but as a *torrente*. Italy quite sensibly defines its streams by the speed with which they descend from the mountains. The *torrente* may be small, but as we've found, it's much more subject to flash flooding after thunderstorms.

The Spluga Pass is thirty kilometres up this road, at a height of two thousand metres. It's one of the oldest invasion routes but very few people take the trouble to enter Switzerland this way now. While it's normally closed by heavy snowdrifts for most of the winter, it's hard driving at any time with many hairpins, tunnels and often landslide blockages.

The reward for this effort is the stupendous view back down the valley from the little settlements along the way— Campodolcino, Pianazzo, Cantoniere di Teggiate. The original village of Cimaganda was built for defence on a ridge of high ground in the middle of the Liro. The collection of poor stone huts still stand there, roofless; the new village on the road is drab and unevocative, but its residents don't have to ford the stream to go to work.

Almost at the end of our climb, we burst upon Lake Montespluga, a tiny crystal-clear pond fed by subterranean springs, in winter a favourite skating rink. From its shores, we had a clear view across to the Suretta, a three-thousand-metre peak wreathed in clouds, exactly on the border. The

Swiss Customs officer was irritable at the trickle of summer traffic, and meticulously checked every document. His Customs post closes at the onset of winter, even though the road may still be open, leaving a strange loophole in the orderly Swiss administration.

But Switzerland was not the objective of this trip, so we hurried into Austria, through the Arlberg tunnel, then turned south up the valley of the Inn, to cross back into Italy over the Resia Pass. The maps also note its other name, the Reschen, a reminder that we were entering a part of Italy that has been Italian only since 1918. To the locals this is not the Alto Adige but Sudtirol. Sixty-five per cent of the population speak Austrian and send candidates of the *Sud Tirol Volkspartei* to the parliament in Rome. The country looks peaceful but there are still residual tensions from being wrenched out of the Austro–Hungarian Empire at the end of the Kaiser's war.

These surfaced in an unexpected way a few years ago when Austrian scientists made off with the remains of Similaun Man, the body of a prehistoric hunter found perfectly preserved in glacial ice for five thousand years, along with his weapons and his rations. The Italians charged that the body was found ten metres inside their territory and accused the Austrians of kidnap.

The Austrians took the remains to Innsbruck for scientific investigation and replied that Italy didn't have the facilities or the skills needed for such an important anthropological examination. Since neither Austria nor Italy existed five thousand years ago, it may be difficult to prove his nationality, but this hasn't stopped the Italians trying. Grasses found in his satchel grow only on Italy's side of the Alps—sure proof, they say, that he was a southern shepherd caught in an early blizzard.

Similaun, one of the highest peaks in the Otzaler Alps, is not far to the east of our route. But at fifteen hundred metres, at the western end of this chain, the Resia is quite a low crossing. It opens immediately into the Val Venosta, the most northerly of Italy's large upland valleys, where the summer air is cool and fresh. Not a kilometre down the road is the artificial lake, *Lago Resia* or (Reschen See, for all the signs are now in two languages) which flooded the village of Curon Venosta. The houses and shops were re-built uphill, but the town hall drowned, and its fourteenth century *campanile* was left to project above the water, a memorial marker of the original site.

The new Curon, with its calming vista of lake and mountains, was the perfect place to stop for lunch. Like Umbria, this is a pork area, but of course the dishes all have an Austrian spin to them—a welcome change from Italian food. We started with their *speck*, the smoked pork that's like prosciutto, but distinctly flavoured with the family's own spice recipe. Then *selchcarree mit kraut*, smoked pork with sauerkraut, and *fastenknodl*, dumplings filled with breadcrumbs and eggs. The Alto Adige is the biggest apple growing area in Europe, so naturally in the Val Venosta apple strudel is the prince of desserts. A meal that would seem far too heavy down on the hot plains carries very well in the high country!

We could have continued down the valley of the Adige to Merano to try the 'grape cure' for which it is famous. The

Merano tourist promoters claim that the radioactive soils of the valley produce exceptional sweetness in the grape and highly distinctive wines, but the experts debunk this theory. It's nevertheless the oldest wine zone of German-speaking Europe, and the area of Italy's finest Rhine-style whites— Gewurztraminer, Riesling, Renano, and Müller Thurgau. Since Roman times, visitors to Merano have alternated between dunking themselves in the rejuvenating spring waters and drinking the wines. Unfortunately we did not have the two weeks recommended for the cure.

Instead, we were headed for the Stelvio, a pass I had always wanted to climb, so we turned up the valley of the Solda, and put the car in low gear at Trafio. The Stelvio has forty-eight hairpins on its eastern (northern) side, more than any other pass in Italy. At each *tornante* there is a number, so you can count your way to the top. There is no room to pass on the corners, but only once did we have to back off, for a camper-van coming down. In seven kilometres, we climbed from one thousand one hundred metres to two thousand seven hundred and sixty metres, and emerged breathless at the tourist kiosks at the top.

For the whole climb, we had been treated to spectacular views off to our left of the four-thousand-metre Ortles massif—the highest in the Dolomites—and the Livrio glacier it spawns. Clinging like a fly to a windowpane, the Livrio refuge for skiers and climbers seemed stuck to the mountain. However did they get the materials up to build it there?

Down the other side of the Stelvio is Bormio, a charming

old town with painted houses in the Austrian style, lying in a basin seemingly besieged all around by mountains. It's a year-round sporting centre; skiers in winter, walkers in summer. We could have lingered for days in Bormio, but we were intent on pushing on to the Gavia Pass and one of those challenging roads where the yellow line on the map becomes narrower and narrower. This started out as an easy run up the Valfurva, but at San Caterina the road forked, narrowed and became very twisted. After a dizzying climb, the country opened out into wide bleak moorlands; the stone refuges dotted along the road attest to the blizzard danger in winter.

These slopes were a battlefield eighty years ago. At the Berni refuge, a granite memorial to soldiers of the Alpine Regiment looks out to San Matteo and its glacier. A young shepherd boy was grazing his cows around the monument and posed for photographs. Over the next month or two, he said, he would be herding them back to their stalls in the Valfurva. At the top of the pass, in clear cool air, where we could see for miles, we found ourselves surrounded by three-thousand-metre peaks—San Matteo, Gavia, Pietra Rossa, Tre Signori and, a little further off, Coleazzo. A high wind whipped cloud around them as in an erotic dance, now concealing, now revealing.

Then came the sharp descent. In seven kilometres, we dropped one thousand metres. Six of them were on a dirt track, barely wide enough for one car, with granite blocks marking the edge of the formation, but no rails to guard against a plunge, who knows how far, into the *Torrente* Frigidolfo. Tyrolese miners hacked out this road, which runs through some terrifyingly rough tunnels of jagged rock. We met an upcoming car in one. Our side rear-vision mirrors hit and we missed scraping the rockface by millimetres. Lovers of mountain driving should note that the Gavia carries a 3-star Michelin rating! It's for drivers, not mere motorists.

Ponte di Legno at the bottom is a mountain resort for the smart and famous, and is the favoured retreat of Umberto Bossi, the demagogic leader of *Lega Nord*. The Northern League looks like a political party, but in reality Bossi is the *Lega Nord*, and his followers seem always to be striving to catch up with his latest direction. He stands for a federated Italy, as a protest against the wealth generated in the productive northern regions being frittered away by the politicians of Rome. But to grab the headlines he shocked the country by demanding the abandonment of Sicily and the complete secession of the north. Then he set up his own 'independent' state of Padania. (The entire area north of, and including the Po valley.) The government has struggled to cope with what is, after all, sedition.

The *Lega* was a vital coalition partner in the government of Silvio Berlusconi, the first in Italy's so-called Second Republic, but Bossi immediately destabilised it and then brought it down. Outside the North, Italy may understand his protest movement but does not support the *Lega*'s erratic policies. We were disappointed that there wasn't a *Lega* rally in Ponte di Legno that weekend. They are spectacular gatherings, designed to re-create (at least politically) the terror of the Lombard invasions. Ten thousand supporters cheer their champions; a thousand red battle standards set fire to the fields around; the amplified threats and promises roll over the town. No one seems concerned that the Party's symbol they carry so proudly—a Lombard knight in full armour, with shield and sword upraised to strike—was pinched from the logo of the Legnano bicycle!

From Ponte di Legno we were to work our way eastwards through the Dolomites. Their jagged peaks, upthrust from coralline formations and then weathered, marked the coast when the sea covered the whole Veneto plain. If nature has made touring rewarding, it has also created its difficulties. The steep mountains mean the roads through the Trentino have had to follow the valleys, and these are never the most direct route. What better time to practice the tongue-twister *Zio Carlo* had taught us to learn to roll our 'Rs':

Trentatre Trentini
Entrarano in Trento
Tutti trentatre
Trotterellando
Thirty-three Trento folk
Enter Trento
All thirty-three
Trotting

Travelling without adventuring is unprofitable, so when we spotted a fairytale castle on a hilltop in the Cavedine valley west of Trento, we just had to investigate. Huge and forbidding, with towers and turrets, its windows covered with dark brown shutters painted with red and white Alpine designs, it looked much more exciting than the *castelli* of Umbria.

There was no notice to say it was private property, or even still inhabited, but I suppose the road would be sufficient deterrent to most. It was just the width of one car, steep, twisting and bounded by waist-high stone walls. We made the final narrow turn, almost at right angles, and came face to face with a huge mediaeval gateway. Two massive wooden doors, three metres high closed the space. There was no sign of life.

I took some photographs, and then pulled on the heavy bell-cord beside the gate. When a man appeared, it was clear that he was not pleased at our arrival.

'This is a private house,' he shouted at me. 'Go back!'

This proved impossible. The car might negotiate the tight turns forwards, but slithering on the smooth stones, it would not do it backwards. There was nothing else for it. With great reluctance, the man swung the big doors open, and signalled that we should drive through, turn around and drive back out again immediately.

What a piece of luck! We found ourselves in a wide circular courtyard, once the life-centre of this fortified dwelling. Around it were ringed the stables, the kitchens, the hay barns and the *stalle* for milk cows and working oxen. Three storeys of living space rose above. A small army could be quartered there in time of need. It was only a quick glimpse, but for a moment we were transported four centuries back in time, when the Trentino was under episcopal governance and castles like this were the homes of feudal lords, vassals of the bishop-prince of Trento. We later learned we had stumbled up to *Castel Madruzzo*, one of the most famous and best-preserved of the dozens that once controlled the valleys and passes of this much-fought-over territory.

Then we were off on a pilgrimage to the front lines of World War I. I have always had an interest in military history and had read with awe of the terrain in which Italians and Austrians confronted each other for three years. The battles of France and Flanders were fought in the mud of the plains; those in the Trentino in snow on slopes of sixty degrees. I hadn't realised the cost of the Great War on this front. It ended the Austrian Empire, it bled Italy economically and collapsed the traditional political system. Five million young Italians were called up, six hundred thousand lost their lives. Most of the rest returned home to unemployment and hopelessness. In its aftermath, Italy fell easy victim to the virus of nationalistic Fascism.

From World War I, Australia has Gallipoli, an heroic defeat and the birthplace of the Anzac legend. Italy has only Caporetto, a national disgrace. Incompetent generals blamed underfed untrained conscripts for cowardice when a German–Austrian attack drove them back one hundred and fifty kilometres. The cost was staggering—twelve thousand killed, two hundred and eighty thousand taken prisoner, another four hundred thousand running away. The name has passed into the language as Italy's Waterloo.

All this took place in the north-east, where Italy was trying to defend its border near the modern-day Slovenia. Further west, in the Trentino, the situations were reversed, for Austria then extended in a big bulge of territory from the

Brenner Pass to Lake Garda. Here, much of the fighting was concentrated on Pasubio, a mountain chain more than two-thousand metres high. In some of the most inhospitable country in Europe, for the last eighteen months of the war, Italians and Austrians fought one of the most incredible battles in history—underground.

We drove first to the Pasubio Ossary. This tapering granite tower stands at the end of Bellavista spur, and looks out over the mountains that were such impossible battlefields. It is both memorial and cemetery, for it contains the remains of the twelve thousand Italians killed in that campaign. The entire area is now the *Zona Sacra*, a national monument area and park. A little museum nearby contains some of the relics—weapons, gas masks, uniforms, miner's tools and the geophones used to listen for the enemy's digging.

But to penetrate the war zone itself, I had to take The Heroes' Road, the *Strada degli Eroi*. Cut to carry wheeled traffic long after the war, the route follows the precipitous mule trail that took supplies to the front. At one point, the road tunnels through an overhang; the mule track, a metre wide, is still there, *outside* the rock! The road widens to the Papa Refuge, built on the site of the old Italian headquarters, where Achille Papa had been the general in command. Today there is a series of well-marked walking tracks leading over the mountains to the Austrian and Italian observation positions. Hikers, however will be standing on top of where the real action took place.

In 1917, when ground offensives had failed, General Papa decided to submerge. Calling up a regiment of engineers and professional miners of the area, he began digging a network of tunnels. His aim was to burrow under the Austrians entrenched on their mountain opposite. Unfortunately, the Austrians had the same idea. As the tunnels approached each other, both sides began setting off explosive charges, to destroy the other's work.

At the museum, I had bought a booklet and maps to understand this strange war. It was clear from these that the Italians' mountain became a gigantic ants' nest with dozens of tunnels running everywhere, but with not much forward progress. The Austrians put all their effort into driving one long adit, deep under the Italians. At 4.30am on 13 March 1918, the Austrians fired the last shot in that war. Fifty thousand kilograms of explosives packed into the end of their tunnel went off in the biggest single bang of World War I. When the dust cleared and the last tongues of flame from burning gases flickered out, the Austrians could see that half the Italian mountain had been blown away. For two days voices of the trapped were heard calling for help; one hundred and twelve are buried there still.

The Austrians lost men too, in a blow-back of flame. It was the end of the war on that front, and the Armistice came seven months later. I felt a chill as I clambered over the rough rocks, not only because of the altitude and the wind. To stand, more than eighty years afterwards, at the entrances to some of those tunnels, on *Cima Palon* and *Dente Italiano* and read the marble memorial plaques that record the fallen and their story, is to feel the full futility of war through one of its most futile battles.

11. DEATH IN ITALY

*'I am not afraid to die. I just don't want
to be there when it happens.'*
Woody Allen

*'Though it will die soon
The voice of the cicada
Shows no sign of this.'*
Basho (1644–94)

'Crimine ab uno, disce omnes.'
('From a single crime know the nation.')
Virgil (70–19BC)

In the family, the event has gone down as 'The Night Father Died'. Like Thurber's droll tale, 'The Day the Dam Broke', it showed how a little misinformation could go a long way.

It started simply enough. One of the light bulbs had blown out and I had been about to replace it. First, however, I went to the lavatory. Downstairs. At the critical moment, I found we were out of toilet paper. Both on the wall holder, and on the reserve spool where normally two or three spare rolls are ready to hand. Our downstairs bathroom is one big room that also houses the laundry; it was impossible to reach the door from where I sat, so the only thing to do was to yell for help. Now I admit that my cry would have been muffled by the closed door and this could have confused the family, but it doesn't really explain what happened next.

Our youngest son Richard was visiting from London at the time. Richard runs in marathons and competes in mountain-bike races. He is in fact the only athletic member of the family, with hair-trigger reactions. For reasons which even he cannot explain, he decided that the call came from upstairs, and that it was a single, final, sharp cry of pain. Certain that some accident had befallen his father, he raced up the stairs two at a time, around the hall and to the bath-room door, which stood open. The moonlight through the window threw an odd shadow on the floor. A moment's pause to make sure there was no movement and then he knew—it was me lying there, and I had been electrocuted.

I could hear all the rushing around over my head, and I was getting pretty annoyed that nobody had come. Then the light went out. Richard had done the sensible thing when someone has received 220 volts and might still be holding onto a live wire—don't touch the body, cut the main power switch for the house. Now there was shouting and running to the front of the house. Then the noise faded as everyone rushed out the door. Was the house on fire? What the hell was going on?

There was nothing else to do. Hitching my pants to my knees, I hobbled through the darkened rooms to the front door—just in time to see our friends the Carinis, Corrado and his wife Graziella, hurrying up the road from their house, white-faced with alarm. And Audrey and Richard running towards them, crying out: '*Goffredo è morto! Goffredo è morto!*'

The Carinis have, from the beginning, been amongst our best friends. They live in Perugia, but at weekends liked nothing better than to escape their eleventh floor apartment to spend the weekend in the clean air of the quiet countryside. They had a little four-room cottage in the jumble of buildings that were once the homes of Varacca's farm labourers. They took us on our first walks over the hills to gather *porcini*, the huge wild mushrooms that flourish in the woods in October and November.

Now, Corrado is warm, *molto simpatico*, but a typical Italian academic, distinguished but quite impractical. A classics professor in Perugia, he writes senior school Greek textbooks and has presented me with his quite magnificent history of Roman literature. No wonder he was white in the face; it would be difficult to imagine a person less able to cope with an electrocuted neighbour.

The situation, still totally inexplicable to me, was now serious. In a few moments the Carinis would be at the doorstep; it was possible they might be more alarmed to find me with dropped daks than dead. I shuffled back to the bathroom, shut the door, and yelled again for someone to come. I figured this was the safest way of ending the game, whatever it was. Afterwards, when we were all laughing, I noticed that Corrado's hands were still shaking. We sat him down and poured him a stiff whisky. He had never been so close to death. And I suppose, like Thurber, I could say we all were both ennobled and demoralised by the experience.

· · ·

Italy is, has always been, and probably will continue to be, a place of violent death. Barzini says Italians fear sudden and violent death above all, but it doesn't seem to stop the senseless killing or the needless dying. During our short time in the country, two of the most horrific of all the many atrocities committed by the Sicilian Mafia have occurred. Theirs is no longer the crude world of the *lupara*, the sawn-off shotgun, or the acid tank that yields the 'white death'—the disappearance without trace. They have experts in electronics who can clone and tap cellular telephones; and they can adapt microwave technology to trigger explosions from a safe distance. With the one, *mafiosi* gather intelligence on their victims' movements, with the other, they can kill without being on the scene.

The first of the massacres (for that is what they were) killed Giovanni Falcone, a leading investigating magistrate too hot on the trail of the Mafia's international links for its comfort. With impeccable timing, one of the Palermo clans blew up two lanes of the autostrada leading into town from the airport exactly one second before Falcone and his escorting convoy reached the spot. At 120 kilometres an hour, their cars ran into a vertical wall of asphalt. His wife and the escorting policemen died with him.

The shockwave of sheer terror at the new power and daring of the Mafia had not dissipated when, two months later, an even bigger bomb detonated in a suburban street of Sicily's capital. Another magistrate, Falcone's friend and collaborator, Paolo Borsellino, was shredded into charred fragments, along with five members of his police escort. With ironic timing, RAI Televideo, the teletext service of the national television service, had just taken off the screen the list of telephone numbers to call to report Mafia activities. The 'Anti-Piovra Index' as it was called, made way for the summer beach reports, listing coastal resorts where it was unsafe to swim because of pollution. The coastline of Sicily was considerably safer than the streets of Palermo, but nothing was going to stand in the way of the sacred summer holidays.

But the Mafia had overplayed its hand. A great shout of rage and grief erupted across the country. The ordinary citizens of Palermo hung bedsheets daubed with messages from their balconies in spontaneous gestures of solidarity against the criminality. 'Falcone and Borsellino—even though you're gone, we will never surrender!', they said, or simply, 'Basta!'—'Enough!'.

Il Effetto Lenzuolo, the 'Bedsheet Effect', as it became known, propelled the government into its most effective action against the Mafia. New powers to the law enforcers, new inducements for *mafiosi* to defect began to pay off. By now there are more than twelve hundred *pentiti*, the supergrasses who have turned State's evidence and with their families have been given new identities in a witness protection programme. Amongst other crimes on which they threw new light, they helped pin the perpetrators of the Falcone and Borsellino murders.

A leading Catholic writer, Vittorio Messori, described the hanging out of the sheets as the symbolism of a new civil religion, a way of exorcising Sicily's devil, the Mafia. But like the devil in all of us, the Mafia will always exist in Italy. The hard heads in the front line of the fight would be happy if they could just cut it down to size, reduce it to the normal dimensions of common-run criminality.

But its organisational ability is terrifying. Although it has largely abandoned its policy of street assassinations of magistrates and policemen, it has now returned to its early roots in extortion. It stands over the squads of street girls from Eastern Europe and Africa, as well as the illegal immigrant tomato-pickers in the south. It runs most of the bootleg speedboat traffic across the Adriatic, importing contraband cigarettes and dumping refugee Albanian families on deserted Italian beaches. It seems to have found life quieter offshore—its main income now derives from business crimes and drug trafficking in countries of the former USSR.

Every Italian knows that Sicily is a different world. Most do not understand it, many fear and shun it. Of all the millions of words that have been written in attempts to explain the phenomenon of the Mafia and its origins in the Sicilian character, none serves better than those of Giuseppe Tomasi di Lampedusa, in his great novel, *The Leopard*, written more than fifty years ago:

'All Sicilian self-expression, even the most violent, is really wish-fulfilment; our sensuality is a hankering for oblivion, our shootings and knifings a hankering for death, our languor, our exotic ices a hankering for voluptuous immobility, that is for death again...From that comes the extraordinary phenomenon of the constant formation of myths which would be venerable if they were really ancient, but which are really nothing but subtle attempts to plunge us back into a past that attracts us only because it is dead.'

Death need not come from criminal activity. A surprising number of young Italians in love commit suicide—together, or sequentially. Jealous husbands kill wives, and vice versa. The electrician who wired our house expired from a heart attack one Sunday morning while on a pig hunt. In charity, his fellow shooters hurried him home to bed—charity, because the law required him to be left lying face down in the mud until the coroner saw him.

Although deplored by the Church, suicide is often seen as the only honourable exit when the law does catch up with illegal activity. The great Montedison scandal, which best demonstrated just how business graft and political corruption intersected, claimed three lives this way. The last of the three to die by his own hand was the head of Feruzzi-Montedison himself, Raul Gardini.

Perhaps I was partly responsible. Only a year earlier, he had been the toast of Italy as his yacht, *Il Moro di Venezia*, raised the country's hopes of winning the America's Cup. The outpouring of patriotic pride in this footballing, cycling but non-sailing nation was so great that the team opened a special fax line in San Diego so Italians could send messages of goodwill and encouragement. Tens of thousands did so.

However, when *Moro* was down 3 to 1, and the end for the outclassed Italian challenger was in sight, optimism dried up. The fax line was free. Tongue in cheek I sent this message: 'Read William Shakespeare's Othello (The Moor of Venice), Act V Scene II Line 266: "Here is my journey's end, here is my butt, and very sea-mark of my utmost sail." Why not suicide now?' Not unexpectedly there was no response, but I have sometimes had twinges that my little literary joke might have put a thought into Gardini's mind.

The greatest cause of sudden and violent death for Italians is their love affair with the motor car. Italy has the highest rate of car ownership in Europe, nearly two per head of population—and some of the most terrible accidents. Most of them are caused by driving too fast, too close to the vehicle in front. Three decades after Ralph Nader's successful crusade in the US against the Ford Pinto for its vulnerable fuel tank, small Italian cars crash and burn at an alarming rate. The rear-end shunt, so picturesquely termed *il tamponamento*, frequently leads to a ruptured tank and fire. If the occupants don't or can't get out, they will be statistics on the news that night, described equally graphically, as *carbonizzati*.

Why then, we asked, don't Italians take car safety seriously? The reckless drivers seem to be acting out the words of a song popular last century:

'*per vedere se poi e tanto difficile morire*'—'just to see if it's so difficult to die.'

Australia has had seat belts in cars since the 1960s. Latching them is now second nature, not to mention compulsory and common sense, for even the shortest trip. At the time we arrived in Italy, seat belts were still compulsory only for front-seat occupants and, as far as we could see, nobody put them on if they could avoid it. This national attitude was turned to profit by the Naples firm that marketed T-shirts with a seat belt printed diagonally across them, to fool the cops at the road blocks.

The first time we took our friends the Ascanios to a concert in the historic *Sala dei Notari* in Perugia, Angela refused to put on her seat belt. Because, she said, quite correctly, the law didn't require it for back seat passengers.

'I am the law in this car,' I replied, 'and everyone wears a seat belt. Just think what would happen,' I went on tactlessly, 'if we hit something, or I had to brake suddenly...I don't want your brains all over the windscreen!'

There was a shocked silence that lasted forty-five kilometres to Perugia. I had broken one of the taboos on death—never to speak of the prospect as near or personal. Which of course is why Italians drive as they do—with verve, skill, speed and complete lack of anticipation. The accident is always going to happen to someone else. And in a country where stop signs are optional extras, pity the poor pedestrian. Zebra crossings may as well have '007' painted on them instead of stripes—they are a licence to kill.

My wife had made the other boo-boo in our first year. She saw some beautiful white chrysanthemums in a roadside stall and bought a bunch for Graziella Carini. Graziella thanked her graciously but made no comment. Later we found out that with the seasons reversed, chrysanthemums blossom here in October, in time for All Souls Day, on 2 November. Every Italian family tries to visit the graves of parents that day, *la commemorazione dei defunti*. White chrysanthemums are only for laying on gravestones, not for the vases of the home, where they are deemed unlucky.

I remember reading some years ago that the Vatican had approved vertical burials in the earth to save space, but most Italian cemeteries continue to be walled cities in which the departed are interred horizontally in concrete compartments. The tiers of tombs, five or six high make a wall like the private boxes at the Post Office, which I suppose they are. Glazed photographs on the travertine ends sealing the tombs identify the incumbents for the relatives, and presumably, the Celestial Postman, when He comes.

At the Paciano cemetery, the *Comune* provides ladders for mourners to fix their flowers at the topmost levels. There is no need for candles—it is now wired so that small red electric lights burn constantly. A fee is charged every quarter for the electricity. When space grew short last year, the *Comune* extended the cemetery and put up public notices inviting the citizens to apply to reserve a space. Serafini, in the office, thoughtfully asked me if we were interested, but I declined. I would prefer an Etruscan cinerary urn but they are no longer on offer. In any case, we hope to be gone before the necessity arises, and a little prize-winning poem by an English school-girl came to mind:

> Let me not die here, Lord
> From this small town
> Heaven would be a culture shock
> And Hell far too exciting.

It is in these rural areas, and especially amongst the aged, that religion still has its ancient hold. In Italy as a whole, the Roman Catholic Church's influence is believed to be dwindling. Although nearly ninety per cent of Italians still define themselves as 'religious', it has been estimated that only four per cent go to confession. The country seems to us more superstitious than religious. Jonathan Keates in his book *Italian Journeys* finds their religion '…a lackadaisical Catholicism, taken out of mothballs at christenings, first communions, weddings and funerals, the religion, in short, of the photo-opportunity'. The fact is that the Italians have learned to make their Catholicism work for them better than most. With the doctrine of original sin providing a convenient admission of human frailty, they know that, should they succumb to temptation, whether in politics, in business or in bed, the soothing rituals of confession and absolution are there to excuse and comfort.

At the first communions, weddings and funerals we have attended, solemnity has been replaced by informality to a degree we found surprising and even disturbing. The Church in its desire to remain relevant in this increasingly secular age, seems afraid of majesty, and pursues informality, but has it gone too far? We found it incredible that people would chatter during a mass, while some wandered out for a smoke. Perhaps as communists they were just there to take a little eternity insurance on the day.

Paciano's is an aged and ageing population. The old widows make their daily pilgrimage to the cemetery and then go home to wait out their time. When we hear the slow tolling of the big bell of the Assumption, answered by its little off-key bell, we know our community has again been reduced by one.

. . .

Ferrara, the Estense city, as it styles itself, is one of the most beautiful, and most beautifully preserved towns in all Italy. None of the tremendous damage wrought by Allied bombing in World War II is now visible. Within its irregular wall, the urban fabric is a harmonious blend of mediaeval and Renaissance that is found nowhere else. Its siting, in the great fertile plain of the Po, permits it a spaciousness denied to hill-towns. The secret of its serenity is its respect for human scale in its buildings of brick and in its streetscapes.

Our first visit there, however, was not the time to take in the splendours of the great moated Este castle, the cathedral with its unique gallery of shops attached to one side, the mediaeval streets of the Jewish ghetto, or the frescoes, paintings and sculptures of the many churches and palaces. Instead of a leisurely sightseeing, we were travelling the three hundred kilometres to attend a requiem mass in the church of *San Cristoforo alla Certosa*, on what was to be the longest and saddest day of our time in Italy.

Aimone Finotti had been a journalist and, at the time of his retirement, a director of RAI, the state radio and television service. He and his wife Marie-Pia bought a house in Paciano with a garden and a small area of olives, and planned to spend a good deal of their spare time here. They were lovely hospitable people, *molto simpatico*, and we were looking forward to seeing much more of them. Aimone is an accomplished musician, playing double bass and vibraphone in an amateur jazz club in Bologna that is good enough to have attracted players of the calibre of Gerry Mulligan as guest artists. Aimone explained that jazz had been banned in Mussolini's Italy, and that The Doctor Dixie Jazz Band was formed in the postwar explosion of interest aroused by the American influence. Its members are doctors, lawyers and other professionals who went to university together; they've now been playing together for more than forty years. Aimone has presented us with all their records and CDs.

Marie-Pia came from a family of doctors in Bologna. That seemed to make it harder to bear the year we returned from our winter away to learn that she had undergone major surgery, but was now at home, dying of cancer. We never saw her again. The long trip to Ferrara with the Ascanios was for our farewell.

The Carthusians established their monastery of *Certosa*—Charterhouse—nearly five hundred and fifty years ago. It lasted until Napoleon's dissolution in 1796, and is now the cemetery for Ferrara and Bologna. The noble semicircular cloister encloses a sweep of immaculate lawn and leads to the church of St Christopher at its centre. I felt a chill as I entered. The church had been built to an experimental plan in the fifteenth century by the Este court architect, Biaggi Rossetti, who was responsible for much of Renaissance Ferrara. It has a narrow single nave, with deep side chapels that had been boarded up for years for restoration work, their treasures and paintings removed to city museums for safe-keeping. I have never seen a church interior so bleak, lifeless and depressing. Just inside the door, only one chapel remained open, and on a plinth rested the casket of Marie-Pia. It seemed so tiny, so pathetic, under the high vaulted ceiling of this cold, bare chamber. We had come to comfort Aimone, but it was he who comforted me.

After the Requiem Mass, three cemetery workers dressed in shirts and shorts and wearing gardening gloves loaded the casket onto a trolley, and we followed it to the monumental cemetery. A truck with gravediggers' shovels pushed through the mourners; there was a long delay, and I couldn't take my eyes off the label *'Depuratore* XT/1' on the end of the coffin. The grave in the family plot was flooded by recent rain, so there could be no interment that day; we had to leave Marie-Pia in the mortuary chapel.

The Italians fortunately didn't seem to be affected, but the muddle and lack of decorum distressed us. It seemed an insulting and unnecessarily insensitive end to the life of a sweet woman. We started on the long trip home depressed and completely wrung out.

. . .

'For the children of Judah have done evil in my sight, saith the Lord…And they have built the high places of Tophet, which is in the valley of the son of Hinnom, to burn their sons and daughters in the fire; which I commanded them not, neither came it into my heart.'

THE BOOK OF JEREMIAH, *Chapter 7, Verses 30 and 31*

We jump back three thousand years in time, to find ourselves in the Tophet, not of Judaeans of Israel, but of Phoenicians, in Sardinia. High on an outcrop of weathered volcanic rock, on the outskirts of Sant'Antioco, archeologists have uncovered the primitive Cemetery of the Infants. Until very recently, they were believed to have been the victims of that very same ritual sacrifice condemned in those words of the Old Testament.

Thousands of lidded terracotta pots contained their ashes; beside each was its *stele*, a miniature tombstone, carved with the figure of a deity, sometimes nude, sometimes cloaked. When they were discovered, the urns were stacked layer upon layer, with a bed of earth between each. Nearly all of them have been removed to museums, but a hundred or two have been left just as they were found, for the visitor to see. Many are intact, complete with handles and lids, but others are only a pile of shards.

It seems that it was the Romans who put around the story that every year the Phoenicians sacrificed the firstborn of the most eminent families to their supreme god, Baal-Hammon, or to Tanit, the mother-goddess to whom they believed everyone returned. It was a persuasive case—after all, the Romans left a comprehensive literature, the Phoenicians did not—so for a long time, this was the accepted wisdom. The fact that the Phoenicians, the greatest mariners of the age at the time of King Solomon, were trading partners of the Israelites (and like them, Semites, descended from Shem, son of Noah), seemed to clinch the matter.

There were doubts and questions. How could a society have afforded to kill every first-born when as it was, only one baby in three survived the first year of life? Then scientific examination of the urns and a closer reading of the *stele* inscriptions revealed that eighty per cent of the charred remains were of stillborn children, or foetuses. Other ashes were proven to be those of lambs, birds and pigs, undoubtedly slaughtered ritually. The Tophet of Sant'Antioco is now known to have been a cemetery for ritual burial, not ritual human sacrifice.

Blood sacrifice is a powerful and suggestive drawcard. The tourist trade would prefer to retain the legend. As we looked down on the scatter of pots among the rocks, I wondered if the racial libel would ever be expunged.

Sant'Antioco, in the south-west corner of Sardinia, was however, only a side trip to satisfy our curiosity about some lesser-known details of this harshly beautiful island. Few tourists venture into the interior for fear of bandits or bushfires, or both. It can be frightening country. Serrated limestone peaks take off precipitously from the valleys and soar thousands of metres into the sky. Under the pitiless summer sun, the streams dry up, and the furnace-wind, the *scirocco*, screams through the trees. Feuds and vendettas continue for decades; policemen are ambushed and shot. The kidnap is alive and well practised on the island. Not long ago criminals seized the little son of a hotel manager—not a wealthy or important man—and demanded a huge ransom for his release. When it was not forthcoming, they cut off a piece of an ear and posted it to his parents, who spent fearful weeks before the boy was returned, otherwise unharmed.

Sardinia was long one of the poorest parts of Italy. But if that other rebellious island, Sicily, can boast a literary genius in Giuseppe di Lampedusa, Sardinia can match it with Salvatore Satta. A notary and jurist, who re-wrote the Italian Penal Code after World War II to remove its fascist aspects, Satta worked for thirty years on a tale of his place. Like Lampedusa's, it was found and published only after his death. 'Nuoro was nothing but a perch for the crows', he wrote, 'its villages as remote from one another as are the stars'. It is a chronicle of the harshness of Sardo life a century ago, but does much to explain the Sardinian character of today. A shudder ran up my spine as I read Satta's account of the vicious sand-storm from the Sahara that devastated the crops for miles around, but did not touch the farm of Don Sebastiano. When he investigated, his sharecropper showed Don Sebastiano what had saved the farm:

'On the closed half of the double doors hung a dog crucified with its front legs stretched apart and nailed into the wood, and its head hanging slantwise on its chest…"He howled for three days, [said the sharecropper] then he died, and the wind that was bending the trees double on the far side of the priest's hillside stopped at once".'

Satta's Sardinia no longer exists in its entirety, but its memory is the reason few 'mainlanders' venture inland to Nuoro today. Unfortunately they miss out on seeing the giant cork oaks with their trunks red-raw after the bark has been stripped. They also miss the *nuraghe*, the thousands of beehive-shaped iron-age dwellings that dot the country. Built without mortar, they are remarkably similar to the *brochs*, the Pictish forts we found years ago at Glenelg, on Scotland's west coast. It would be interesting if there were a link.

To 'mainland' Italians, Sardinia means coast—transparent warm water lapping little sandy beaches hidden between granitic promontories, many of them accessible only from the sea. Certainly some of the most ruggedly beautiful boating, swimming and aqualung waters in the world. These coasts have also inspired a strong environmental movement for the protection of the rich bird life of the *stagni*, the swampy fresh-water coastal lagoons. The pink flamingoes that fly every year from South Africa to nest in the *stagni* have become one of the island's symbols and most important attractions.

On that coast, the little seaside resort of San Teodoro, once a fishing village, but now dependent on tourism, at first seems an unlikely centre for a renowned marine research institute. But *l'Istituto delle Civiltà del Mare* is leading the battle to have some of the coastline's most precious areas saved from development as a national marine park. Every year, to promote its conservation message, the Institute hosts an important international festival of films on marine subjects, called 'Dolphins of the Tyrrhenian Sea'. The dolphins are real—a pair sculptured in solid gold by a local artisan, mounted on a block of Sardinian granite, and worth fifteen million *lire*.

The festival was the reason we were in Sardinia. I was there to accept the dolphins on behalf of Australian filmmakers David Parer and his wife Elizabeth Parer-Cook for their brilliant documentary on killer whales, narrated by David Attenborough, 'Wolves of the Sea'. The invitation had come about in a strange way. Liz had telephoned me as ABC correspondent in Italy to ask my help to interpret the ambiguous messages they were getting from San Teodoro about their entry in the festival. Across the language barrier, the organisers seemed to be anxious to know if David and Liz would be there to present their film. They would not tell David and Liz if it was a prize-winner, but there was no money in the ABC's budget for a flight from Melbourne to Sardinia anyway.

A quick telephone call to the organisers at the Institute and a little reading between the lines made everything clear. 'Wolves of the Sea' would be awarded the golden dolphins, but only if someone was there to receive them. I was asked to go as their proxy. It was a proud moment, on a balmy night in the public square of San Teodoro to see the film 'Wolves' projected to hundreds of people on a giant screen, and to then receive the trophy and the citation from leading actress and environmental campaigner, Lea Massari.

Getting the precious dolphins back to Australia was a little more nerve-wracking. We kept them at Varacca until we were returning for Christmas, then swaddled them in clothing in our hand luggage so they would never be out of our sight. Liz and David came to collect them personally at Mosman. They were already working on their next nature film, 'Mysteries of the Ocean Wanderers'; the golden dolphins of the Tyrrhenian Sea were the best Christmas present they could have had.

12. THE CRISIS OF SEX

'Sexuality is the lyricism of the masses.'
Charles Baudelaire

'There is no greater nor keener pleasure than that of bodily love—and none which is more irrational.'
Plato

When we tuned in to Italian television, we found one of the most popular programs on the commercial networks was *Striscia la Notizia, Skim the News*, a zany send-up of the day's doings. Apart from its irreverent humour, a large part of its appeal lay in the startling way in which late news was delivered to the two comic presenters. Bikini-clad girls on roller skates zoomed down a ramp that was an extension of the news desk and squatted, their plump thighs at eye level, to hand over the hot items. To an outsider, it was a startling (but relatively mild), example of the sexism which pervades the Italian media—television, cinema, magazines and much of the advertising.

How, one might ask, does a matriarchal society which still reverences the Madonna, permit the top-rating *Amateur Strip Show* with its total nudity, to go to air? Why do advertisers of products as diverse as computers and shampoos feel it so necessary to slip a bare breast or two into their contrived scenarios? And how does a nubile female, clad in animal skins and reaching through the bars of her cage, sell more cheese? Even worse, how could a Catholic country permit a blasphemous Last Supper, with topless girls as disciples, to go to print to sell 'Jesus' jeans?

The annual displays of semi-nudity by the rich and famous on summer beaches, all faithfully recorded in the popular magazines, may seem surprising, but at least they are based on equality—the Italian Constitutional Court ruled that women have as much right as men to bare their chests. And every year, celebrities compete to do so. The ambivalence in the Italian attitude to their womenfolk has always perplexed foreigners and it puzzled me. More than twenty years ago, H. V. Morton observed: 'Italy is a country where women allow men to believe themselves to be strong and masterful'. Many centuries earlier, Robert Burton wrote in his *Anatomy of Melancholy*: 'England is a paradise for women and hell for horses; Italy a paradise for horses, hell for women'.

Although the rest of the world may have moved on to liberation and equal opportunity, little has changed in Italy. It is tempting to play the amateur psychologist. Was it Renaissance art, with all those depictions by the masters of the Annunciation, the Adoration and of course, the *Pietà*, which locked both men and women into their roles for the next six hundred years? The Vatican still adamantly refuses to concede equality for women, let alone any part in the Church's decision making.

While history records a number of women of great talent who exercised considerable power, many more seem to have ruled from behind the scenes. The manipulative approach may have been the shrewd (and possibly the only) way for women on this peninsula to gain power in earlier times, but it may also have condemned them to a subservient position completely inappropriate for the new millenium.

The conditioning process starts from birth, with the spoiling of the child. We have a friend who teaches English to Italian secondary students after school. At the end of one class, she said to a sixteen-year-old boy:
'Well, you'd better run—you'll have time to help your mother with the washing up.'
A mortal insult!
'I have never washed a dish in my life, and I never will!' he replied.
Our friend however had the perfect riposte: 'As somebody who's always talking about wanting to marry an American girl in preference to an Italian, you'd better think again—something's gotta give!'

This reinforcement of male superiority has had dramatic and devastating effects on career prospects for Italian women. There are successful, highly visible and articulate women in Italy. The talented Milanese architect Gai Aulenti created the brilliant Musée d'Orsay from a condemned Paris railway station and will now re-build the burnt-out La Fenice theatre in Venice; Rita Levi di Montalcino is a Nobel Laureate in chemistry; and the culinary reputation of Lorenza de' Medici of Badia di Coltibuono extends worldwide. Italy has a higher proportion of women parliamentarians than either Britain or Australia; Susanna Agnelli was made Foreign Minister. But nearly all such outstanding women are professionals, are members of wealthy, and therefore independent families or, like the large number of top class women winemakers, come from the land, perhaps even of the old nobility. Elsewhere, career progression is slow indeed. Penetration of the higher echelons of the public service, and of business enterprises, is far below the levels achieved in the United States or Australia.

I had reason to look into these aspects of Italian social life for an article I was writing for an Australian magazine. In the offices of Italy, women seem to be not only second-class citizens, but also distracting sexual objects. A conference in Modena on sexual harassment in the workplace was told that one worker in two complained of molestation in one form or another. The most revealing finding from a survey of five hundred women was that *le molestie sessuali* was most frequent in the public service. In the factories, heavy attention and *manomorta*, the expressive term 'dead hand' for 'touching-up', was less common. Sadly, the Modena conference rephrased Mozart: in the office, *Cosi Fan Quasi Tutte*—almost anything goes.

More recently, an official government survey lasting three years confirmed that things were really worse. Sampling women between 14 and 59 years of age, it found:

- 4% of all Italian women had suffered sexual violence;
- 700,000 had suffered rape or attempted rape;
- 22% of the rapes were by strangers, so the greater proportion were by friends, acquaintances, husbands or other family members;
- only 1.3% of the attempted rapes and 32% of rapes were reported.

These figures are remarkably similiar to findings in other western countries, indicating that in Italy too, the historically sacrosant family life is shattering.

In the absence of effective legislation against sexual harassment, it needs inventiveness to deal with transgressors. In Naples, a policeman who demanded sexual favours from a Colombian migrant because her papers were not in order, was charged with, and convicted of, extortion. Attacks on women are now amongst the most frequent in Europe. As the grim statistics mounted, the scream of outrage against rape reached a crescendo. Since the 1930s, rape, under Italian law, was defined as a 'crime against morality'. After sixteen years of trying, the Chamber of Deputies, the lower house of parliament, finally won overwhelming support for a 1979 bill to make rape a crime against the individual—only to have it blocked in the Senate. Women senators were amongst its fiercest opponents, defending, they said, the autonomy of their chamber! The new law on sexual violence did not get onto the statute books until 1996.

Traditional sexual morality seems increasingly in short supply as the secularisation of society accelerates. A massive survey commissioned by the Conference of Italian Bishops and published as a book, *La Religiosità in Italia*, confirmed the Church's waning influence on Italian mores. Homosexuality, masturbation, cohabitation, contraception, divorce, premarital sex—behaviour that the Church has always considered gravely sinful—now rank at the bottom of the table of comportment meriting popular disapproval. And the population growth is now negative.

Is it a sense of male inferiority that so many men support the increasing numbers of brothels, the '*case chiuse*' or 'closed houses', present in every town (to the rage of local residents and the frustration of the authorities)? It's a huge trade, and now the illegal immigrants—from Nigeria, Tunisia, Sri Lanka, Yugoslavia, and Russia—seem to have driven the Italian street girls off their pitches. On a twenty-five kilometre stretch of country road I counted nineteen prostitutes, three-quarters of them black. At night, their roadside fires attract the men like moths, and give the girls their nickname, *lucciole*—fireflies.

But what of the men? The carefully-nurtured reputation of the Italian male as a great lover is also increasingly being revealed as a myth. Swaggeringly self-confident towards foreign females in the *piazza* (as many a bruised tourist buttock will confirm) the young Italian male seems even less able to cope with the company of women than the legendary Australian beerkeg bore. On Sunday mornings, you will see him with his crowd of male friends in the street, strutting and chatting away the hours until *mamma* has made the pasta and is ready to preside at her *pranzo*.

We went to dinner one night in a restaurant at Lucca. Suddenly a powerful motorcyle engine roared in the night air. The door burst open, and there stood the local Hell's Angel—all black leather and studs. Talk stopped. Forks hovered in mid-air. Then a little voice from the kitchen broke the tension.

'Luigi, you naughty boy, where have you been? I told you to get home before this!'

His shoulders dropped and he slunk out the back, his great moment of *machilismo* over.

An Italian journalist, Piero Ottone, who writes a perceptive weekly column called 'Vices and Virtues', sees the Italian male and Italian masculinity in crisis. He lays much of the blame on the excesses of mother love, and believes maternal protectionism and solicitude are now on the increase again.

'A mother who smothers her son is conditioning him to see himself as the centre of the universe…Then, when the world treats him badly, it is a tragedy.'

It also seems a tragedy to me that so many Italian women happily and unnecessarily enslave themselves to their children, long after they reach adulthood. Our friend Angela cannot go on holidays until she has finished all the ironing for her thirty-year-old sons. That, to me, is a perfect definition of *Mammismo*. It took a woman writer, Barbara Grizzuti Harrison, to put it more bluntly: 'In a country of Madonnas and *bambini*, mothers have their sons by the balls.' Perhaps the only revenge of the Italian male is to portray all women—his mother excepted, of course—as sex objects.

13. Autumn—stop-work orders

Suddenly, as if a switch has been thrown, the sun is losing its heat. It is still officially summer, but the next of the seasonal changes, which I find so sharply dramatic, is under way. It's a relief. The *Scirocco* has been scorching the countryside and suffocating its people. No wonder Norman Douglas called the wind 'the withering blast whose hot and clammy touch hastens death and putrefaction'.

Sometimes it dumps a fine golden dust that was once Sahara sand onto everything. In years when the wind is strongest, the whole of Sardinia, being closer to Africa, can take on a pale yellow tint. The high pressure systems which have dominated the weather charts for months gradually weaken, and lows start to move down into Italy's latitudes. We watch them from above, through the genius of satellite photography, and from below, here at Varacca. The clouds themselves seem confused at the change they are bringing. At three different levels, they move in opposing directions, opening and then closing windows on the blue. Often, towards the end of the day, they confuse the sunbeams. The light, shafting through the gaps, is diffused into brilliant rays that spray the countryside. Immediately when I first saw the spectacular effect, I realised that the old masters did not invent those beams of light they painted streaming from boiling clouds, illuminating the Madonna and Child—they gave us celestial photographs. So I call them 'Jesus skies' and hope nobody find this blasphemous.

The farmers are harvesting the last of the summer crops. The *mietitura* of the sunflowers is underway, the huge lumbering headers trundling back and forth across the fields, leaving the stalks trampled and askew behind them. The dried seed heads go to big mills in the north, but the *Oleificio Pacianese*, the cooperative oil mill on the corner of our road, is already preparing its plant for the start of the olive season in November.

Over the hill, the melon crop has already been taken off, but the mile-long strips of black plastic through which the plants poked their heads, have to be torn up and dumped. Down on the flat, the last capsicums and tomatoes are being crated for market by lines of itinerant workers.

The wheat and barley fields are now bare, dotted with straw bales waiting to be carted off to storage. Some are cubes, but these days more and more are *rulli*, or cylinders—the latest and most fashionable shape. Paciano has just accorded them official recognition by introducing the '*Corsa dei Rulli*', a race in which sturdy young men of the village roll them up the steep slope of the Viale Roma. If the warm weather holds, there will be time for a third or even a fourth cut of the lucerne before it's ploughed in to enrich the soil.

Suddenly the birds appear out of the bush to attack the late fruit. We defend our fig trees with strips of plastic film and sardine-tin lids tied to the branches, but this works only if there is a breeze. We wish for wind, or my wife's jam-making will be the poorer. I read somewhere that the true fig-eater is supposed to be *Sylvia bori*, the English Garden Warbler, but even consulting my big bird book, *Uccelli Europei*, I can't tell whether he's the real culprit. It doesn't really matter. As the local saying goes,

'*Ogni uccello di settembre è beccafico*'—'In September, every bloody bird is a fig-eater!'

For the local grape growers, the matter is more serious. The September partridges get up very early in the morning to attack the bunches, and return for more in the evening. It used to be a fairly level playing field, for the shooters would get up before the partridges. Now, with the decline in hunting, we still hear the shotguns the first weekend in September, but the balance has been tipped in favour of the bird, and against the vigneron.

...

The lack of action on the road continues to niggle us. 'Our' road, as we defiantly call it, is still gazetted as a *strada comunale*, and the *Comune* seems in no hurry to transfer it to us. Until it does, it will not accept any development application for retaining walls, fences, gates and paths. It is another perfect 'catch-22' situation.

I had tried every angle of persuasion, but the council would not budge.

'How can you have two roads?' I had asked Mayor Alfonso one day. 'One of them is closed and disused, and part of it should rightly belong to us. The other is built on private land, is in daily use, yet is not formally acquired or gazetted? *Non è giusto!*'

He shrugged: '*Pazienza!*'

'Patience' is the standard Italian reply to avoid explaining why any service cannot be performed within a normal time. Italian literature is full of proverbs extolling its merit. St Francis, Italy's patron saint (who was of course an Umbrian) himself gave it his benediction with: 'Patience is an act of perfection and proof of virtue.' *Pazienza* is now so entrenched as an excuse that Italians joke about it, and use the exhortation ironically. Italy's Charlie Chaplin, the beloved Neopolitan comic actor Toto, poked fun at its usage by turning a proverb on its head with his quip: 'Every limit has its patience!'

One day I took another tack with Alfonso:

'Is there any doubt at all that the old road will be transferred to us?'

'None whatsoever.'

'Then, to allow us to get on with our *sistemazione*, why not give us provisional permission to develop, and confirm that when you get around to arranging the formal transfer?'

Alfonso had some very good bureaucratic reason why this could not be done, but it was not very convincing. So I had gone back to Gabriele Tomassoni, the technical officer and our bête noir.

'Why all the delay?', I asked.

'The problem is, the *giunta* has not yet authorised the *frazionamento*. We have to survey the area involved, create a new parcel of land and register it in Perugia. Then we can transfer the old road to *Signora* Biavati, and she can give it to you.'

'How long, Gabriele?' (It was then June. I knew that registration of a *frazionamento* normally can be achieved in a few months at most).

'*In breve tempo*', he said—by September or October.'

He was making it up as he went along. It took Paciano council more than four years. We have often pondered the reason for its passivity. Certainly, there were some costs involved— for the survey and the notary act—and the Council was poor. In any case, the sums would not have been large, and I would gladly have paid them to accelerate the process.

I would certainly have offered and, indeed, even insisted if I had known how the years would drag on. It was never suggested to me, however, that I should. Perhaps in an Italy by then obsessive about official corruption, there was a fear that this would have been interpreted as *tangenti*, a bribe? Another possible, more sinister reason had suggested itself as I began to have trouble with our neighbour, Cerimonia. From the moment he had learned that we had legal rights to that part of the old road in front of our house, and would be enclosing our property, his former friendliness turned to enmity.

Gian-Carlo Cerimonia had bought his little cottage and come to live in Paciano when he retired from his clerical job in the Buitoni pasta factory in Perugia. He has been blind in one eye since he was a boy, the result, he says, of an injury caused by a German bayonet during the war, but he would never explain how it happened. He was, and is still, an unreconstructed communist. He has lived with Bruna, unmarried, for forty years. This excites no interest whatsoever today, but began as a deliberate gesture against the Church at a time when such protests were daring indeed in Italy. With age, his attitude to the Church may have mellowed. We notice that Don Rossi, the parish priest, comes and blesses his house every Easter.

He and Bruna live comfortably on their state pensions, and grow much of their own food in their well tended garden. When we first met him, Gian-Carlo was pulling snails off his trees and stamping on them as he named them: 'Thatcher!' 'Bush!' 'Kohl!' 'Mitterand', and then slightly more kindly, 'Kruschev!' We thought it slightly bizarre, but put it down to a horticultural way of saying 'A plague on all your houses!'

At that stage the Cerimonias had two cocker spaniels and three cats (one of which had been found abandoned in the culvert outside our house and taken in). The dogs had a predisposition to canker and cysts. Whenever their condition became really bad, Gian-Carlo would visit old Doctor Agostini in the village for a prescription for antibiotics. I don't believe the health department ever knew that its free pensioner terramycin and penicillin were going to the dogs.

Gian-Carlo is, I suppose, basically a kindly man, but with an enormous chip on his shoulder. When we were restoring, and for the few years afterwards, he was most hospitable. We always brought them presents when we arrived back from

Australia, and imagined we would have a good neighbourly relationship in our tiny hamlet.

Unfortunately, things did not work out that way. It was not long before we discovered that he regarded us as his trophies. A close association with the foreigners raised his local status, but the price of friendship turned out to be acceptance of his superior knowledge in everything. The more we went our own way, especially in making friends of whom he did not approve, the more I became a *'fascista'*. Eventually he tried to forbid the other Italian neighbours to speak to us. When we had our boundaries pegged by the surveyor, Cerimonia appeared and disputed with him what was our land. From that day he hardly spoke to us, except to shout abuse, and is likely to spit on the ground if we should happen to pass on the street. The saying, 'Good fences make good neighbours' definitely did not seem to apply in Italy. It's a tiny shadow on our happiness.

Cerimonia was second cousin to Mayor Alfonso. He was constantly complaining to him that we were alienating land that should be part of the 'common court' of Varacca. To change the rules would, of course, have meant reneging on its agreements, and the *Comune* was not about to subject itself to a legal fight. But we always felt that Alfonso was dragging his feet on the issue; and the longer it took, the more inconvenience we suffered.

As the months and years went by, the catalogue of explanations, excuses and broken promises mounted. We joked about it constantly with our Italian friends. They were sympathetic but also angry—they were obviously embarrassed for Italy.

It was frustrating, but there was no use becoming paranoid over it. We decided that the reason for the delays was probably just the old Italian problem, inefficiency. What we were experiencing was a microcosm of what was happening across the country.

When we talked to *Zio* Carlo about the problems with Cerimonia and the council, he smiled and triumphantly quoted another of his proverbs: '*Chi ha la terra, ha la guerra.*' Property ownership has always been a potential battleground in Italy.

Domenico, the *Vigile*, became quite concerned at the friction. The idea of not getting on with your neighbour, not by any means unknown in Australia or Britain, seemed definitely upsetting here. He tried to explain that some Italians became consumed with envy and a sense of inferiority when confronted with foreigners, and counselled me not to descend to Cerimonia's level.

After two years alternately waiting and pestering, Tomassoni finally promised that the road transfer would be through by the end of that second summer. So we booked a builder to make the terraces and steps. When October came, there was another set of excuses—nothing had been done. Confronted with the choice of cancelling and therefore inconveniencing the builder, who would have had no other work, or just going ahead, we decided to take the bit between our teeth.

This time we used a local *muratore*. Luciano Torrini now lives in Castiglione del Lago, but he was born at Pietreto, where his mother, old Enrica, was still living, in her eighties. Luciano and Francesco Montioni together built a small chapel at

Pietreto, in memory of Enrica's husband, Pietro. It is constructed of local stones which were gathered in the fields and, appropriately, is dedicated to St Peter. Every June, on the Feast of St Peter and St Paul, the two families host a festival at Pietreto. At their own expense, they cook for and serve all comers, and Francesco's cellar provides the wines. I was a little worried that Luciano would be working without a building permit, but he was unconcerned. There was no love lost between him and Paciano; his phrasing of his attitude to the *Comune*—as far as I could tell—lay somewhere between 'jump in the lake' and 'get stuffed'.

Audrey and I had spent endless hours designing the steps at the front door and in the angled space between the house and the new terrace. They were to be terracotta *gradini*, handmade in the traditional style. For these we had to go to Castel Viscardo, a little mountain village not far from Orvieto, and about fifty kilometres away. There, in a simple primitive shed, in incredible heat and discomfort, workmen were pushing clay into wooden box-moulds with their bare hands, tamping and trimming it as their forefathers had done for centuries.

The only modern touch was a huge gas-fired kiln in the corner, where the trays of moulds were loaded after they had dried on racks for days. We made two round trips with our little trailer to carry the steptreads home, stacked on edge and packed with cardboard. At four thousand *lire* each, we couldn't afford to break any.

Like all Italian *muratori*, Luciano loves to pour concrete. Sixteen cubic metres of the stuff went into the retaining walls and the terrace, a grossly excessive amount. For a few happy hours, the builders had the excitement of blocking the road with a massive mixer truck. From the rear, the operator extended a long hydraulic arm high over our hedge; a rubber hose bigger than an elephant's trunk spewed the slop into the formwork. I saw statistics that Italy pours something like two million tons of concrete for every man, woman and child in Italy, every year; and that doesn't count concrete mixed on the job by builders. No wonder environmentalists are concerned at what they term the 'crust of concrete' spreading over the country!

Luciano was just finishing the terrace, but had not yet started on the stairs when Domenico arrived. I suspected that Cerimonia had tipped him off, but by then any such speculation was academic. Naturally he wanted to know if I had a building permit for the work that was going on in front of his eyes; he looked very sceptical when I put my tongue in my cheek and told him I didn't need one, as it was really only a continuation of the work on the house.

Sure enough, the next day he was back after checking the records.

'Mi dispiace, Goffredo', he said. 'Non c'è autorizzazione per questo lavoro—devi sospenderlo subito.'

To get a stop-work order at this point was highly inconvenient. For three years the steps at the front door had been temporary—a couple of concrete blocks. We were in sight of having proper stairs, with a stack of gradini costing one and a half milione waiting to be laid. The situation called for drastic action. I telephoned Alfonso. Of course he knew all about Domenico's stop-work order.

'Non preoccupavi, Goffredo', he said, 'non è grave!'

This was a relief, as I thought a summons or a fine might follow. But while he insisted that no further work be done across the 'road', it would be permissible to make the stairs, as they would be on our existing land. This was a very satisfactory compromise for us, since Luciano had completed all the work except the steps! So he finished the job, and for the first time since we had arrived, all our friends were able to enter the house without risking a sprained ankle. I knew we had joined the ranks of *abusivo* builders, but it wasn't really our fault. When we heard no more from the council, all worry slipped from my mind.

. . .

The change of seasons brings terrifying electrical activity. As well as being highly volcanic and seismically unstable, Italy suffers from being one of the most lightning-prone countries in the world. The clash of the weather fronts produces towering cumulonimbus clouds that generate the most spectacular multi-million volt discharges. The electricity supply system cannot cope. There is a loud bang, and the two circuit-breakers in the house trip out. Everything stops. Occasionally, with an extra heavy discharge, the main circuit-breaker in the meter box outside shuts down the whole house. Power can be restored by a push of the button, but the first time it happened, I waited several hours, assuming it was just ENEL losing power to the whole district, as so often occurs.

It's more serious if the charge comes down the telephone line. Our electrician had installed a double fuse on the line, but one day the lightning bolt was so close that a huge electrical surge blew them out, then jumped down the line to destroy our fax machine and three telephones. The same shock took out the masthead amplifier on our television antenna, leaving RAI-UNO reduced to a moving pointillist painting in black and white. We now pull out the telephone plugs at the first sign of a thunderstorm.

The lightning problem is now regarded so seriously that the government has legislated to require protection systems in all new buildings. It has gone further, with one of its favourite retrospective clauses. At every house sale, the documentation must include a lightning risk assessment report. Every region is rated according to its riskiness; if the house risk comes in above the factor for the region, the sale cannot go through until lightning arrestors are installed.

We got to know all this from Giampietro Favero, our Roman friend, who is a member of the international committee on lightning and lightning protection. We had met Giampietro and his charming wife Nanni under what were initially somewhat embarrassing circumstances. (Nanni is not her real name. She is a Milanese, but the family have simplified her difficult Lombard name to Nanni and as 'familiars' we may now use it too.)

The old house on the hill, off the *Via degli Etruschi* towards Moiano and Chiusi, was being restored. I had photographed it when it was a romantic ruin, so when we were passing one Saturday afternoon it seemed a good idea to have a look at what was being done to it. We were deep inside, amongst beams and props when we heard a car draw up outside. As we clambered out over the piles of building materials, a large Pavarotti-like man with a fierce expression advanced towards us. A woman we took to be his wife was just getting out of a car with Rome number plates. Obviously these were the owners—we had been caught red-handed! I thought quickly. The only thing for it was what the military call a pre-emptive strike.

'Is this your house?' I asked him before he could say a word.

'*Si.*'

'*Complimenti!…una bella casa!…un bel restauro!*'

The ice was broken, he beamed at the praise, and led us proudly on a tour, upstairs and down.

Giampietro is an electrical engineer with his own consulting business in Rome. He has had some prestigious projects, including the complete electrical and electronic designs for some of the *palazzi* that front Rome's *Piazza di Venezia*. It was when I asked about the thick electrical cabling I saw poking out of the roof that he explained about the lightning risk, and how to guard against it. Those spikes attached to church steeples and the parapets of public buildings are now *passè*, it seems. They may attract and conduct the lightning away, but the latest technique is to circle the roof of a building with a continuous band of conducting metal, and link it to earth.

'Do you have any idea what the risk is to your house?', he asked.

Since I didn't, he offered to come and define it for us. Starting with the plans, he measured the roof height and the distances from all the surrounding buildings, and then estimated the slope of the hillside. A few weeks later, he was back to present a detailed report, complete with a computerised calculation of the risk factor for the house. Fortunately, it fell below the standard level set for Umbria, so we were not obliged to install a protection system. It need not be as complicated as his, Giampietro explained—it would be sufficient to use the house guttering as the electrical armature, and connect it firmly to earth.

We share many family moments together on their weekend visits to the countryside. In winter, we sit around the fire in his lounge room and roast chestnuts. In the spring, we go off together to Montalcino, where Giampietro has identified the winery of the Baricci family as producing the best Brunello in the district. We have a tasting in the cool, cool cellar. Not very satisfactory, because in April, even cupping the glass between our hands, we cannot get enough warmth into the wine to bring out its full flavour. But we buy a few cases to see us through the year, and later find that at the right temperature, it opens up superbly.

The *vendemmia* has begun around Paciano. We have learned to be especially careful on the roads at this season. As the grapes are picked, they are hurried off to the Trasimeno Wine Co-operative in Castiglione del Lago in every available vehicle. Tractors, trucks and the little Piaggio three-wheelers, the *Api*, are liable to shoot out onto the road from a farm track without warning. Nearly every year, someone is skittled.

Will anything ever replace the *Ape*, we wonder. (The *Ape*, or bee, is the companion to the *Vespa*, or wasp, and is the agricultural version of the famous motor scooter.) It is cheap to buy and cheap to run. Its 50cc motor and low gearing give it a maximum speed of forty kilometres an hour (which makes it a menace on the roads), but it is light enough to traverse ploughed fields and clamber up steep slopes. At the grape harvest and the olive picking, they are so grossly overloaded with the big wooden trays that the drivers in the cramped cabins steering with handlebars, not a wheel, can't see other traffic.

Now it's time to go across to Pietreto to help Francesco press his grapes. He doesn't grow his own, because like us, he has no south-facing slopes. Instead, he buys them in, choosing the best from around the district. Francesco is an absolute stickler for following all the *contadino*'s ancient rules on timing. He leaves the *vendemmia* until the very last moment to make sure the grapes get the last sun of the season. He will quote an old proverb:

> *Di settembre e d'agosto*
> *bevi vino vecchio*
> *e lascia stare il musto*
> In September and August,
> drink the old wine
> and let stand the must

It's a very long day, picking all morning, then back at his *cantina* in the afternoon tipping the heavy boxes of fruit into the screw press. I am grateful that the romantic treading of grapes has long since passed into history. Now an electric motor turns a big augur in the bottom of the trough, a blower expels the stalks and a pump sends the juice and skins down into the vats in the cellar below.

We press enough to make about twelve hundred litres of wine. Francesco's idea had been to make all the house wine for their restaurant. After the first successful year, the health authorities moved in, demanding that he register as a vintner. On his small scale, he could not afford to pay another raft of taxes, so his wine is now only for his own use, and his friends.

The day always ends with a big family dinner. Audrey may bring a pavlova (which always excites attention), but the rest is *Umbra genuina*. There is always a big plate of mixed cold meats—*salame, prosciutto, capacollo*—a dish of Giuseppina's home-made pasta, perhaps spaghetti with the ubiquitous tomato sauce, or if she has time a *pasta al forno* (which we would call *lasagna*), fried meats or an ox-tail stew, a big bowl of mushrooms and *insalata*. Francesco plies us incessantly with his *rosso* and *bianco*. All old wine, as the proverb instructed, from his cellar of ten thousand bottles. The second part of the wine year is nine months away. The following June we will go again to help bottle the vintage but, faithful to the traditions, only at full moon and with no storms about.

Over dinner, we get to talk about local problems. Francesco starts to bemoan the state of the road. The *Comune*, having initiated the restaurant project, has left it to languish at the end of the badly-made road it pushed through the Biavati lands. There is no passing traffic; even if a hungry traveller finds his way up to *Il Casale*, the state of the dusty rutted road is enough to deter return visits. We come from a country of action, so I suggest what is needed is a petition, pointing out the dangerous state of the road for the increasing traffic, and requesting that it be sealed. To my surprise, Francesco is enthusiastic. I'm surprised, because we've found Italians all too ready to grumble about situations, but content to remain convinced that nothing they can do will ever change things.

I wrote out the *supplica*, Francesco corrected my Italian and then toured the district collecting signatures. Most people had never seen such a document, some were even a little fearful of possible repercussions, but Francesco, the ex-*Carabiniere* was not standing for any nonsense.

'*Sta zitto—firma!*'…'Shut up and sign!' I heard him say to Cerimonia.

At the end, we had thirty-four signatures; everyone who used the road signed and Francesco presented the petition to the *Comune*. Two years later, the jeremiahs looked as if they'd been proved right. No acknowledgement and, of course, no action.

14. ETRUSCAN BRONZES AND ITALIAN TRACTORS

Like a *tegole* from the sky, a letter came from Sydney from a friend of a friend who was writing a mystery novel that revolves around those Iguvine tablets found at Gubbio, the modern Iguvium, in far northern Umbria.

'Could you help with information about the latest research on the Etruscans of Gubbio?' was the request.

After our early experience of Audrey's icy accident, the very mention of Gubbio sets off bad vibrations in this house. However, I'm a sucker for real-life mysteries. I'd always been curious about those strange bronzes covered with a mix of Etruscan and Latin script. Why had scholars experienced so much difficulty making head or tail of them? Doing a little research for our friend would satisfy my curiosity too. I quickly found it didn't involve another visit to Gubbio (to my wife's relief), only an interview with Professor Francesco Roncelli, head of the Department of Historical Sciences of Antiquity in the University of Perugia.

Le Tavole Iguvine are seven bronze tablets now on public display in the Gubbio Museum in the Consul's Palace. They had been discovered in an underground cavern among the ruins of the town's Roman theatre in 1444, and have been accurately dated to 200BC. It's known that they contain the rites of a mysterious Iguvium brotherhood of priests known as the *Fratres Atiedii*. One part of the mystery lies in interpreting their meaning and purpose; the other in the tantalising story that originally there were not seven tablets, but nine.

The existence and loss of the other two tablets can be traced to a single source—a Renaissance scholar, Leandro Alberti. In 1550, he wrote that ten years earlier, two tablets had been sent to Venice for interpretation. There they had been either lost or stolen, but in any case, never returned to Gubbio. Scholars have been searching for them for centuries in the hope they can throw light on the other seven. Our friend was constructing her novel around their disappearance and a fictitious re-discovery.

Professor Roncelli had good news and bad news. The two 'missing' tablets had not been found (leaving the novelist wide scope for historical embroidery). However, the current thinking among Etruscan scholars was that there had never been nine tablets, only seven. Alberti's story is perhaps a furphy.
'Why can't the tablets and, for that matter, the Etruscan language itself, be accurately translated?' I asked. It was a question that had always puzzled me.
'We have never found a "Rosetta Stone" with the same text in Etruscan, Latin and Greek' was the response. 'The Iguvine

Tablets were incised at the time the Etruscan Federation was in decline, its civilisation becoming increasingly Romanised. The writing is a mixture of both languages, with many words merely religious incantations and others indecipherable that were most likely dialect.'

I asked Professor Roncelli about the legend that they had once hung in a temple to Jupiter high up in the Apennines of which no trace remains. He shrugged.

'There is no evidence. What we can say from the blank spaces left on each side of some tablets is that they were probably carried by an acolyte, like a missal, for a priest to read from. The writing on the reverse is upside down, perhaps so they could be flipped over.'

In the eighteenth century, when excitement about the tablets was at its peak, a number of counterfeits appeared on the market to supply the demand for the missing two. I reflected that discovering them in a novel would be quite harmless, and for all of us, much more enjoyable.

After this historical diversion, we could relax and enjoy the tranquillity of warm autumn days, putting out of our minds the need to prepare for the approaching winter. The ancients' saying, *'Per San Donato l'inverno è nato'*, was too pessimistic for us. No sooner had they got to the feast of Saint Donato on 7 August—at the height of Summer—than they were worrying about winter coming!

The birds had been telling us the good times could not last, but we pretended not to hear. We would sit late over dinner on the terrace, watching the swallows and swifts come wheeling around in their thousands. Each night around sunset they would be looking for a safe resting place, ready to resume their migration to Africa early next morning. Some tucked themselves up warmly in the dense wisteria foliage over our pergola; they were always gone by the time we were up next day. Good quiet guests—except for their droppings all over the chairs and tiles.

The little birds were going, but the birdmen were still coming—from all over Europe. Just across the fields, at Panicarola on the flat land between Paciano and the lake, is one of the most important parachuting schools on the continent. The European free-fall championships are sometimes held there—teams of eight somersaulting and holding hands from three thousand metres before opening their multicoloured nylon blossoms and flaring out to a walk-on landing.

The school and its airstrip base at Panicarola were founded by one of the outstanding industrialists who helped re-build postwar Italy, Ferruccio Lamborghini. It was 1946, and the vast plains north of Bologna and Ferrara were littered with the tanks the Germans had abandoned in their retreat. Thirty year-old Lamborghini stripped them, and started building crawler tractors from their parts. Today, all over Italy, his cream and black tractors are the Rolls Royces of agricultural machinery.

Lamborghini was always passionate about speed. One day he drove one of his Ferraris to Maranello to complain to Enzo Ferrari himself that the brakes were inadequate.

'They're not as good as the brakes on my biggest tractor', he told Enzo. Provocation indeed! The old man, whose nickname 'The Dragon' was well-earned, berated him:

'You think you can improve one of my cars—prove that you can make a better one yourself!'

So he did. The Lamborghini Miura became the fastest and most desirable sports car in the world. The name came from the breed of the fiercest fighting bulls of Spain; the charging bull was Lamborghini's logo—he chose it deliberately to challenge the prancing horse of Ferrari. But Ferruccio Lamborghini was always looking for a new challenge. He sold the sports-car business, and bought three hundred hectares beside Lake Trasimeno to show Italians how to make wine. He built an ultra-modern winery with all the temperature-control technology that the best Australian wineries use. The back-label on every one of the million bottles a year he produced proclaimed immodestly: 'All my life, I have striven to produce the best—this is my wine.'

We went to see the winery, and there was Ferruccio, shirt-sleeves rolled up, driving a tractor—a muscular little man, intensely active despite his age. His leathery face relaxed into a smile at my interest in his story. He hopped down to show us through the little museum he had built beside his villa, *La Fiorita*. In it was an example of every Lamborghini car he had built—from the Miura and the Espada to the Uracco and the Jalpa. In pride of place was the mythical Countach, the first production sports car in the world capable of exceeding three hundred kilometres an hour.

But his real pride was the collection of tractors, for they represented his beginnings. He led us to a little orange machine, the first tractor he had built, more than forty years earlier. 'It took me a long time to track it down', he explained, 'and when I did, the old farmer wouldn't sell it to me. He was still using it, after all those years. Eventually though, the cunning peasant mind came into play. He wouldn't sell it, but he would swop it for my latest, biggest model.' He laughed. 'That's how I got it back.'

In Italy, powerful personalities like Lamborghini are surrounded by their own legends. One day he discovered that one of his early wives (he had three in all) had taken a lover. So he borrowed a bulldozer from a friend, waited half an hour for the couple to get into their rhythm, then demolished the house around them!

Coming to Umbria had added twenty years to his life, he told us, but a year later, he was dead from a heart attack at seventy-six. The day of his funeral, burglars ransacked his villa, taking everything of value. He left the car and tractor museum to his son, who moved it to the tractor plant at Modena; the Panicarola buildings seem forlorn without it. Lamborghini's name lives on—in the country club he established on the estate, in his wine, and on those thousands of cream and black machines ploughing the rich fields of central Italy.

15. Winter—cold winds and olive milling

'A sad tale's best for winter.
I have one of sprites and goblins.'
William Shakespeare, *The Winter's Tale*

That arctic blast—the *Magistralis Ventus* or 'Master Wind' that once made the Caesars button up their togas, but now better known by its Provençal name, the Mistral—blows straight down the Val di Chiana. With its arrival we knew that soon enough, autumn would turn to winter in Umbria.

In the municipal offices in Paciano the air was suddenly chill, but not from the Mistral. A bundle of documents had landed with a thud on Mayor Alfonso del Buono's desk. Forty-four *denunce* or summonses against citizens of Paciano for various infractions of the law. The word spread like wildfire—so many people were in trouble. Domenico Verga, the *Vigile*, had just been doing his job, but very assiduously. It had taken him two years to gather all the evidence, and one of the summonses was for me.

There are several meanings to the word *denuncia;* most times it means simply and innocuously a 'report'. But there is also a more ominous translation—'a charge against'. It is ominous because unlike an Australian summons, a *denuncia,* once issued, cannot be withdrawn. I had always got on well with Domenico, but his arrival in town had been greeted with cold suspicion by many citizens. Unlike Franco Boldrini, his predecessor, he was seen as an outsider. Although he lived in Paciano, he was born in Sicily (in fact, in Corleone, the very epicentre of Mafia influence, which may be responsible for an over-compensating zeal) so, like us, would never be really accepted. He had done his military service in the *Carabinieri,* and had then become a *geometra.*

With these credentials, the town immediately saw Domenico as the new sheriff riding in to clean up Dodge City. In no time at all, parking areas had been defined and Pacianese who had been used to leaving their cars any-old-how in the street were getting tickets for stopping in 'no standing' zones.

My friends pointed out delightedly that in Italian, *verga* means a rod or cane.

'What's wrong with that?' I asked. The symbolism seemed appropriate for a *vigile* even if it was a little fascist.

'Aha!' they replied. 'You do not know that in *gergo* (slang) it is a vulgar term for the *pene,* the, er…male member.' Vulgarisms seem to cross all boundaries.

'Well, in my country', I replied, 'we would simply say he was a prick'.

Francesco Montioni, who was at that stage running a few saddle horses he hoped to hire out to tourist pony-trailers, was outraged that Domenico had put up signs at the town gates—'horses prohibited'. Not, as Francesco said, that anyone would want to ride a horse down Paciano's brick-paved streets, which made it absurd to plaster the town gates with such signs. Much of the charm of Paciano's *centro storico*, the ancient town centre, lies in the way the necessary intrusions of modern life have been so successfully subdued. No neon, no billboards, no advertising projecting or dangling overhead. But soon official signs were proliferating everywhere.

In a town that is only a couple of hundred metres long, it is not difficult to find the post office, Ivana's pharmacy or Enzo's barber shop. Paciano had already won an 'Ideal Village' award in a competition sponsored by the European Economic Community, but Domenico was not satisfied. He seemed to think it needed a forest of *cartelli* on every corner to make it a model town.

I suppose it is hypocritical of me to complain of this defacement because it was Domenico who had shown most interest when I arrived back from Sydney with the street signs proclaiming Mosman's link with Paciano. Mosman Council had developed the idea of making their presentation to Paciano a little too enthusiastically for my liking. I was left to struggle to the airport with a package more than a metre and a half long and weighing thirty-five kilograms. It needed a baggage trolley all on its own, and only Alitalia's goodwill towards the sister-city relationship saved me from an horrendous excess baggage charge. The airline carried them free. Then at Rome airport a forceful Alitalia hostess helped me get them past suspicious

Customs officers who refused to believe a passenger would be arriving with road signs as part of his luggage.

The signs read: 'Gemellata con Mosman, Sydney, Australia'. In one corner is Mosman's coat of arms with its whale, in the other the logo of 'Sydney 2000', proclaiming the Olympiad at the threshold of the new millennium. We had thought this would be good publicity for the Games, but it had caused some problems. Sydney's Olympic Committee had refused to release the colourful transfer of the city's Olympic bid because of a copyright issue, so we had an artist paint it by hand on each sign. Domenico organised council workers to erect them on the three roads leading to the town, with the result that I am kept busy explaining to locals and visitors the origins of the link between a Sydney municipality and an Umbrian hilltown.

Any excitement about the *gemellagio* was far from everyone's mind however when Domenico's summonses reached the mayor. When I arrived in his office, Alfonso had Gabriele Tomassoni with him, and they were looking glum. I tried to joke that all those fines would make the council rich, but failed to amuse them.

'*No, no, molti guai!*' said Alfonso.

He could accurately foresee the backlash from the citizenry who would blame him for their misfortune.

The offences cited by the *Vigile* were mostly technical breaches, petty stuff that a dilatory council in a tolerant society had up until then overlooked. They included letting a house to tourists without a permit, and installing aluminium windows in a building zone where only wooden frames were allowed. David McTaggart, the Greenpeace man, had converted a cow-shed into an apartment without permission. Petty breaches they might be, but Domenico was clearly serving notice on the Mayor that the law was the law in Paciano too.

Some people later alleged angrily that Domenico had gathered his evidence by gaining access to their houses on other pretexts and talked of legal action for abuse of office. But as so often happens with Italian talk, nothing came of it. My offence, of course, went back to that day years earlier when Domenico had issued his stop-work order. The *denuncia* stated that I had breached Italy's Civil Code by conducting unauthorised building work on a communal road. It would be more than a slight understatement to say that I was angry and exasperated at this new turn of events.

'This is *scandaloso*! You are responsible for putting me in this position. What about the fact that the *Comune* has dragged its feet for nearly four years in transferring the road to me?' I demanded.

'No excuse.' Alfonso shrugged. 'And even if we could make the transfer today, it's too late. The *denuncia* has been issued, a copy has gone to the magistrates.'

'So what am I supposed to do?'

'Well, we think we can bring it under the *condono* legislation, but we're not sure—you had better talk to your lawyer.'

When I took this sorry story to our friends the Ascanios, *Zio* Carlo was sympathetic, but had another of his proverbs ready to warn me:

'Chi va in mano all'avvocato

spende l'ultimo ducato'

'If you put yourself in a lawyer's hands

You can watch your money run out like sands'

We had always been leery of getting caught up in the Italian legal system—it would probably be as inefficient and even more costly than the medical system, we thought—but now we had been dragged into it, and needed help. Fortunately we did know an *avvocato* who had given us some advice when our dispute with Cerimonia had looked like boiling over.

Giuseppe Marruco has his *studio legale* in Orvieto, that wonderful Etruscan and mediaeval city perched high on a *tufa* mountain and, for my money, the most beautiful town in Umbria. Approaching from the west across the valley on the Lake Bolsena road, the afternoon sun on the mosaics of the cathedral lights up the facade in a sheet of golden flame. The exterior is constructed in alternating bands of black and white marble, because Lorenzo Maitani, the first of the thirty-three architects who laboured for over three hundred years to build it, was Sienese, and copied the style of his home town *duomo*.

Marruco had been the *pretore*, or lower court magistrate, in our neighbouring town of Città della Pieve before going into private practice, so he knew the law from both sides. He is young, calm and competent. We certainly needed a calming influence when we arrived, hot and apprehensive in his office in the ancient street of merchants.

We were caught like a rabbit in a trap, he explained as he read the Civil Code to us. The law ordained one outcome and one outcome only for *abusivo* development on public lands such as a council road—immediate demolition.

'Surely there are extenuating circumstances in our case', I argued. 'The road is disused, the *Comune* is obligated to transfer it to us and agrees it will do so, but has procrastinated.'

'Unfortunately', explained Giuseppe gravely, 'the law provides no scope for arguing such an explanation. The case will be declared proven by the facts and the magistrates are not permitted to consider anything in mitigation.'

I knew it was useless to butt my head against such a situation, nevertheless I felt my anger rising at the injustice. Then it occurred to me—the rabbit need not break the trap, it just has to prise open the jaws a little to remove its foot. It may be left with a limp, but it will escape.

'The *Comune* thinks it can be handled under the new *condono* legislation', I said. 'That would involve a financial penalty, but avoid the stupidity of demolition and having to start all over again.'

The Italian government had just introduced the latest in its series of postwar amnesties on building infringements. The penalties were fixed by the national parliament, but this time the individual *comuni* would retain the monies collected. I began to suspect that Domenico's coup against the forty-four offending *cittadini* had been expertly timed to benefit Paciano's coffers. As Marruco worked his way through a close reading of the legislation, it became clear that the *condono* could be the escape route, but it would be tricky. The law spoke only of the amnesty extending to illegal building. Strictly speaking, we had not 'built', and nowhere did it say that developments such as terracing were included. On the other hand, nowhere did it say that they were not! It was another example of the loose drafting that has been responsible for so many loopholes in Italian law. Marruco undertook to recommend to Paciano council that it could validly excuse my illegal development by payment of a *condono* penalty. But he would also warn it to hurry up and complete the transfer of the road. Relief!

Marruco explained to us that the law was a mess, full of pitfalls, because much of the Civil Code was still as originally drafted in the middle of last century. The real danger for people like us, he said, was the complete absence of any system of legal precedents in Italy, so every case had to be argued afresh. This could drag on for years, and often did, through court after court, or until the money ran out! I began to understand how lucky our escape had been.

There was much to do, however, before I was out of the woods. First came a telephone call from Brigadiere Paladina, in charge of the local *Carabinieri*. As a matter of course, the magistrates had sent the *denunce* for investigation. Would I come up and make a statement? Of course I had to admit the offence, but it was a heaven-sent opportunity to put the *comune* in the hot seat by telling the whole pathetic story. I hoped the message would get through to the magistrates.

Then I needed to engage a *geometra* to prepare the document for submission to the council, seeking the *condono* indulgence.

It was a little alarming to see this was headed: *'Dichiarazione Sostitutiva di Atto di Notorietà'*. I knew that I had been naughty, but it seemed a bit hot to call it a 'notorious act', the literal translation. I rushed home to consult my large Sansoni dictionary, and was pacified. An *'Atto di Notorietà'* is merely an attested affidavit.

Finally, we had to pay the penalty, two million *lire*, nearly two thousand Australian dollars. All the paperwork had taken a great deal of time, and the deadline for payment was at hand. It fell on a Saturday. That morning I went to the local post office with my deposit form neatly filled in, to hand over the money. *Crisi!* There was a power blackout, so the machine that stamps the receipt wasn't working. This was the last straw. I was desperate.

'Can't you do it by hand?'

No, it wasn't permitted, so they couldn't take my money.

I had only half an hour till midday to make the payment, or miss the *condono* deadline. If I waited at Paciano, and the power wasn't back on before the post office closed for the weekend…! Into the car and off to Chiusi, where I made it with five minutes to spare. A week later, bowing as it usually did to an avalanche of protests, the government announced that the deadline had been extended by three months.

· · ·

November is one of the most variable months of the calendar, often confounding the forecasters. The saints' days that stand like milestones guiding the *contadino* through the rural year are surrounded by a forest of proverbs reflecting this uncertainty. The freeze can come early:

> *Per tutti I santi*
> *la neve è sui campi*
> *per I morti*
> *la neve è negli orti*
> By All Saints Day (November 1)
> the snow is on the fields;
> by All Souls' Day (November 2)
> it's in the kitchen gardens

The days are short. We look down from our hill at the tractors hurrying over the fields to finish the sowing. If this year it was sunflowers, next year will be wheat and barley. There is no time to waste, not two weeks to the feast of St Martin. Will we get a respite from the cold? In our very first year, *Zio* Carlo had explained that at this time, before plunging into winter's depths, everyone hopes for that brief burst of warm weather known throughout Europe as the Saint Martin Summer. He is fond of quoting:

> *L'estate di San Martino*
> *dura tre giorni e un pochinino*
> A St Martin Summer will seem quite poor
> count three days only, very little more

It was beginning to strike me that most of these proverbs looked on the gloomy side of life. It's all too clear that they enshrine mediaeval memories, in this case of a capricious climate that could and did bring famine, pestilence and death.

The Benedictine monks of the area left their own testimony to the struggle for life in centuries past:

> *'La carestia è sempre presente. La fame e le sue fedeli compagne, le epidemie, bussano sovente alla porta del contadino. In alcuni anni I monaci patiscono la fame come I fedeli.'*
>
> 'Famine is always with us. Starvation and its faithful companions, the epidemic diseases, often knock on the peasant's door. Some years the monks suffer too, going hungry along with the faithful.'

No famine today. We make the most of the few days of sunshine and clear skies St Martin lends us with our last luncheons for the year on the terrace. Then we take down the big umbrella and pack the chairs away. Before long, it will be time for the olive harvest, very likely in freezing conditions.

Olives are grown in Italy further north than Umbria, but we have come to the conclusion that *olivicultura* on these hillslopes above three to four hundred metres is risky. The proof came in the bitter winter of 1985–86. Nearly half the olive trees in Umbria were killed off by a heavy snowfall followed by a thaw, then while everything was still dripping wet, a black frost, ten degrees below zero, froze all the moisture solid, crushing the life out of the trees.

This was before our time, but more recently, all Umbria was blasted by the *buriana*, an icy wind direct from Siberia, dropping our temperature to minus 17 degrees. The bark split and burst under the pressure of the freezing sap, killing the branches slowly, and giving us a heavy pruning job the next year. When we planted our little *campo*, they told us that olive trees never die. Well, it's only true in warmer climes. They are drought-resistant, but definitely frost-sensitive.

Hill culture of olives has two big advantages, however. Here, we are free of both the *tignola* moth and the olive fly, *mosca olearia*, which attack the fruit, and we don't get the *muffa* or spotty mildew. All three reduce the yield and spoil the taste. The cooler drier air in the hills enables us to avoid using insecticides and also produces fruit with a very low acid content. This is why the three upland regions of Umbria, Tuscany and Liguria are renowned for their *'extra vergine'* oil, with acidity well under the one per cent threshold.

One of our house guests left us, as a parting gift, a slim new book called simply, *The Oil*. It's the history of *l'olio d'oliva*, the story of its spread throughout the Mediterranean, its production and uses over six thousand years. I found references from *The Iliad* and *The Odyssey*; quotations from Pindar, Pliny, Plutarch and Catullus. All bear testimony to the very special, almost mystical importance attached to the oil of the olive. Here in Paciano, that tradition lives on. To have one's own *oliveto* is not merely important in producing oil for the household, which on average uses between fifty and one hundred litres a year, it is prestigious. We certainly got local credit for our little plot of fifty trees. 'You will be self-sufficient', everyone told us. They were also pleased that we had recognised, and adopted, their values.

The culture is kept alive in the family, and taught in Paciano's school. At the town's annual olive festival I found this little poem, written by an eight-year-old girl:

Mentre il bosco
arde d'autunno
nei colori di fuoco
brilla
sotto un tiepido sole
il verde argenteo
dell' antico ulivo
e una carezza di pace
si posa sui colli

While the woods flame
in their autumn colours
the silvery green of the ancient olive
sparkles under a tepid sun
and strokes the hills
with a caress of peace

Exquisite! It is just like that.

What the ancients knew from experience, modern scientists have proven with their chemical analysis—olive oil is good for the health. Containing no cholesterol, it is the best form of fat to use to avoid heart disease, and it reduces gastric acidity. Because it is high in unsaturated fatty acids, it is the centre-piece of the popular Mediterranean diet. Our light Umbrian oils are among the most unsaturated oils in Italy.

None of this makes up for the fact that olives have to be picked in bitter weather. 'Picking' is the wrong term. Olives are stripped from the tree and allowed to fall into large nets, eight to ten metres square, spread out below. I was amazed to find how rough an olive tree is. Those leaves shimmering in the slightest breeze give an impression of lightness, delicacy, fragility. In fact, the leaves are coarse, the branches are rough, and twigs grow out higgledy-piggledy to tear at the fingers. When the air temperature is around five degrees, hands quickly become numb, but when it snows it becomes truly painful.

Some people use gloves, there is even a hand tool like a small rake, but the purists, the traditionalists, use their bare hands. So do I. Not by any means because I am anxious to martyr myself in the traditionalist's cause. No, I quickly found my own, least painful method. It's an action like milking a cow that forces the olives from their stems by finger pressure instead of ripping them off. It does less damage to the tree and eliminates a lot of leaves and twigs, all of which have to be taken out before processing. My neighbours don't understand why I do it that way, but then this isn't a dairy zone; none of them has ever milked a cow.

The feast of Saint Catherine is the next seasonal milepost. 'You must not start to pick before *Santa Caterina*', we were told, very early on. But by the saint's day, 25 November, the first snowfalls of the winter may be dusting the hillslopes. *Per Santa Caterina la neve alla collina* the proverb warns!

Our trees were heavy with fruit, although they were only young. Two years of constant care—weeding, watering, organic fertilising—was paying off. I was waiting obediently for the end of November when, a few days before St Catherine's we saw the long-range forecast, via our satellite receiver. A massive cold front was approaching Spain; we calculated it would reach Italy in three days.

We had invested in the satellite system out of disgust at Italian television's coverage of world events. The Gulf War, as everyone knows, was conducted in English. In Italy, the war's progress was virtually unintelligible, because Norman Schwartzkopf and Colin Powell didn't speak Italian. We couldn't understand what was happening from the scrappy and disjointed series of truncated reports which had to be delayed until translations could be superimposed. Tuned simultaneously to two satellites, we enjoy about forty television and twenty radio channels, with FM quality stereo sound. All free.

The choice of harvest time—between that decreed by the *contadino* regimen of the traditional church calendar and that suggested by modern meteorological help delivered by satellite—was an easy one for me to make. We started picking. Almost alone in the district I thumbed my nose at Catherine's rule. On the third day, as I was balancing on a swaying ladder four metres above the ground, the snow began to fall. I had nearly finished, but there was an excruciating hour as the snow turned to freezing water on my hands. Red and raw, my fingers had as much feeling as a robot's. I got the last basket filled and climbed stiffly down. We dried those final few kilograms of olives on old towels on the kitchen table—moisture on the fruit induces mould and ruins the taste of the oil. Our neighbours had to wait another week or more for dry weather.

A few kilometres along the San Donato road from us, Dr Maturi, a Milan stockbroker, had shrewdly taken advantage of European Union subsidies to plant fifteen thousand new olive trees. Euro-money also financed his own mill. In time, *'Le Balze'* should be a model farm, but his trees were still small; until his own crop increased, he had spare capacity and invited me to press our olives there. Most cooperative mills, like Paciano's, use heat to extract the oil and the yield may be a little greater. But the best oil is 'first press, cold press', meaning no heat, and no re-treating of the residues left from the primary extraction.

The *'Le Balze' frantoio* is spotless as a Dutch dairy. I lugged my boxes of fruit to the scales, and tipped them down a chute into a washing machine. Then two giant millstones revolving in a steel basin began to crush everything—skins, pulp and seeds. The technique has not changed in two thousand years, except that today an electric motor drives the stones around, instead of a donkey. In an hour, the beautiful colours of our fruit—purple, olive green and black—were gone; the greasy brown paste under the stones resembled nothing so much as baby's poo.

The milling may be ancient technology, but from there on it's all modern applied-science. Maturi may be a financier in Milan, but here in Paciano he is *'il professore'*. I still don't know whether he is really a professor of anything, but in Italy, this rarely matters, the title is the thing. Agnelli of Fiat is known simply as *'Avvocato'*, De Benedetti of Olivetti as *'l'Ingenere'*.

The professor seated himself at what looked like a giant gramophone turntable, and carefully adjusted his white cap. Playing a foot pedal like an organist, he extruded a wide strip of my olive poo like toothpaste onto a woven nylon mat as the turntable made one revolution. The mat, with a hole in the centre like a record, was whisked away by a workman and stacked on a steel spindle two metres high. The process was repeated, over and over, and the stack rose steadily. Three mats, then a flat steel disc, another three, another disc, until the whole assembly, thirty discs high, was wheeled into an hydraulic press.

Over two hours, at a pressure of four hundred kilograms per square centimetre, every last drop of moisture was wrung from the paste. I watched as the glistening liquid carrying its little bubbles of oil ran down the mats into the tank below. It was dirty brown, the colour of sump oil. Maturi read my thoughts. 'It's still a messy mixture of oil, water and vegetable stain. Now we will separate it for you.'

He turned on the centrifuge, a large high-speed motor-driven version of the cream separator I used to crank by hand on my uncle's farm on the Darling Downs. I waited impatiently. For twenty minutes nothing emerged but a stream of the brown waste liquid being spun off. Then from the topmost spout came first a trickle, soon a steady flow of our own oil—pure, intense green in colour, with its astringent fruity fragrance. Maturi shook my hand.

'Your first oil—*complimenti!*'

It was a proud moment, like a first vintage, but there was still a little ceremony to come. In a corner of every *frantoio* there's a hearth with a fire burning. The professor had bread ready for the ritual end to the pressing. We toasted it and poured on the new oil. The taste was *piccante*, peppery—not as smooth as it would be in three months time—but the experts around me judged it a good vintage. And then the analyst in the back room came out with the figures—a yield of nearly twenty per cent, amongst the highest ever known in the district. In all, twenty-four litres, enough for ourselves and some to take back to family and friends in Australia.

Francesco Montioni, who was waiting to mill his olives, produced a bottle of his wine. We drank to my oil, and the end of another year's work.

. . .

Leone Cruciani, a *contadino* of Marsciano, just across the Tiber valley from Assisi, bought his first car in 1973, at the age of fifty-three. It was a two-door Fiat 126, bodywork the colour of our new olive oil, motor in the rear, 600cc and 23 horsepower, the size of a decent motor-cycle engine. He kept it well, and fifteen years later passed it on to his son, Stefano. I know all this because my wife and I were sitting in it, driving home to Paciano from Perugia and all the information was there in the papers in the glovebox. We had just sold our own car, and had got ourselves caught up in another one of those hilarious adventures that seem to happen only in Italy.

In its day, a Fiat 126 offered economical motoring for a thrifty *contadino* and his family, a comfortable step up from the *Vespa* and *Lambretta* scooters that made Italians mobile after World War II for the first time in their lives. Just over twenty years later, however, it had fallen well behind current motoring standards. Although everything worked, and seat belts had been fitted to conform to the new law, there was no heating, the suspension transmitted every ripple in the bitumen to the seat of the pants, and the roaring engine behind seemed to be trying to get to us through the back seat.

It was freezing in the car. Our heavy coats were so bulky we had difficulty doing up the fixed seat belts, and then we couldn't move. We possibly looked like Ma and Pa Kettle going to town. The situation was so incongruous we nearly ran off the road laughing. The problem was that we had sold the Peugeot too quickly. It had been good to us—comfortable, reliable and, with a turbo on the diesel motor, as quick as we needed. But after four years and eighty thousand kilometres, it was time to change before expensive maintenance caught up.

We had ordered a new car and, finding trade-in prices derisory, set out to sell the Peugeot ourselves. We advertised it in Perugia's free classified newspaper, *Cerco e Trovo* or *Find & Seek*. My expansive glowing description produced just the buyer we needed—a professor of Perugia University whose own Peugeot had been shortened by a metre in a *tamponamento* sandwich. His was the middle car in a motorway pile-up. He was delighted to acquire a car better than his own; the brief haggling yielded us a price almost twice the trade-in value. But he needed it immediately.

So we were whirled off first to an *agenzia pratica automobilistica*. The business of transferring the registration of a car is so difficult that it is best handled by a specialist—just one example of the parasitic service industries that thrive on Italy's bureaucratic complexity. Next, to the notary's office. As a property, a motor car's change of ownership must be notarised, simply to make sure both parties are in full agreement! It was dark, seven o'clock at night and the office was crowded with people arranging everything from house purchases to marriage licences. The notary, a portly self-important fellow, brushed all these people aside and bore down on me. He could see I didn't belong.

'*Signor*...ah...Look...' (nobody can pronounce Luck) 'Do you understand Italian?', he boomed.

'*Abbastanza bene*'—'well enough', I replied.

'Are you selling this car to Professor Bucci?'

'*Sì.*'

'And is the price fifteen million *lire*?'

'*Sì.*'

'*Benissimo, buon natale!*' and shaking my hand, he turned and went back to his desk.

In all my life, I had never seen a fee of five hundred dollars earned so quickly. No wonder Christmas greetings were early that year.

Professor Bucci had brought his wife, elegant in a mink coat, for the inspection of the car and the conclusion of the deal, and now they were anxious to get home with their new toy. But first, there were civilities. He took us across the road to a bar for a cup of coffee, and invited us to come and visit them at Città di Castello. The professor dropped us off at Renzo's garage. For the first time we were passengers in our own car— no, it wasn't ours any longer, the speed of the transaction had confused us. It was Renzo who for a small payment had checked and accredited the Peugeot's mechanicals, so he kindly lent us the little Fiat for three weeks of agony until our new car was delivered.

Italy and Italian motor cars have come a long way in the last twenty-five years. One of the latest Fiat advertisements says proudly, 'No Italian boy grows up wanting to be a train driver!' I bet he did in the days of the 126!

16. The road resolved and ghosts exorcised

'Eppure si muove'
Galileo Galilei

Things have always moved slowly in Italy. It took the Vatican exactly three hundred and fifty-nine years, four months and nine days to rehabilitate Galileo. On 31 October, 1992, I had driven over to Sarteano to order some more of the green stone from Monte Bianco for our terracing and stopped at Chiusi on the way home to buy a newspaper. There in *La Repubblica* was the amazing headline: *'Il Vaticano cancella la condanna di Galileo'*. Amazing, because I knew well enough the story of the old man's imprisonment and interrogation by the Inquisition. That he had been forced to abjure his heretical support of Copernicus' observation that the sun, not the earth, was the centre of our universe, (the Church still backed Ptolemy's geocentric theory of the universe). But I had forgotten that Galileo was still, officially, *'un penitenziario della Santa Inquisizione'*.

Despite Einstein, Neil Armstrong and the Vatican's own two superb observatories—in Tucson, Arizona, and *'La Specola'* at Castelgandolfo—the man who perhaps more than any other could claim to be the father of physics was only now being re-admitted as a legitimate son of the Roman Catholic Church. So, when Galileo muttered his rebellious (and some say, apocryphal) phrase, 'Nevertheless it does move', he should have meant not just the earth.

In a way, it was entirely appropriate that heliocentrism should have been recognised in 1992. That year, all of us in Italy were starting to believe *'eppure si muove'*, as the political dam holding back the floodwaters of corruption began at last to crack. Like the unravelling of a sweater, the revelation of Italy's massive political corruption scandal began with a single loose thread.

Laura Sala was the estranged wife of Mario Chiesa, President of *Pio Albergo Trivulzio,* the biggest old people's home in Milan. One day, she complained to the authorities that her alimony payments had stopped. It was an unimportant civil matter, so the complaint was filed away for investigation one day. Not long afterwards, Luca Magni, a small businessman who supplied meat to the PAT went to the magistrates to report that Mario Chiesa was extorting bribes from him to renew his supply contract. I don't understand why, but somehow the magistrates connected the two reports and pounced.

In a classic sting, they equipped Magni with a hidden telecamera, a microphone-pen, and an envelope containing seven million *lire* (about six thousand Australian dollars) in marked notes. When the *Carabinieri* barged in, Hollywood style, moments later, to find the envelope in Chiesa's desk drawer, and Chiesa trying to flush the notes down the toilet, the game was up. The magistrates hadn't expected what happened next, though. Mario Chiesa confessed to siphoning these and other bribes through a secret Swiss bank account to political parties. And no doubt in the hope of saving some of his own skin he plaintively told his interrogators: 'But everyone does it!' and named names. The magistrates took the thread and pulled …and pulled.

The unravelling skein led to the Milan city council, present and past mayors, national politicians and cabinet ministers, and the secretaries and treasurers of all the main political parties. Ultimately, more than four thousand people were investigated, hundreds were arrested, dozens were processed in courtroom trials televised live to the nation. Three prominent businessmen committed suicide. Antonio di Pietro, the policeman-become-magistrate who had bugged Magni to catch Chiesa, became a national hero feted around the world, later leveraging his popularity into a political career. Three years later the leading Danish and Swedish newspapers awarded di Pietro their annual Freedom Prize. Completing the circle, so to speak, he gave the one hundred thousand Danish Crowns that went with the award to the *Pio Albergo Trivulzio* of Milan.

When I first came to Italy, I had wondered how the political parties could afford all their conventions; every few months, each one attended by thousands of supporters. They didn't seem to decide anything and increasingly looked to me like junkets at the seaside for the faithful. Di Pietro solved that little mystery for me. The 'Rimini Reunions', as I dubbed them, turned out to have been funded by the payments extorted from virtually all the major corporations, in return for fat contracts or favourable political action. Unmasking Milan as *Tangentopoli* or 'Bribe City' blew the cozy arrangements of decades to pieces. It destroyed the Christian Democratic Party which effectively had ruled Italy for forty years, and annihilated its political ally, the Socialist Party. The Socialists went from bonanza to bankruptcy in one year. No more conventions.

As the sensational exposures continued, I could almost feel the shudder of excitement that ran through the nation. Suddenly Italy accelerated out of its political torpor. At last, it seemed, there was hope that corruption was out and clean politics was in. A referendum on electoral reform was proposed and carried by a huge majority; the proportional voting system which had encouraged the plethora of splinter parties was largely, but not completely, abandoned in favour of the British 'first past the post' system; in the subsequent elections, a new right-wing coalition government was swept into power with a mandate for businesslike administration and clean hands. Italy's 'Second Republic' was proudly launched.

The whiff of change in the air even reached Paciano. Up on the noticeboard at the Comune went a call to citizens to a public political meeting. Four parties were to contest the next council elections; they had been summoned to present their policies and programs and to face the public's questions. It wasn't exactly an American-style presidential debate, but the

Pacianese had never heard anything like it. In the first place, Italian politics had always been run on ideology, not on policies; programs were something to be developed after the election, so a party could be safe from any audit of promises. In the second, in this Communist heartland, nobody had ever thought of challenging the entrenched Partito Communista Italiano, now the Democratic Left.

A hundred of us crowded into the basement room of the council chambers. More surprises were in store. The chairman, who was not a candidate, announced that each party would be given five minutes to explain its policies; members of the public could then ask questions, but not make speeches; there would be a final period for each party to reply and sum up. Time limits would be strictly enforced. And they were. The smartest of the parties distributed leaflets explaining themselves; the speeches were concise, the questioners controlled. It was the only Italian meeting I have ever attended that was run by rules—and it was a great success.

The general shift to the right in Italian politics was not however the only reason for the flowering of new parties in Paciano. They were also launching on a groundswell of opinion against *Il Sindaco*, Mayor Alfonso del Buono. Alfonso was universally blamed for those forty-four *denunce*. It was his lackadaisical administration and his procrastination hidden behind an authoritarian leadership style, people said, that allowed Paciano to fall victim to the crusading *Vigile*. Of course this was not entirely true or fair, but there had to be a scapegoat (Italians always have a scapegoat), and del Buono was the *capro espiatorio*. He announced to the meeting that he would not be standing again. And when he tried to make a speech justifying his administration, the chairman curtly cut him down under the rules. There was a ripple of applause.

The new Mayor was a thirty-one year old employee of the Trasimeno Cooperative Society, Roberto Lombrici. A fortnight after the elections, I called on him to offer my congratulations…and, I have to admit, to try to suss out what the change in office would mean for us. It was a pleasant surprise. '*Signor* Luck', he said, 'I know all about your troubles with the road. There are many things in Paciano that have been put aside as "too hard", your road is one of them. I am sorry it cost you the *condono* fine, but I cannot reverse it. But I can promise that the transfer will be made *al più presto*.'

I had been hearing these nice promises for five years—how long was 'as soon as possible'? I decided to reserve judgement, but I was wrong. Within three months the *Comune* had surveyed and registered the stretch of old road as a new subdivision and prepared the transfer documents. I felt as if a huge weight had been lifted when Audrey and I signed them in the office of *Dott.* Giuseppe Ventura, the *Comune*'s notary, in Castiglione del Lago. Another two months and they were formally inscribed in the *libri catastali*, the Land Registry records in Perugia. The petty little area that had caused so much heartburn, one hundred and sixty-five square metres in all, was finally ours. I was at last legally free to erect the driveway gates and the last panels of fencing, shutting out stray dogs and the giant porcupines that like to gobble up any fallen hazelnuts.

I took Gino Caviglioli, the *fabbro*, our designs for automatic gates that had been pigeon-holed for years, and called up our *muratore*, Luciano Torrini, to be ready to install them. Approval by the *Comune* was immediate; in no time at all, with a little more concrete, the final paving was completed and the gates responded to our radio commands. At last, the project was complete.

Italy's new coalition government collapsed within a year because of petty bickering within and assault from without; before long the prime minister, his brother and several of his business managers were indicted for corruption and tax evasion. They claimed a political witch-hunt, and not without justification. Italy's Magistracy and Judiciary are institutionally politicised, so any decision may be impugned as lacking impartiality. The prospect of stable, economically responsible government retreated several years, the movement for constitutional reform shifted down into low gear and Italy returned to yet another period of its favourite diversion, political controversy. It was as if the whole country had frightened itself with the pace of sudden progress, and needed to catch its breath.

In our municipal elections, the addition of a couple of councillors from one of the reformist parties did nothing for the stability of Paciano's *Consiglio Comunale*. A deep split developed over the future of Domenico Verga, the *Vigile*, when the old faction tried to force him out. The move was eventually defeated with the support of a public petition. I added my name to those who believed that Paciano needed a fearless independent sheriff to keep it honest—even if it hurt from time to time.

. . .

We consummated the link between Paciano and Mosman on a windy November day that set the strings of Australian flags fluttering merrily in the central *piazza*. Jim Reid had flown in especially with the illuminated Friendship Agreement, prepared in both languages. The Pacianese crowding into the council chambers had never before seen the mayoral splendour of ermine-fringed robes and glittering chain of office he brought for the occasion. Since Italy voted out the King after World War II, officials in this republican state have had to be content with a tricolor sash over the shoulder with a bow at the hip—so the more corpulent mayors look like giant Easter eggs.

The Australian Ambassador Rory Steele presided over the little ceremony; Roberto Lombrici who had the honour of signing on behalf of Paciano had *spumante* ready, and everyone drank to the common principles and commitments now binding two communities twenty thousand kilometres apart. The document recorded that:

'...Paciano has a recorded history of more than one thousand years; Mosman was an early settlement in the young nation of Australia nearly two centuries ago, although aboriginal people inhabited its lands well before Europeans arrived. Mosman is surrounded by water in the beautiful harbour of Sydney; walled hill-town Paciano lies in green Umbria, a land-locked region of Italy. Both are today pledged to the love of nature…' and concluded: 'NOW THESE PRESENTS confirm the establishment of a Friendship Agreement between the *Comune* of Paciano and Mosman Municipal Council, to promote a greater awareness of our links of friendship, and to foster a better understanding of our culture, our system of education, sports, tourism, environment, business and lifestyles.'

Then, at last, it was time to exorcise the ghost of Domenico Liscio. We had been at Varacca long enough for the house to be known as ours, not his; after all, he had not lived in the place for nearly fifty years. I went back to my *fabbro* Caviglione, who patiently cut the letters for a nameplate out of sheet steel, to be attached to one of the massive brick entrance pillars Luciano Torrini erected in that burst of 'illegal' building. It seemed so long ago.

The Pacianese certainly don't think of me as a *padrone*. I don't act like one of their arrogant landowners, or carry myself like one of Italy's phony counts. They have seen me labouring like any *contadino* to develop the property, as any Australian home-owner does, my wife working alongside me. Our house is large, but it is still an old farmhouse, so I proposed to call the place *Casa Fortuna*, a nice wordplay on my name, I thought, and an appropriate continuation of local tradition.

But the locals would have none of it. They saw that in restoring the biggest and most important house in the derelict little hamlet of Varacca, encouraging others to follow, we had helped turn over the peasant page in Italian history. So the plate reads, not *Casa*, but *Villa Fortuna*. It has a happy sound. The house is good for another couple of centuries. Long after we are gone, its name will be a reminder of the Australian who came from so far away to restore it, the last *contadino* of Varacca. And I will always remember how fortunate I was to have found it in that fog, to have crowded all its experiences into the last corner of my life.

EPILOGUE

The reader may have been surprised that this story conveyed a somewhat different view of Italy to the popular one of the Italophile who commonly eulogises the food, the design flair, the *simpaticissimo* nature of the people. In fact, the Italians are their own sternest critics so, as a footnote, I offer a small selection of Italians' self-criticism from my reading of the books, newspapers and magazines of my time in their country.

'I don't like this Italy. Not at all. I find it burdened with the same defects as ever. Theatrical, inaccurate, fatuously carefree, verbose, unfair, always ready to shift the blame to "others"—anyone else. More than that, with some worse defects: The aggressive uncouthness aggravated, if not actually introduced by television. And there is always our animal wiliness, the cult of the "private" hypocrisy; the myopic turning everything to one's own benefit, at the expense of the general interest. Which, in the long run, would have been to their interest also, all things considered. And why do we show off everything we own—the car, the house in the country, the yacht, the cellular phone, if not because of our radical insecurity. It's true, sometimes we are surprised, in a positive way. As a matter of fact, Italy never ceases to surprise us. But more often it surprises us in the negative. With that "stupid intelligence" of ours that no, really doesn't please me.'

INDRO MONTANELLI, *Journalist*

'Italy is not a civilised country…In Italy, replying to a letter is not considered a rule of good manners, it is optional. Therefore if the letter we receive does not interest us, the tendency is to ignore it, or throw it in the bin…'

PIERO OTTONE, *Columnist*

'An Italian nation does not exist.'

NORBERTO BOBBIO, *Philosopher*

'I believe that the greatest obstacle (to finding a national identity) is the habit of thinking small. On one side I would say narrow-mindedness and selfishness, on the other, acceptance, a passive attitude. And this is terrible.'

IRENE PIVETTI, *Parliamentarian/Journalist*

'To govern the Italians is not difficult, it is useless.'

BENITO MUSSOLINI, *Dictator*

'The Italian democracy carries within its body an unresponsive and evil opposition; there is a part of the Italian population that dislikes and distrusts it.'

GIORGIO BOCCA, *Journalist/Author*

'We have swept out the old corruption, but we have not fundamentally changed the body.'

ROMANO PRODI, *Prime Minister*, 1997

'We are authoritarian to the bone: and by heredity, by custom, by education are induced too much to give orders and too much to obey.'

GIUSTINO FORTUNATO, *Writer*

'Semi-Christians, who accept neither religiousness nor the absence of God; scepticism if not cynicism…and what is the scepticism of the Italians? It is the incapacity to commit oneself strongly to certain moral values.'

PIER VINCENZO MENGALDO, *Critic and lecturer*,
University of Padua

'On the one hand, Italy appears relatively peaceful and prosperous enough, even well-oiled and fat, on the other it confirms itself as the eternal country of melodrama and play-acting, considered abroad as tradionally dishonest.'

CARLO DIONISOTTI, *Emeritus Professor of Italian Literature*,
London University

'Italy is a country that has been immersed for years in a sort of "omertà" (conspiracy of silence).'
UMBERTO ECO, *Semiologist*

'Honesty in Italy is a vice; one may practice it—but only with caution, hiding it.'
ITALO CALVINO, *Author*

'The only stable thing here is instability.'
SUSANNA AGNELLI, *Foreign Minister*, 1996

'Things are tragic but not serious.'
ENNIO FLAIANO, *Playwright* (d.1972)

'In Italy only plumbers understand the time-value of money.'
ENZO BIAGI, *Journalist*

But let the sharp Italian tongue have the last word about all of us—the visitors in their country:

'The foreigners in Italy rest content in their national virtues. Everything in their house is correct, orderly, irreproachable. Once here amongst us, they amuse themselves contemplating our picturesque confusion, our theatrical unreliability. They bask in their exhausting virtue and in the process profit from it by feeling themselves superior. What a wonderful thing a trip to Italy is!'
LUIGI BARZINI, *Journalist/Author*

GLOSSARY OF ITALIAN WORDS APPEARING IN THE TEXT

a fuori — outside, in the open

abbastanza — sufficiently

abbronzatura — suntan

abusivo — unlawful, unauthorised

aglio — garlic

albergatore — hotel-keeper

allora! — well then!

altro — (an)other

Ambasciatore — ambassador

amico(ci) — friend(s)

anagrafe — demographic registry

analcolico — non-alcoholic

ape — bee (also, the 3-wheeled truck)

armadio — wardrobe

asino — ass

atrofia — atrophy

atto di notorietà — affidavit

autorizzazione — approval

autostrada — motorway, turnpike

avvocato — lawyer, advocate, counsel

ballare — to dance

barra — bar, lever

basta! — enough!

battuto di caccia al cinghiale — wild boar hunting in progress

beccare (buscarsi) — to cop (slang)

bel paese — the fair country (Italy)

bella figura — a good impression

bene — good, well

benzinaio — service-station keeper

bere — to drink

bianco — white

bistecca — (beef) steak

bocca — mouth

bollo — stamp, seal

bosco — woodland, scrub

breve — short, brief

brigadiere — sergeant

bruschetta — basically, toast with olive oil

buon — good

buona cucina — good food

camino — fireplace

campanile — belltower

campo — field, paddock

cantare — to sing

cantina — cellar, wine store

caparra — deposit, down-payment

carattere — character

carbonizzato — burnt to death

carciofo — artichoke

cardo — thistle

carta — paper

carta da bollo — stamped duty paid paper

cartello — notice, poster, sign

casa — house

casa chiusa — brothel

cassazione — quashing, annulment

castello — castle

catasto	land register/registry office
cenere	ash, cinders
centro storico	the old town centre
certificato di residenza	
	residence certificate
certo!	certainly!
Certosa	Carthusian monastery
chiesa	church
cicoria	chicory, endive
cielo	sky, heaven
cima	peak, summit
cinghiale	wild boar
cinquanta	fifty
cittadino(a)	citizen, local inhabitant
civiltà	civilisation
cocomero	watermelon
codice fiscale	fiscal card
collina	hill
colonico	share-farmer's (adj)
combattere	to fight
commemorazione	remembrance
complimenti!	congratulations!
compromesso	preliminary contract
comunale	communal
comune	council (n) common (adj)
Comunità Montana (di Trasimeno)	
	public works dept, Trasimeno region
condono	amnesty, pardon, remission
condottiere	mercenary commander
contadino	farmer/peasant/countryman
conto	account, reckoning, bill, cheque
conto corrente postale (CCP)	
	post office current (giro) account
contorno	vegetable, side-dish
contrada	town quarter, ward
coppa	cured neck of pork
coppo	curved capping roof tile
cornacchia	crow
corpo	corps, body
corsa	race (competition)
cotto	cooked; here, fired clay floor tiles
credere	to believe
creta	chalk/clay (as in Tuscan hills)
crisi	crisis
cucchiaia	
	tablespoon, dipper, scoop, bucket
cucchiaino	teaspoon
cucchiaio	spoon
cucchiaione	tablespoon, ladle
cucù/cuculo	cuckoo
danno	damage, injury
defunto	dead, deceased
dente	tooth, jagged peak
denuncia	report, return, summons
denunciare	
	to report, lay information against
depuratore	purifier
dichiarazione	statement, declaration
disastro	disaster, accident, fiasco
dispiacere	to be sorry
documenti!	your identification!
dogana	Customs (house)
duca	duke
ducato	
	ducat (old Italian gold coin), money
duce	leader, chief
duomo	cathedral
ecco fatto!	that's done!
ente	corporation
entrare	to enter
enuresi	enuresis, bed-wetting
erba	grass, plant
eroe	hero
esposto	exposure, statement of fact
estetica	aesthetics
ettaro	hectare
fabbro	blacksmith
faciloneria	easy-goingness
ferro battuto	wrought iron
festa	holiday, festival
fidarsi	to trust (reflexive)
finocchio	fennel
firmare	to sign
fiscale	fiscal, tax (adj.)

fiume	river
fonte	spring, source
forestale	forest, forestry (adj.)
forestiero	
stranger, foreigner(in the same country)	
Formula Uno	Formula I (G.P.)
fortuna	luck
fortunatissimo	very luckily
fossa	pit, grave
fossa biologica	septic tank
fosso	ditch, drain
frantoio	crusher, olive-press, oil mill
frazionamento	subdivision
fruttuoso	fruitful, abundant
fungo(ghi)	mushroom(s)
fuoco	fire
fuori legge	illegal
gattopardo	leopard
gemellagio	twinship, twinning
genuino	genuine, authentic
geometra	surveyor, draughtsman
gergo	slang
girasole	sunflower
giunta	
municipal council management committee	
(in)giusto	(not) fair, just, legitimate
gonfalone	
standard, processional banner	
gradino	step
graffitisti	graffiti writers
gramigna	couch grass
granaio	granary, loft
granturco	Indian maize, corn
grave	serious
guaio	misfortune, trouble
guardare **(intorno)**	to look (around)
Guardia di Finanza (GdF)	
Italian tax & finance police	
guarire	to heal
guerra	war
il	the, on the (in a document)
immobili	real estate

imposta sul valore aggiunta (IVA)	
tax on the added value (VAT/GST)	
imprenditore	entrepreneur
incalcolabile	inestimable
incendio	fire
incontro	meeting, encounter
inquinamento	pollution
insalata	salad
integrale	wholemeal
inverno	winter
istrice	porcupine
iustitzia	justice
ladro	robber, thief
lasciare	to leave
lavorare	to work
lavoro	work
lega	league
legarsi	to be bound
legge	the law
lenzuolo	(bed)sheet
leone	lion
levito	rising
loggia	verandah, porch
lucciola	firefly
lupa	wolf
lupara	sawn-off shotgun
machilismo	machismo
maddonina	little madonna
mafiosi	members of a Mafia clan
mais	corn
mammismo	mother domination
mano	hand
mattone	brick
Mazzini Giuseppe,	19thC republican
meglio	better
melanzana	egg-plant, aubergine
mezzadria	share farming (system)
mietitura	harvesting, reaping
milione	million
minestra	soup
molestia	annoyance, molestation
molto	very, a lot, many, much

morto	dead
mosto	must (in wine-making)
motore elettrico	electric motor
motorino	light motor cycle
multa	fine, penalty
muratore	mason, bricklayer, builder
naso	nose
natale	birth (adj.)/Christmas
nato(a) a	born at
'Ndrangheta	the Calabrian mafia
nera	black
ninnananna	lullaby
non c'è	there is not
nord	north, northern
notaio	public notary
notaro	councillor of old Perugia
notturno	night-time (adj.)
nulla osta	no objection, impediment
nuraghe	prehistoric Sardinian hut
obbedire	to obey
oleificio	oil mill
oliveto	olive grove
olivicoltura	olive growing
onorario	honorary
operaio	worker
oro	gold
orto	kitchen (vegetable) garden
padrone	proprietor/employer
palazzo	palace; now any large building
palio	banner, as prize in a contest
pallamaglio	pall-mall (antique croquet)
pasticceria	pastry shop
pastore	herdsman, shepherd
patente	driving licence
patto	pact/agreement/contract
pazienza	patience
pazzarello	a madcap
pazzo	mad
pecorino	sheepmilk cheese
pene	penis
pensione	boarding house
pentiti	supergrasses

pentito	sorry, regretful, penitent
peperone	capsicum, chilli
permesso di soggiorno	permit to stay
piano	slow, slowly
piazza	town square
piede	foot
pietra serena	Umbrian sandstone
piovoso	rainy
più	more
Po' del Vento (abbr. podere)	
	Windy Farm (now a road name)
podere	estate, farm, holding
Polizia	the state police
pomidoro	tomato
porco	pig
porta	gate, door
pozzo	well
prato	meadow, grassland, lawn
prendi!	take! (imperative)
preoccuparsi	to be worried, concerned
pretore	magistrate, lower court judge
prezzemolo	parsley
primavera	Spring
primo piatto	first course
problema	problem
pro-loco	local promotion committee
procrastinare	to put off, postpone
Procura	Power of Attorney, proxy
Pronto Soccorso	Casualty Department
quasi	almost
quercia	oak
querela	legal action, suit (eg. for libel)
questo	this (one)
Questura	police headquarters
raccolta	harvest
ragione	reason, justification
rastrella	rake
razionalismo	
	functionalism (architectural style)
recupero	recovery, restoration
restauro	restoration
ricordare	to remember

rocca	fortress, stronghold
Romagnolo	of/from the Romagna Region
rosso	red
rullo	roll
sacra	sacred
sagra	festival, feast
sala	hall
salsiccia(ce)	sausage(s)
sambuco	elder (tree)
sangue	blood
scandaloso	outrageous, shocking
scavatore	digger, back-hoe, JCB
semplice	simple
sempre	always
setola	bristle
si	yes
signora	woman, lady, Mrs
signore	man, gentleman, Mr
Signoria(e)	Lordship(s)
simpatico	nice, pleasant, likeable
sindaco	mayor
sistemazione	layout, development
sole	sun
sono	I am/they are
sospendere	to suspend, stop
sostitutiva	substitutive
sottoscritto	undersigned
spingere	to push
squadra	group, team, squad
stagno	lagoon, pond
stalla	stable, cowshed
stare	to stand, stay
strada bianca	white (gravelled) road
straniero	foreigner (from abroad)
studio	professional's office
subito	immediately
supplica	petition
tacco	heel
tamponamento	plugging, so a rear-end collision
tara	hereditary flaw
targa	number plate
tartufo	truffle
tavola	table
tegola	flat pan roof tile
tempo	time/weather
terra	ground, land
terrazza	terrace, verandah, patio
terreno	soil, earth, land
ti	you, (thou)
tornante	hairpin bend
Torre d'Orlando	Roland's tower
torre	tower
torrente	torrent, flood
torta	cake, tart
tossicodipendenza	drug addiction
trave	beam, girder
trentatre	thirty-three
Trentini Trento	Trento people
tufa	calcium carbonate rock
tutela	protection, tutelage
tutti	everyone, all
uccello	bird
uguale	equal, the same
ultimo	last, final
unità	solidarity
uva	grape
vecchio/a	old
ventoso	windy
vendemmia	grape harvest, vintage
vespa	wasp (also, the scooter)
Via degli Etruschi	The Etruscan Road
vigile	local policeman
vino	wine
Volkspartei	People's Party
vuole	wishes
zappa	hoe
zappatore	hoer
zio(a)	uncle (aunt)
zitto!	shut up!
zolla	clod, turf, rootball of earth
zona	zone, region, area
zona occupata	occupied (danger) zone

A SELECTION OF READINGS IN ENGLISH AND ITALIAN

- Books in Italian
∞ The Longmans **History of Italy** series

Alighieri, Dante **The Divine Comedy** (Oxford University Press, 1993)

Andreotti, Giulio **Lives** (Sidgwick & Jackson, 1988)

Bartlett, Vernon **Central Italy** (B.T. Batsford, Northumberland Press, 1972)

Barzini, Luigi **The Europeans** (Simon & Schuster, 1983; Penguin,1984)

Barzini, L. **The Italians** (Hamish Hamilton, 1964; Penguin, 1991)

Belloc, Hilaire **The Path to Rome** (Penguin Travel Library 1988)

Bertoldi, Silvio **Dopoguerra** (Rizzoli, 1993) •

Bocca, Giorgio **La Repubblica di Mussolini** (Mondadori, 1997) •

Bocca, G. **Storia dell'Italia Partigiana** (Mondadori, 1997) •

Bocca, G. **Italiani Strana Gente** (Mondadori, 1998) •

Borghese, J. Valerio **Sea Devils** (U.S. Naval Institute Press, 1995)

Bosi, Roberto **L'Olio** (Nardini,1996) •

Calvino, Italo **Adam, One Afternoon** (Minerva, 1992)

Calvino, I. **Italian Folktales** (Harcourt Brace, 1980; Penguin, 1982)

Calvino, I. **Marcovaldo** (Minerva, 1993)

Calvino, I. **Our Ancestors** (Minerva, 1992)

Carpanetto, Dino **Italy in the Age of Reason 1685-1789** (Longman, 1987)∞

Cavallaro, Felice **Mafia Album** (RCS Rizzoli Libri, 1992) •

Cervi, Mario **Salo Album** (RCS Rizzoli Libri, 1995) •

Ciano, Galeazzo **The Ciano Diaries 1939-1943** (Doubleday NY, 1946)

Ciano, Edda Mussolini **My Truth** (William Morrow NY, 1977)

Clark, Martin **Modern Italy 1871-1982** (Longman, 1987)∞

Cochrane, Eric **Italy 1530-1630** (Longman, 1989)∞

Cornwell, Rupert **God's Banker** (RCS Rizzoli Libri, 1992)

Costanzo, Maurizio **Un paese anormale** (Mondadori, 1999) •

Cresciano, Gianfranco **The Italians In Australia** (ABC Enterprises, 1985)

Crivellari, Domenico **Venice** (Gruppo Editoriale Electa, 1982)

De Felice, Renzo **Mussolini il Duce—Gli Anni di Consenso 1929-1936**
   (Einaudi, 1996) •

De Felice, R. **Mussolini il Duce—Lo Stato Totalitario 1936-1940**
   (Einaudi, 1996) •

De Felice, R. **Mussolini L'alleato—L'Italia in Guerra 1940-1943**
   (Einaudi, 1996) •

De Felice, R. **Mussolini L'alleato—La Guerra Civile 1943-1945**
   (Einaudi, 1996) •

De Felice, R. **Rosso e Nero** (Gruppo Editoriale Fabbri, Bompiani, 1991) •

de Rosa, Peter **Vicars of Christ** (Crown Publications, 1999)

del Corto, Giovan B **Storia della Val di Chiana** (Arnaldo Forni Editore, 1985) •

Dessaix, Robert **Night Letters** (Arcadia Books, 1998)

Douglas, Norman **Scirocco** (Marlboro Press, 1994)

Dulles, Allen **The Secret Surrender** (Weidenfeld & Nicolson, 1967)

Eco, Umberto **Apocalypse Postponed** (British Film Institute Publishing, 1994)

Eco, U. **Travels in Hyperreality** (Minerva, 1995; Harcourt Trade, 1990)

Falessi, Cesare **Balbo, Aviatore** (Arnaldo Mondadori Editore, 1983) •

Festuccia, Luciano **The Lands & Castles of Trasimeno**
   (Cornicchia Grafiche, Perugia, 1987)

Frei, Matt **Italy—The Unfinished Revolution** (Mandarin, 1996)

Friedman, Alan **Agnelli** (Harrap, 1988)

Gilmour, David **The Last Leopard** (Quartet Books, 1988)

Goethe, Johann W. **Italian Journey 1786-1788** (Penguin, 1970)

Guareschi, Giovanni **The Don Camillo Omnibus** (The Readers Book Club, 1956, by arrangement with the original publishers, Victor Gollancz)

Guerri, Giordano B. **I Fascisti** (Mondadori, 1996) •

Guerri, G. **Gli Italiani Sotto La Chiesa** (Mondadori, 1997) •

Guerri, G. **Io ti Assolvo** (Mondadori, 1998) •

Harrison, Barbara G. **Italian Days** (Houghton Miffin, 1995)

Hay, Denys/Law, John **Italy—Age of the Renaissance 1380-1530** (Longman, 1989)∞

Haycraft, John **Italian Labyrinth** (Penguin, 1992)

Hearder, Harry **Italy—Age of the Risorgimento 1790-1870** (Longman, 1983)∞

Hellenga, Robert **The Sixteen Pleasures** (Sceptre, 1995)

Hibbert, Christopher **Garibaldi & His Enemies** (Penguin, 1987)

Hibbert, C. **Mussolini** (The Reprint Society, 1963)

Hibbert, C. **The Rise & Fall of the House of Medici** (Penguin, 1979)

Hobday, Peter **In the Valley of the Fireflies** (Penguin, 1995)

James, Henry **Italian Hours** (Penguin Classics, 1995)

Joll, James **Europe since 1870** (Penguin, 1990)

Keates, Jonathan **Italian Journeys** (Heinemann, 1991; Picador Pan 1992)

Keates, J./Cornish, J. **Umbria** (Philip's Travel Guides, 1991)

Kelly, J. N. D. **Oxford Dictionary of Popes** (Oxford University Press, 1988)

Lamb, Richard **War in Italy, 1943-45; A Brutal Story** (J.Murray, 1993)

Lamb, R. **Mussolini and the British** (J. Murray, 1997)

Lampedusa, Tomasi di G. **The Leopard** (Reprint Society/Wm Collins, 1961)

Landon/Norwich **Five Centuries of Music in Venice** (Thames & Hudson, 1991)

Lapucci/Antoni **I Proverbi dei Mesi** (Garzanti Editore, 1985) •

Larner, John **Italy—Age of Dante & Petrarch 1216-1380** (Longman, 1983)∞

Lepre, Aurelio **Mussolini l'Italiano** (Mondadori, 1997) •

Levi, Primo **The Sixth Day and Other Tales** (Abacus, 1991)

Levi, Carlo **Christ Stopped at Eboli** (Penguin, 1990)

Littlewood, Ian **Venice, A Literary Companion** (J. Murray, 1992)

Livy, Titus **The War with Hannibal** (Penguin, 1970)

Luraghi, Raimondo **Resistenza Album** (Rizzoli, 1995) •

Lyttleton, Adrian **The Seizure of Power; Fascism 1919-1929** Weidenfeld
& Nicolson 1987

Malony, John N. **The Emergence of Political Catholicism in Italy**
(Croom Helm, 1977)

Mate, Ferenc **The Hills of Tuscany** (Flamingo, 1999)

Mawer, Simon **A Place in Italy** (Sinclair Stevenson, 1992)

Mayes, Frances **Under the Tuscan Sun** (Bantam, 1998)

Mayes, F. **Bella Tuscany** (Bantam, 1999)

Menzies, Y. M. **Living in Italy** (Hale, 1991)

Montanelli, Indro **Eppur si muove** (Rizzoli, 1995) •

Montanelli, I. **Storia d'Italia—La Guerra Civile** (Rizoli, 1998) •

Origo, Iris **The Merchant of Prato** (Penguin, 1992)

Origo, I. **War in Val d'Orcia** (Century Hutchison,1985; Allison & Busby, 1999)

Origo, I. **Images and Shadows** (J. Murray, 1998)

Parks, Tim **Italian Neighbours** (Mandarin, 1993)

Parks, T. **An Italian Education** (Minerva, 1997)

Pasolini, Pier P. **A Violent Life** (Carcanet Press, 1996)

Pasolini, P. P. **Roman Nights & Other Stories** (Quartet Books, 1994)

Petacco, Arrigo **La Nostra Guerra 1940-45** (Mondadori, 1997) •

Pisano, Giorgio **Le Ultime Cinque Secondi di Mussolini**
(Il Saggiatore, 1996) •

Plumb, J. H. **The Italian Renaissance** (American Heritage Publishing, 1993)

Pope-Hennessy, John **The Piero della Francesca Trail** (Thames & Hudson, 1993)

Raw, Charles **The Money Changers** (Harvill, Harper Collins, 1992)

Regolo, Luciano **Il Re Signore** (Simonelli, 1998) •

Ricci, Nino **Lives of the Saints** [aka The Book of Saints]
   (Minerva, 1991)

Richardson, Emeline H. **The Etruscans** (University of Chacago Press, 1976)

Robb, Peter **Midnight in Sicily** (Duffy & Snellgrove, 1996)

Rocca, Gianni **L'Italia Invasa** (Mondadori, 1998) •

Rostovtzeff, Michael **Rome** (Oxford University Press, 1960)

Runciman, Steven **The Sicilian Vesper**s (Cambridge University Press, 1992)

Sandwith, Francis **Camera & Chianti** (Nicholas Kaye, 1955)

Satta, Salvatore **The Day of Judgment** (Collins Harvill, 1987)

Serafini, Remo **Castiglione del Lago & Paciano** (Editore di Grifo
   Montepulciano, 1989) •

Sforza, Count Carlo **Machiavelli** (Greenwood Press, 1976)

Simon, Kate **A Renaissance Tapestry** (Harrap, 1988)

Simonetti, Gualtiero **Erbe di Campi e Prato** (Arnaldo Mondadori
   Editore, 1986) •

Stendhal **A Roman Journal** (Charterhouse of Parma)

Sterling, Claire **The Mafia** (Grafton Books, 1991; Everyman's
   Library, 1992)

Tompkins, Peter **The Other Resistance** (RCS Libri e Grandi Opere, 1995)

Twain, Mark (S.Clemens) **The Innocents Abroad** (Oxford University
   Press, NY, 1997)

Vasari **Lives of the Artists**—2 Vols (Penguin, 1987)

Unsworth, Barry **After Hannibal** (Hamish Hamilton, 1996)

Ward, William **Getting it Right in Italy** (Bloomsbury, 1990)

Willey, David **God's Politician** (Faber & Faber, 1993)

Winstone, H. V. F. **Uncovering the Ancient World** (Constable, 1993)

Yallop, David **In God's Name** (Corgi, 1987)

In the Kitchen

Anderson, Burton **The Wine Atlas of Italy** (Mitchell Beazley, 1992)

Bugialli, Guiliano **The Taste of Italy** (Conran Octopus, 1986)

Cornish, Elizabeth **Cooking with Pasta** (New Burlington Books London, 1987)

David, Elizabeth **Italian Food** (Barrie & Jenkins London, 1987)

de'Medici, Lorenza **The Villa Table** (Pavilion Books London,1993)

de'Medici, L. **Italy the Beautiful Cookbook** (Child & Assocs. Publishing, NSW 1988)

de'Medici, L. **The Renaissance of Italian Cooking** (Trafalgar Square, 1998)

della Croce, Julia **Pasta Classica** (Chronicle Books San Francisco, 1987)

Dolamore **The Essential Olive Oil Companion** (Pan Macmillan Australia, 1993)

Famularo/Imperiale **The Joy of Pasta** (Barronís Educational Series NY, 1983)

Gray, Patience **Honey from a Weed** (Macmillan, 1990)

Harris, Valentin **Recipes from an Italian Farmhouse** (Conran Octopus, 1989)

Hazan, Marcella **The Classic Italian Cookbook** (Macmillan, 1990)

Hazan, M. **The Second Classic Italian Cookbook** (Macmillan, 1986)

Hazan, M. **Marcella Cucina** (Macmillan, 1999)

Ital-Aust Womens Assn **Buon Appetito— Regional Italian Recipes** (NSW State Library,1994)

Ross/Waterfield **Leaves from our Tuscan Kitchen** (Penguin Handbooks, 1979)

Santolini, Antonella **Umbria in Bocca** (Edikronos Palermo, 1985)

About the author

After twenty-six years in journalism, in which he broadcast the news to outback Queensland, trained the first indigenous journalists in Papua New Guinea, dodged petrol bombs in Northern Ireland and reported on Australian business, Geoffrey Luck spent more than a decade in the clandestine world of headhunting. Italy beckoned as a quiet retirement, but over the next ten years he founded an olive grove, restored a derelict *casa* and found some of the best human interest stories of his career. He set the stories down here, in *Villa Fortuna*—named for the home he and his wife Audrey restored in Varacca, a tiny hamlet of Paciano, Umbria, where they still live today. As an ABC radio correspondent, he broadcast regularly on Italy for national radio, and especially for Italian Australians.